HISTORY OF AMERICAN
THOUGHT AND CULTURE

Paul S. Boyer, General Editor

Facing page: "Behold! a Fabric now to Freedom rear'd," etching from *The Columbian Magazine,* 1788. The pediment is faced by an American eagle with a ribbon reading 'E Pluribus Unum'. On top of the temple are statues of Freedom (with the liberty pole and cap), Justice (with the scales), and Peace (with a palm). Clio, the muse of history, kneels beside Columbia to inscribe the message ("We Are One"), delivered to her by Concord, who holds a copy of the United States Constitution. (Prints and Photographs Division, Library of Congress.)

Behold! a Fabric now to Freedom rear'd,
Approv'd by Friends, and ev'n by Foes rever'd;
Where Justice, too, and Peace, by us ador'd,
Shall heal each Wrong, and keep ensheath'd the Sword.
Approach then, Concord, fair Columbia's Son;
And, faithful Clio, write that 'WE ARE ONE'.

Design'd by G.T.   Trenchard Sculp.

Also by Michael Kammen

Selvages and Biases: The Fabric of History in American Culture (1987)

A Machine That Would Go of Itself: The Constitution in American Culture (1986)

Spheres of Liberty: Changing Perceptions of Liberty in American Culture (1986)

A Season of Youth: The American Revolution and the Historical Imagination (1978)

Colonial New York: A History (1975)

People of Paradox: An Inquiry Concerning the Origins of American Civilization (1972)

Empire and Interest: The American Colonies and the Politics of Mercantilism (1970)

Deputyes & Libertyes: The Origins of Representative Government in Colonial America (1969)

A Rope of Sand: The Colonial Agents, British Politics, and the American Revolution (1968)

Editor

The Origins of the American Constitution: A Documentary History (1986)

The Past Before Us: Contemporary Historical Writing in the United States (1980)

"What is the Good of History?" Selected Letters of Carl L. Becker, 1900–1945 (1973)

The History of the Province of New-York, by William Smith, Jr. (1972)

The Contrapuntal Civilization: Essays toward a New Understanding of the American Experience (1971)

Politics and Society in Colonial America: Democracy or Deference? (1967)

Sovereignty and Liberty

Constitutional Discourse in American Culture

MICHAEL KAMMEN

THE UNIVERSITY OF WISCONSIN PRESS

The University of Wisconsin Press
114 North Murray Street
Madison, Wisconsin 53715

The University of Wisconsin Press, Ltd.
1 Gower Street
London WC1E 6HA, England

5 4 3 2 1

Printed in the United States of America

Library of Congress Cataloging-in-Publication Data
Kammen, Michael
    Sovereignty and liberty.
    (History of American thought and culture)
    Includes bibliographical references and index.
    1. United States—Constitutional history.
2. Political culture—United States—History.
I. Title. II. Series.
KF4541.K35   1988   342.73′029   88-40200
ISBN 0-299-11730-8

for Douglas Anton Kammen

Contents

Illustrations

Acknowledgments

NUMEROUS INDIVIDUALS and institutions contributed in countless ways to the making of these essays. Consequently I welcome this chance to recognize their assistance without implicating them in my own sins of omission or commission. Readers will discover that out of sight (momentarily) scarcely means out of mind. Those persons and organizations who are "responsible" for particular pieces — as sponsors or hosts, or as the editors of earlier versions — are thanked in the notes that explain the provenance of each chapter. The appreciation expressed here pertains to the process whereby connected explorations came to be collected into a kind of constitutional cartography: a map of my own vocational odyssey, as it were, during the recent Bicentennial.

More than fifteen years ago an eccentric and Francophile Oxford don made an observation of which I am fond: "Le plaisir de l'amour est dans la chasse," Richard Cobb recalled. He then added this donnish note: "The same can be said of the process of historical research, of the accumulation of evidence from original resources and of the publication of that evidence as a form of historical wealth."

La chasse, in my case, has been cheerfully assisted by several very able Cornell undergraduates, Laura Dick and Matthew Berger in particular, because they worked with me so diligently as research aides during the period 1983–87; and less directly by dozens of others who took my upper-level seminar on aspects of American constitutionalism, served as sounding boards for some of this material, and mutually shared creative explorations of their own. I appreciate their intellectual sustenance, just as I do the substantive support that comes from the Colonel Return Jonathan Meigs Fund at Cornell.

Bruce Kennedy, an outstanding reference librarian at the Cornell Law Library, came to my rescue more than once. In fact, I imposed upon him for help more times than either one of us might care to recall.

Jackie Hubble, Marianne Christofferson, and Cathy Hendley typed and then patiently retyped several versions of these essays with precision and good cheer. Anne Eberle made the index with intelligence and dispatch, as expected. I'd like to believe that all four recognize my affection as well as my praise. But with *la chasse,* one never knows.

Colleagues and friends read various essays and made suggestions for their improvement. Although I failed to follow *all* of their directions, my odyssey would not have reached port without their generous guidance. Thanks be to Morton Keller, Walter LaFeber, Herbert I. Lazerow, Richard Polenberg, Joel H. Silbey, S. Cushing Strout, and Robert H. Wiebe.

At the University of Wisconsin Press there are good people who care less about odysseys and more about authors. I am one of their bookmaking beneficiaries. Special gratitude, once again, to Allen N. Fitchen, a director who puffs laconically and keeps faith; to Elizabeth Steinberg, a beloved editor who bothers to consult and who keeps a writer on his toes; and particularly to Paul Boyer, who happens to be Series Editor for the History of American Thought and Culture volumes, but is also a superb scholar, critic, friend, and man of amazing grace.

The book is dedicated to a blithe spirit who recently completed his own, rather remarkable, fourteen-month odyssey around the world. That venture—philosophic as well as geographic—took him through the dry and rainy seasons in Java, the steamy jungle of Sumatra, and then across the dense yet dazzling interior of Kalimantan (once known as Borneo). His safe return to Ithaca is the true odyssey for which a Te Deum is due; so this book is for him, with a father's fond salute.

Above Cayuga's Waters   M.K.

Sovereignty and Liberty

"It is obviously impracticable in the foederal government of these States; to secure all rights of independent sovereignty to each, and yet provide for the interest and safety of all—Individuals entering into society, must give up a share of liberty to preserve the rest."

The President of the Constitutional Convention (George Washington) to the President of the Confederation Congress (Arthur St. Clair), September 17, 1787.

"The present Confederation may be compared to a *hut* or *tent,* accommodated to the emergencies of war—but it is now time to erect a castle of durable materials, with a tight roof and substantial bolts and bars to secure our persons and property from violence, and external injuries of all kinds. May this building rise like a pyramid upon the broad basis of the people! and may they have wisdom to see that if they delegate a little more power to their Rulers, the more liberty they will possess themselves, provided they take care to secure their *sovereignty* and *importance* by frequent elections, and rotation of offices."

An editorial in the Philadelphia Independent Gazetteer, *June 27, 1787, and widely reprinted in the newspapers of ten states during July 1787.*

"Every word of [a constitution] decides a question between power and liberty."

James Madison, "Charters," an essay written for The National Gazette, *January 19, 1792.*

Introduction

SOVEREIGNTY AND LIBERTY have long been vital concepts in the continuum of human perceptions concerning the nature of political authority and the quest for freedom. For many centuries, sovereignty in the Old World was metaphorically represented by a sphere: on ceremonial occasions, a medieval or Renaissance ruler held in the left hand an earthly sphere of sovereignty, usually a golden orb or globe, symbolic of an imperial authority so comprehensive that it covered the known world.[1]

Ever since the era of the American Revolution and constitution-writing, however, the theory of sovereignty in the United States has called attention to compartmentalization rather than comprehensiveness. We understand federalism in terms of sovereignty divided and distributed to several levels of government. We remember popular sovereignty and state sovereignty as concepts for which Americans have been ready to shed blood—their own as well as the blood of fellow countrymen

---

1. Georges Duby, *The Age of the Cathedrals: Art and Society, 980–1420* (Chicago, 1981), 14; Paul R. Baker, *Richard Morris Hunt* (Cambridge, Mass., 1980), 186; Franz Georg Kaltwasser, ed., *Das Evangeliar Heinrichs des Löwen und das mittelalterliche Herrscherbild* (Munich, 1986), plates 12, 14–16, 18, 21, 25–26, 28.

and other races living in exotic places. The concept of sovereignty has given rise to sanguinary conflicts in diverse spheres.

It should come as no surprise that sovereignty and liberty have often co-existed in a state of tension. As Supreme Court Justice Robert H. Jackson explained in an interview more than four decades ago, "Your view of the Bill of Rights and the balance that must be drawn between authority and liberty, between stability and progress, will affect your decision."[2] Nevertheless, the tension between sovereignty and liberty has frequently been a creative one because both qualities are deemed essential in achieving social harmony. While our desire for human services and security justifies government, our passion for freedom generates liberty as a value that really matters — one that motivates men and women, and has discernible consequences.

Maintaining an ideal equilibrium between sovereignty and liberty is never easy. The most appropriate balance, moreover, has varied in accordance with changing situations. Although liberty was cherished more than sovereignty in 1776, altered circumstances in 1787–88 elicited an adjustment in American concerns. Consequently several aspects of sovereignty achieved prominence in the arena of political ideas when the United States Constitution came to be written and ratified. The precarious relationship between sovereignty and liberty in 1787 is the subject of the epigraphs that precede this introduction.[3] They indicate the extent to which the framers of the Constitution, as well as their contemporaries, concerned themselves with the goal of securing liberty by means of a sensible distribution and configuration of sovereignty.

Members of the founding generation were persuaded that they pursued a distinctive mission, and that their new nation had a special des-

2. Quoted in Sidney Fine, *Frank Murphy: The Washington Years* (Ann Arbor, Mich., 1984), 154. For Franklin Delano Roosevelt's observation about the problem of balance at the time of the Sesquicentennial in 1937, see his "Address on Constitution Day": ". . . the Constitution guarantees liberty, not license masquerading as liberty." Samuel I. Rosenman, comp., *The Public Papers and Addresses of Franklin D. Roosevelt*, 6 (New York, 1941), 366.

3. The first two quotations will be found in Merrill Jensen, ed., *The Documentary History of the Ratification of the Constitution*. Volume 1, *Constitutional Documents and Records, 1776–1787* (Madison, Wis., 1976), 305; and John P., Kaminski and Gaspare J. Saladino, eds., *The Documentary History of the Ratification of the Constitution*. Volume 13, *Commentaries on the Constitution: Public and Private*, 1 (Madison, Wis., 1981), 148.

tiny. Consequently a recurrent theme in this volume concerns the contribution of constitutionalism to the development of a sense of American exceptionalism. That notion has been much discussed (and frequently criticized) during the past decade. In my view, however, insufficient attention had been devoted to its origins and evolution.

While similarities between constitutional perceptions in the United States and elsewhere ought to be noticed, and have been, I am much more impressed by the continual sense of difference—in political assumptions, institutional arrangements, and values—and by the cultural implications (including ambiguities) that have arisen from the belief that the framers created a distinctive system of government well-suited to the character, or "genius," of a society unlike any other the world had ever known. The intellectual atmosphere of that perspective permeates the discourses described in these essays. Inevitably, perhaps, mixed feelings about the proper function of public opinion profoundly shaped the changing perceptions of American constitutionalism *and* exceptionalism.

On February 6, 1788, as the constitutional ratifying convention of the Commonwealth of Massachusetts neared completion, John Hancock, its presiding officer, rose to speak. He had said little during the course of debate, and remarked that "all the ideas appertaining to the system [the United States Constitution], as well those which are against as for it, have been debated upon with so much learning and ability, that the subject is quite exhausted."[4]

Similar sentiments must inevitably enter the mind of any author with enough temerity to emit yet another work concerning American constitutionalism. Can there conceivably be anything left to say? I believe that there is, obviously, and that it arises from the polemical patterns that have trailed in the wake of the contested situation witnessed by John Hancock two hundred years ago.

Although the conflict between Federalists and Anti-Federalists gradually subsided, others of a more enduring nature emerged. Perhaps their persistence helps to reinforce the conviction expressed by Johan Huizinga, the great Dutch historian, that "human thinking vacillates be-

4. Bernard Schwartz, ed., *The Roots of the Bill of Rights* (2d ed.; New York, 1980), 3:711.

tween antinomies, that is, that man is constantly forced to admit the validity of seemingly opposite points of view."[5]

The principal issues and problems discussed in this book have been subjects of on-going contestation in the extensive arena of American constitutionalism. Those issues endure, in part, because certain words and phrases persist in our political discourse long after their meaning has lost its original reference and implications: sovereignty and liberty, republicanism and federalism, are just four from an array of concepts that have had more complex etymologies than most of us, including scholars, ordinarily acknowledge.

Do such shifts really matter beyond the groves of academe and the graveyards of jurists whose spirits await their own Judgment Day? I am persuaded that they should matter profoundly to concerned citizens, for the fundamental reason that life in a republic entails rights as well as responsibilities. James Madison conveyed much of the rationale in an essay first published in 1792.

> A republic involves the idea of popular rights. . . . And a confederated republic attains the force of monarchy, whilst it avoids the ignorance of a good prince, and the oppression of a bad one. To secure all the advantages of such a system, every good citizen will be at once a centinel over the rights of the people; over the authorities of the federal government: and over both the rights and the authorities of the intermediate governments.[6]

Some of the contested relationships explored in these essays involve the comparative significance and connectedness of events, such as the perennial question of continuities versus discontinuities in American political thought between 1776 and 1788, a question that energizes chapters one and two especially. Whereas John Adams felt certain that the days of early July 1776 "will be the most memorable Epocha in the History of America,"[7] George Mason of Virginia wrote the following from Philadelphia to his son on June 1, 1787:

5. Karl J. Weintraub, *Visions of Culture* (Chicago, 1966), 210.

6. "Government," *The National Gazette*, Jan. 2, 1792, in Gaillard Hunt, ed., *The Writings of James Madison*, 6 (New York, 1906), 82.

7. John Adams to Abigail Adams, July 3, 1776, in L. H. Butterfield, ed., *Adams Family Correspondence* (Cambridge, Mass., 1963), 2:30.

The revolt from Great Britain, & the Formations of our new Governments at that time, were nothing compared with the great Business now before us. There was then a certain Degree of Enthusiasm, which inspired & supported the Mind; but to view, thro the calm sedate Medium of Reason, the Influence which the Establishments now proposed may have upon the Happiness or Misery of Millions yet unborn, is an Object of such Magnitude, as absorbs, & in a Manner suspends the Operations of the human understanding.[8]

When we recall that in 1776 Mason wrote the Virginia Declaration of Rights and played a key role in drafting his state's first constitution, and that John Adams wrote the Massachusetts constitution of 1780, the contrasting character of their judgments is intriguing.

We should also reflect upon the relationship between those momentous decisions made two hundred years ago and the complexities of our own world today. When Hugh Williamson of North Carolina urged the voters of his state to ratify in 1788, he used this metaphor:

We have a common interest, for we are embarked in the same vessel. At present she is in a sea of troubles, without sails, oars, or pilot; ready to be dashed to pieces by every flaw of wind. You may secure a port, unless you think it better to remain at sea.[9]

Are we, too, drifting on a sea of troubles? If so, are we likely to locate a pilot, or even a sheet anchor, amidst the political conflicts and constitutional creativity of the founders who met at Philadelphia in 1787 and then in various state conventions throughout much of 1788? Although we may lack a consensus concerning the meaning for our own time of what they said (and left unsaid), can we at least agree upon the major implications of their assumptions and solutions?

The documentary record of the framers' deeds and thoughts is voluminous. Consequently, one possible (yet unappealing) response to our "sea of troubles," constitutional and otherwise, can be found in a self-deprecating observation made by Frederic William Maitland, the emi-

8. Mason to George Mason, Jr., June 1, 1787, in Robert A. Rutland, ed., *The Papers of George Mason, 1725-1792* (Chapel Hill, N.C., 1970), 3:892-93.

9. Williamson, "Remarks on the New Plan of Government," printed in *The State Gazette of North Carolina* (1788), in Paul Leicester Ford, ed., *Essays on the Constitution of the United States Published During Its Discussion by the People, 1787-1788* (Brooklyn, N.Y., 1892), 405.

nent Victorian historian of English law, about himself and his work: "I can only shovel evidence into heaps and chuck it at the public."[10]

Perhaps that worked for Maitland; but I believe that the historian's vocation calls for a combination of description, documentation, explanation, and interpretation. It most certainly requires selectivity of the sort that might enable a concerned citizen to make informed judgments and decisions. What was said and done in 1787–88 *does* matter to us two hundred years later. What was said and done in 1787–88 has been acted upon, explicated, and reinterpreted ever since. That entire process constitutes what we mean by constitutionalism; and the on-going imperative of reinterpretation gives rise to what we call the "living constitution" (see chapter five especially). Participation in that process is not the exclusive province of jurists, lawyers, or scholars. Justice Louis D. Brandeis said it all in a single sentence: "The greatest menace to liberty is an inert people."

Reinterpreting the Constitution has been required by the evolving circumstances of national life; hence all of the essays that follow have as their common focus the cultural nature of change in discourse concerning American constitutionalism. The alterations that I have chosen to examine are fundamentally conceptual: the character of popular as well as state sovereignty, and the political implications of shifts in the perception of those concepts; the manifold notions of personal liberty and their relation to the emerging belief in a constitutional right of privacy; the development of public opinion, and more particularly the attitudes that judges have held concerning the role that public opinion should or should not play in American constitutionalism; the genesis and transformation of the concept of a living Constitution in the United States, along with the ideological conflicts concerning that concept at the time of the Bicentennial; the frequency with which certain key words recur in American constitutionalism, and what those patterns of repetition may signify.

A few concluding thoughts may be appropriate about the illustrations in this book. They are intended to indicate traces of constitution-

10. C. H. S. Fifoot, *Frederic William Maitland: A Life* (Cambridge, Mass., 1971), 273–74.

alism in the realm of material culture and the decorative arts. I use the word "trace," however, in the sense suggested by definition number two in the *Random House Dictionary of the English Language*: "a barely discernible indication or evidence of some quantity, quality, characteristic expression, etc." Traces of constitutionalism in American art are not exactly abundant, which is paradoxical when one considers the centrality of constitutionalism itself in American culture. It seems highly symptomatic that late in 1787 George Washington observed to an English friend that Robert Edge Pine, the painter, was struggling to complete a historical painting of the Constitutional Convention.[11] Yet Pine had encountered no difficulty rendering on canvas the signing of the Declaration of Independence in 1776.

By contrast the French, who wrote and discarded constitutions helter skelter following their great Revolution, created all sorts of icons and erected various monuments and statues to both particular and abstract aspects of constitutionalism during the course of the nineteenth century.[12]

Attempts to portray the two concepts featured in this volume have been extremely disproportionate: very little on sovereignty *per se* contrasted with vastly more that allegorizes liberty, justice, and Magna Carta.

If, however, we conceive of the Constitution itself as an instrument responsive to issues of American sovereignty that were so vital two centuries ago, then the iconography of the Constitution, its creators and custodians, becomes a means of signifying sovereignty on canvas, in wood, and by means of the imprimatur of popular prints.

Seventy-five years ago Justice Oliver Wendell Holmes observed that "life is painting a picture, not doing a sum." I would only add, in this context, that liberty provides us with the opportunity to choose either or neither. Sovereignty, in turn, gives shape to the conditions of our freedom. And the inexorable nature of change urges us to appreciate

11. See Washington to Catherine Macaulay Graham, Nov. 16, 1787, in John C. Fitzpatrick, ed., *The Writings of George Washington*, 29 (Washington, D.C., 1939), 316.

12. See Maurice Agulhon, *Marianne into Battle: Republican Imagery and Symbolism in France, 1789–1880* (Cambridge, 1981), 79, 85, 101, 173, 175, and passim; Brian C. J. Singer, *Society, Theory, and the French Revolution: Studies in the Revolutionary Imaginary* (New York, 1986); and Lynn A. Hunt, *Politics, Culture, and Class in the French Revolution* (Berkeley, 1984).

the subtle transformations that time has wrought in both sovereignty and liberty for public culture in the United States.

Contemplating such matters can be humbling, may even reduce us to quiescent reflection, for as Plato put it in the *Laws*: "as the years go by, time will change and even reverse many of your present opinions. Refrain therefore awhile from setting yourself up as a judge of the highest matters." Aye.

One

Rethinking the "Fountain of Power"

Changing Perceptions of
Popular Sovereignty, 1764–1788

I

TWO WORDS were especially pervasive in American political discourse during the Revolutionary era: liberty and sovereignty. Although writers and orators constantly invoked both concepts, I would suggest that in 1775–76 liberty supplied the dominant concern, with sovereignty somewhat secondary—a relationship that would gradually be reversed by 1787–88. In order to appreciate this significant shift, we need to notice that changes also occurred in the dominant view of human nature (encoded in the concept of Virtue); in the degree of confidence that people placed in legislative bodies; but above all, in deceptively veiled alterations in the meaning ascribed to popular sovereignty.

In theory, at least, sovereignty and liberty should have been benignly compatible notions: taken together they constituted a whole concept. In reality, however, the two co-existed in a state of tension; and that strain increased steadily between the Declaration of Independence and promulgation of the federal Constitution. As the need for adjustments in the distribution of power between state and national levels of government became evident, the perceived role of liberty in a republican system became increasingly ambiguous. Many believed that liberty would need to be partially restrained in order to avert disorder, or worse still, anarchy. Yet sovereignty also required redefinition—and redistribution too—in order to obviate tyranny and corruption, particularly in legislative bodies.

Above all, however, those who hoped to supplant the weak Confederation government with one having more national energy were obliged to circumvent state sovereignty by means of renewed emphasis upon popular sovereignty: the people as constituent power; the people meeting in extraordinary conventions; the people acting, in the words of James Madison (speaking at the Philadelphia Convention), as "the fountain of all power." Madison urged his colleagues to require ratification by special conventions rather than by the existing state legislatures precisely because the new Constitution, nearly completed, would redistribute sovereignty in ways somewhat disadvantageous to the states.

> The powers given to the Genl. Govt. being taken from the State Govts the Legislatures would be more disinclined than conventions composed in part at least of other men; and if disinclined, they could devise modes apparently promoting, but really thwarting the ratification. . . . The people were in fact, the fountain of all power, and by resorting to them, all difficulties were got over. They could alter constitutions as they pleased.[1]

The basis for Madison's rationale was more expedient than populistic. Practical politics dictated that the likelihood of ratification would be considerably enhanced if vested interests could be bypassed. Doing so might best be legitimized by invoking popular sovereignty. So James Wilson's draft Preamble, which quite logically began with "We the States," gave way to a high-minded subterfuge, "We the People." At first glance, then, it looks as though popular sovereignty achieved its apogee in 1787 when the delegates declared that they acted in the name of the sovereign people. (But see figure 13.)

If we think hard about it, however, we ought to know better; and the most astute iconoclast concerning this matter has been Edmund S.

---

1. Max Farrand, ed., *The Records of the Federal Convention of 1787* (2d ed.; New Haven, Conn., 1937), 2:476.

Morgan, who periodically reminds us that as a people we naively (though conveniently) subscribe to a national creed based upon a considerable set of political fictions. "Our own favorite fiction," he writes, "the sovereignty of the people, the fiction that people are masters of their governors, has lasted now for three centuries and gives no signs of giving up the ghost."[2]

Although Morgan has provided an invaluable service by exposing the casuistry of some resounding rhetoric in 1787–88 (among the most voluble and enduring too), his insistence upon Federalist fiction-writing, and our subsequent self-deception, seems to me to have gone too far in two respects: first, by minimizing the heartfelt sincerity of many American advocates of popular sovereignty, especially between 1764 and 1780; and second, by disregarding the diversity of opinion concerning popular sovereignty during the 1780s and thereby failing to take into account a transition in attitude symbolized by a shifting set of metaphors, whereby the image of a fountain of power received plausible competition from the image of power as a pyramid.

It is my belief that the competition between these two metaphors in 1787–88, and beyond, was indicative of a deep dualism in American political thought — one that persists to this day — and consequently that we are obliged to raise a series of questions about the trajectory of "popular sovereignty" in American minds during the quarter-century of the Revolutionary era: Was it *always* a deceptive device, a "political fiction"? Did its meaning remain constant? If and when it acquired multiple meanings, in what manner and why did they diverge?

I shall argue that apparent continuities have concealed substantive changes that are both real and revealing; that one finds sincerity and casuistry in roughly equal portions, depending upon when and to whom one listens; and that James Wilson's vision of a pyramid of power eventually became more plausible than a fountain of power (so ubiquitous an image circa 1776) because the pyramid metaphor managed to com-

2. Morgan, "The Great Political Fiction," *New York Review of Books,* March 9, 1978, p. 13; Morgan, "Government by Fiction: The Idea of Representation," *The Yale Review* 72 (Spring 1983): 321–39; and Morgan, *Inventing the People: The Rise of Popular Sovereignty in England and America* (New York, 1988), chs. 10–11. On pp. 254, 258–59, and 268 Morgan provides material and explication that support the central contention of my essay.

prehend two separate senses of sovereignty in a single and relatively simple image: the people as constituent power at the broad base of a republican polity, and the partial subordination of state sovereignty in a new configuration that James Madison (and others) liked to call "partly national and partly federal."

Neither popular sovereignty nor state sovereignty ceased to compel attention in 1787–88. Far from it. But each one would be diminished as a result of the new Constitution and the government to which it gave rise. Much of the rhetoric of 1764–76 lingered on because it had acquired immense popularity as well as persuasive credibility. It became less logical after 1787, however, because its applicability to the national political scene was less appropriate. Its persistence thereby created a curious discrepancy in American discourse between public realities and what Professor Morgan has designated as "political fictions."

Most of us are likely to agree that those fictions have served Americans fairly well over the past two centuries: in terms of stability, as a partial basis for consensus and as a coherent national ideology. I wish to suggest, however, that once upon a time such fictions compelled widespread assent simply because they seemed profoundly true. Under republican regimes, where else could power originate than from the consent of the people? During the years from about 1765 until 1785, popular sovereignty appeared utterly compatible with individual liberty because the power of the people as a collective force would shield free individuals from governmental tyranny.

Gradually, however, Americans came to recognize that an overbearing majority of the people might pose just as great a threat to liberty as tyrannical officials. When that shock of recognition took hold, the meanings ascribed to sovereignty, to liberty, and to republicanism all required adjustment. The process of reformulation began in 1787. It has not yet run its course. Given the nature of the concepts themselves, and given the dynamics of change in a free society, perhaps it never will.

II

I cannot say whether popular sovereignty is most sensibly referred to as a theory, a concept, or simply a shifting set of attitudes. In any case, its core (like the tightly wound inner sphere of a baseball) included the following during the Revolutionary era: a belief that public authority and the legitimacy of governmental actions originate in the people-at-large; that those people, when "rightly informed," will perceive a situation accurately and take the proper course of action;[3] and that, as Tom Paine put it, there could be "no majesty but that of the people, no government except that of its own representatives." In 1780 Paine would make the central point about as succinctly and emphatically as it can be made: that there should be "no such thing . . . as power of any kind, independent of the people."[4]

Having defined our designated concept, and having placed it chronologically, we must begin to move both backward and forward in time: backward in order to locate the origins of popular sovereignty, and to understand why sovereignty, in general, became such a burning issue during the 1760s and '70s; forward in order to ascertain the changes in meaning and application that popular sovereignty underwent during the years after 1776.

The basic ingredients of popular sovereignty had been around for quite some time prior to that date. They simply had not congealed into the particular configuration that they would take in Revolutionary America. They lacked the propulsive circumstances of that era; and they had been articulated by only a small number of people at any given time. We can find a few components in the contractual nature of Puritan theology, especially in what the Puritans called the church covenant and the social covenant, which were significant in the forming of congregations and the organization of new towns. We find ingredients, too, in the Great Awakening—the religious revivals of the 1740s and later, when

3. The necessity for the people to be "rightly informed" is one of the most critical, yet commonly neglected, ingredients of popular sovereignty. In 1769, for example, George Washington wrote to George Mason (about proposed opposition to the Townshend Duties) that it would be possible to control purchases "if the Gentlemen in their several Counties wou'd be at some pains to explain matters to the people, & stimulate them to a cordial agreement." Robert A. Rutland, ed., *The Papers of George Mason, 1725–1792* (Chapel Hill, N.C., 1970), I:97–98.

4. Quoted in Jack P. Greene, "Paine, America, and the 'Modernization' of Political Consciousness," *Political Science Quarterly* 93 (Spring 1978): 85, 89. For Robert R. Palmer's important essay on "The People as Constituent Power," see Jack P. Greene, ed., *The Reinterpretation of the American Revolution, 1763–1789* (New York, 1968), 338–61.

ministers became more responsive to their parishioners and when so many new communities came into existence.[5]

We also find elements in the heritage of English political thought, especially from the Civil War of the mid-seventeenth century, and from theorists who wrote about "popular government" between the 1650s and the 1750s.[6] We can see even more important seeds in the evolution of colonial institutions. The nature of representation in the assemblies, for example, expanded geographically as well as demographically, developed residential requirements for delegates, and often resulted in the issuance of binding instructions from their constituents. The *practice* of colonial politics reveals these ingredients most clearly; for as Landon Carter complained bitterly to his son, winning election to the House of Burgesses in Virginia required a gentleman to "kiss the arses of the people."[7]

Although all of these factors may have been present by the close of the French and Indian War, only the intense agitation of rebellion, like a capacious cocktail shaker, would blend them into a mixture palatable to most American patriots. In his political pamphlets of 1764 and 1765, for example, James Otis of Massachusetts dealt explicitly with issues of sovereignty, but he was not quite ready for the radical understanding of popular sovereignty that would be widely accepted a decade later. Otis emphasized obedience. As one scholar has written of him, "the basis for the obligation of obedience was found in the initial act of consent by which the community-at-large empowered the sovereign to act as an agent for the entire realm; and that obligation remained

5. See William G. McLoughlin, "'Enthusiasm for Liberty': The Great Awakening as the Key to the Revolution," *Proceedings of the American Antiquarian Society* 87 (1977): 69–95; Perry Miller, "Jonathan Edwards and the Great Awakening," in Miller, *Errand Into the Wilderness* (Cambridge, Mass., 1956), 153–66.

6. See J. G. A. Pocock, ed., *The Political Works of James Harrington* (Cambridge, 1977), 389–566; and Paul K. Conkin, *Self-Evident Truths* (Bloomington, Ind., 1974), 18–25.

7. See Bernard Bailyn, *The Origins of American Politics* (New York, 1968), 82, 84; John C. Rainbolt, "The Alteration in the Relationship between Leadership and Constituents in Virginia, 1660 to 1720," *William and Mary Quarterly* 27 (July 1970): 411–34; and Gary B. Nash, "The Transformation of Urban Politics, 1700–1765," *Journal of American History* 60 (December 1973): 605–32.

in force so long as the sovereign wielded its power with the *intention* of promoting the common good."[8]

Between 1765 and 1775 the ingredients made a volatile mix. In December 1765, for example, as the Stamp Act crisis reached furious proportions, the people of New London, Connecticut, declaring "that every form of government rightly founded, originates from the consent of the people," asserted that it is the people who set limits in any constitution, and that when those limits are exceeded "the people have a right to reassume the exercise of that authority which by nature they had before they delegated it to individuals." Such statements echoed and re-echoed throughout every colonial city and hamlet. The citizens of Worcester, Massachusetts, put it quite bluntly in the spring of 1775: the commonwealth should have a government in which all officials were "dependent on the suffrages of the people for their place and pay."[9]

But not so fast. Before moving beyond independence, we ought to clarify two points. The first is that American politicians had had to break through the crust of an exceedingly venerable tradition, and managed to do so in less than two decades with considerable originality and power.

It had been widely accepted in Western thought for a very long time that sovereignty within any political system was, first, indivisible, and, second, sifted down from the top. For the colonial assemblies somehow to divide and share sovereignty with the King and Parliament was inconceivable to the British; but to the colonists it seemed, increasingly, both natural and inevitable. The breach in 1775–76 occurred, in one sense, because the idea of dividing sovereignty was anathema to

8. Bernard Bailyn, ed., *Pamphlets of the American Revolution, 1750–1776* (Cambridge, Mass., 1965), 1:424; James R. Ferguson, "Reason in Madness: The Political Thought of James Otis," *William and Mary Quarterly* 36 (April 1979): 196–97. (Ferguson's italics.)

9. Quoted in Merrill Jensen, *The Founding of a Nation: A History of the American Revolution, 1763–1776* (New York, 1968), 125, 293, 509, 625. See also Rhys Isaac, "Dramatizing the Ideology of Revolution: Popular Mobilization in Virginia, 1774 to 1776," *William and Mary Quarterly* 33 (July 1976), esp. 364, 367, 369, 374, 377, 380–82; and Dirk Hoerder, "Socio-Political Structures and Popular Ideology, 1750s–1780s," in Erich Angermann et al., eds., *New Wine in Old Skins: A Comparative View of Socio-Political Structures and Values Affecting the American Revolution* (Stuttgart, 1976), 41–65.

George III and his ministers. It made sense to the Americans, however, partially because it was expedient and desirable by the 1770s, and partially because the structure of American politics had been highly decentralized and localized from the beginning.

The colonists had long inhabited a world in which power was parcelled out at various levels: imperial, provincial, county court or town meeting, parish or congregation. The "invention" of federalism in 1787 was simply the formal culmination of tendencies that had been underway for more than five generations. A pluralistic people scattered across a vast landscape found itself quite comfortable with the notion of divided sovereignty.[10]

The second point to be clarified is that even in the years 1774–87, the years when popular sovereignty became a standard refrain sung by a swelling chorus, even then there were doubters and cynics — enough to help justify Professor Morgan's caustic label, "the great political fiction." Leaders constantly reminded the people that they were sovereign. "It is your greatest Glory," one statement ran, "that you give Being to your Legislature, that from you they receive their political Existence." Spokesmen said what needed to be said in order to maintain control of a given situation; but we know from private correspondence and from overt behavior that the Whig elite, while accepting popular sovereignty in theory, did not intend to implement it any more fully than they had to.[11]

Having acknowledged the presence of cynicism and self-interest, however, we are equally obliged to recognize the deeply felt commitment to popular sovereignty that peaked between 1775 and 1780. We find it in May 1776, for example, when a committee of the Continental

10. See J. G. A. Pocock, *The Machiavellian Moment: Florentine Political Thought and the Atlantic Republican Tradition* (Princeton, N.J., 1975), esp. 368, 397, 409, 481, 525; Bernard Bailyn, *The Ideological Origins of the American Revolution* (Cambridge, Mass., 1967), 202–29; Gordon S. Wood, *The Creation of the American Republic, 1776–1787* (Chapel Hill, N.C., 1969), 362–89.

11. Isaac, "Dramatizing Ideology of Revolution," 376; Jensen, *Founding of a Nation*, 697; Morgan, "Great Political Fiction," 17. Clinton Rossiter made the point very well: "Conservatives considered the doctrine of popular sovereignty a useful notion that was not to be applied too literally in concrete situations. Radicals were inclined to accept popular sovereignty at face value." Rossiter, *Seedtime of the Republic: The Origin of the American Tradition of Civil Liberty* (New York, 1953), 427.

Congress called for new elections to state constitutional conventions with the proclamation that "the right of framing . . . is and ought to be in the People." Most of the original state constitutions and declarations of rights reaffirmed that statement. It was no fiction when George Mason wrote the following sentence for Virginia's Declaration of Rights in 1776: "That all power is vested in, and consequently derived from, the People; that magistrates are their trustees and servants, and at all times amenable to them."[12]

The Declaration of Independence twice invoked popular sovereignty. First, following the litany of abuses by King George III, it asserted that "the Legislative powers, incapable of Annihilation, have returned to the People at large for their exercise." And second, the delegates made it explicit when they declared the colonies independent "in the Name, and by Authority of the good People of these Colonies. . . ."[13]

Given the tendency in recent years to minimize the impact of John Locke on American Revolutionary thought, it seems pertinent, in passing, to observe that in Locke's work the people do become the supreme power when government disintegrates or is actually dissolved. American awareness of that belief may help to explain the growing frequency of references to and quotations from Locke between 1764 and 1776, and then once again in 1787.[14] (See also figures 4, 5, and 8.) It is too rarely noted that Thomas Jefferson commissioned a copy of Sir Godfey Kneller's famous portrait of Locke in the Royal Society, and that Jefferson's copy

12. Bernard Schwartz, ed., *The Roots of the Bill of Rights* (2d ed.; New York, 1980), 2:234, 237, 248, 303. See also Anon., *The People the Best Governors: Or a Plan of Government Founded on the Just Principles of Natural Freedom* (1776), in Charles S. Hyneman and Donald S. Lutz, eds., *American Political Writing during the Founding Era, 1760–1805* (Indianapolis, Ind., 1983), 1:390–400; Willi Paul Adams, *The First American Constitutions: Republican Ideology and the Making of the State Constitutions in the Revolutionary Era* (Chapel Hill, N.C., 1980), 50, 84, 135–37; Ronald M. Peters, Jr., *The Massachusetts Constitution of 1780: A Social Compact* (Amherst, Mass., 1978), 2–3, 5.

13. Merrill Jensen, ed., *The Documentary History of the Ratification of the Constitution.* Volume 1, *Constitutional Documents and Records, 1776–1787* (Madison, Wis., 1976), 74, 75.

14. Adams, *The First American Constitutions*, 139; J. G. A. Pocock, *The Ancient Constitution and the Feudal Law: A Study of English Historical Thought in the Seventeenth Century* (Cambridge, 1957), 236; Bailyn, ed., *Pamphlets of the American Revolution*, 1:434–35; Schwartz, ed., *Roots of the Bill of Rights*, 3:641; Jensen, ed., *The Documentary History of the Ratification of the Constitution.* Volume 2, *Ratification of the Constitution by the States: Pennsylvania* (1976), 472, 586.

has occupied a place of honor in the parlor at Monticello ever since he returned home from France in 1789.

III

During the decade that followed independence, well-meant reiterations of the conventional formulation continued to be voiced in newspaper squibs, sermons, and private correspondence. Surely Jefferson did not believe that he was perpetuating a fiction when he wrote the following to Richard Price, a leading English libertarian, in 1785: "The happiness of governments like ours, wherein the people are truly the mainspring, is that they are never to be despaired of."[15]

Indications did begin to appear, however, that some concerned citizens wondered whether popular government might need to be countermanded by various measures — used in moderation, to be sure — such as balanced government with clear separation of powers, an elitist upper house, a stronger executive with veto and appointive powers, and a life-tenured judiciary (all provisions of the Massachusetts constitution of 1780 which the electorate there had approved). A New Hampshire newspaper noted in 1783 that power in the hands of the people's "immediate representatives" in the lower houses of the legislatures was fundamentally no less dangerous than power in the hands of governors, senators, and judges.[16]

By the mid-1780s a variety of practical political problems elicited statements about popular sovereignty that were tainted either by self-interest or else by the onset of a new constitutional realism. Quarrels between groups of frontier settlers and land speculators in western North Carolina (the state of "Franklin") and in the unsuccessful Transylvania Colony (located in what became Kentucky) produced conflicting asser-

15. Jefferson to Price, Feb. 1, 1785, in Julian P. Boyd, ed., *The Papers of Thomas Jefferson,* 7 (Princeton, N.J., 1953), 630–31; Catherine L. Albanese, *Sons of the Fathers: The Civil Religion of the American Revolution* (Philadelphia, 1976), 41–43; Adams, *The First American Constitutions,* 129, 148.

16. Oscar and Mary Handlin, eds., *The Popular Sources of Political Authority: Documents on the Massachusetts Constitution of 1780* (Cambridge, Mass., 1966); Adams, *The First American Constitutions,* 125–26; Wood, *Creation of the American Republic,* 453.

tions about the relative merits of a popular referendum versus a less democratic way of choosing legislators based upon North Carolina's constitution.[17]

By that time, however, because the established states had selected some form of settled government—all variations on a single-minded republican theme—discussions in which "sovereignty" figured had less to do with the empowering will of the people and more to do with the apportioning of authority between state governments and the Confederation Congress.[18]

It was precisely that dual usage of sovereignty—and the potential for ambiguity between the two forms of emphasis—that prompted self-serving invocations of popular sovereignty by the Federalists in 1787. Support for state sovereignty and popular sovereignty need not conflict, and from 1776 until 1786 they rarely did. Nationalists at the Philadelphia Convention, however, changed all that. We know that Gouverneur Morris deliberately wrote the Preamble ("We the People" rather than "We the States") in order to undercut traditional claims by the thirteen sovereign polities. *Federalist* number 45, written by Madison, declared with facility that, "as far as the sovereignty of the States cannot be reconciled to the happiness of the people . . . let the former be sacrificed to the latter."[19]

From the Anti-Federalist point of view, such arguments (including Hamilton's in *Federalist* number 78 that judicial review would help to protect popular sovereignty as a reality) really amounted to sophistry. The Anti-Federalists insisted that the proposed redistribution of power within a "consolidated" union genuinely jeopardized liberty at the grassroots level. Luther Martin of Maryland, for example, pointed out that in 1776, "when the states threw off their allegiance to Great Britain, they had become independent of her *and each other.*" (My italics.) He explained that the people preferred "the Establishment of themselves into thirteen separate sovereignties instead of incorporating themselves into one."[20]

17. Richard B. Morris, *The Forging of the Union, 1781–1789* (New York, 1987), 225–26.
18. Adams, *The First American Constitutions,* 50.
19. Morris, *Forging of the Union,* 289–90; Jacob E. Cooke, ed., *The Federalist* (Middletown, Conn., 1961), 309.
20. Frederick R. Black, "The American Revolution as 'Yardstick' in the Debates on the

Before we plunge more fully into uses and applications of the concept in 1787–88, however, it should be noted that pointed references to *popular* sovereignty now become less common than they had been between 1775 and 1780. Taking all eighty-five numbers of *The Federalist,* for example, the unmodified word "sovereignty" appears thirty-three times; there are numerous references to state and national sovereignty; but none at all to popular sovereignty *per se,* though twenty-six usages of "popular government" or "popular assemblies" do appear.[21]

In *The Complete Anti-Federalist,* moreover (a thorough five-volume compilation), primary references to popular sovereignty occur rather casually in the *Letters of Cato* and the *Letters of Centinel.*[22] In fact, relatively few references to "sovereignty" appear in any form!

Even so, a fair number of speakers and writers discussed popular sovereignty in 1787, though they did so in diverse ways ranging from absolute sincerity to cunning casuistry. To those who were sincere, popular sovereignty was scarcely a "fiction." As Timothy Pickering, a Federalist, wrote privately:

> The *people* of the United States form *one nation* — that tis evidently their interest and desire to continue *one nation* — altho' for the more easy and advantageous management of the affairs of *particular districts,* the people have formed themselves into 13 seperate communities, or states; that the *people* of these distinct states, having certain common & general interests, it is obviously necessary that one common & general government should be erected, to manage those interests for the best good of the whole; that as all power resides originally in the *people,* they have a right to make such a distribution of it as they judge their true interests require.[23]

Other exuberant declamations do, on the other hand, seem to deserve Professor Morgan's designation as political fiction. I have in mind,

---

Constitution, 1787–1788," *Proceedings of the American Philosophical Society* 117 (June 1973): 175, 177.

21. See Thomas S. Engeman et al., eds., *The Federalist Concordance* (Middletown, Conn., 1980).

22. Herbert J. Storing, ed., *The Complete Anti-Federalist* (Chicago, 1981), 2:107, 138–39.

23. John P. Kaminski and Gaspare J. Saladino, eds., *The Documentary History of the Rati-*

for example, the rhetorical question posed by Philadelphia poet Francis Hopkinson: "What is the object exhibited to our contemplation?" he asked in 1788. "A WHOLE PEOPLE exercising its first and greatest power— performing an act of SOVEREIGNTY, ORIGINAL, and UNLIMITED."[24]

Speaking at South Carolina's ratifying convention in May 1788, Charles Pinckney fairly observed that "all the states have adhered, in their forms, to the republican principle, though they have differed widely in their opinions of the mode best calculated to preserve it."[25] Divergent views of the most suitable means to make republicanism operational lay at the heart of differences between advocates and opponents of the Constitution concerning popular sovereignty. Among the Anti-Federalist polemicists, for example, "Brutus" differentiated the diverse meanings of popular sovereignty under despotic government, democracy, and republicanism. "Centinel" insisted that republican government could exist only where citizens were virtuous and where property was equally divided: "in such a government the people are the sovereign and their sense or opinion is the criterion of every public measure."[26]

By contrast, "A Freeman," writing in the *Pennsylvania Gazette* early in 1788, asserted that the proposed Constitution did not threaten popular sovereignty because it provided explicit safeguards for republicanism.

> The states can alter and amend their several constitutions, provided they do not make them aristocratical, oligarchic or monarchical—for the foederal constitution restrains them from any alterations that are not *really republican*. That is, the sovereignty of the people is never to be infringed or destroyed.[27]

fication of the Constitution. Volume 14, *Commentaries on the Constitution: Public and Private,* 2 (Madison, Wis., 1983), 201. For comparable statements, see ibid., 84, 86, 203, 400, 444; and James Wilson, in Farrand, ed., *Records of the Federal Convention,* 1:179.

24. Hopkinson, *Account of the Grand Federal Procession, Philadelphia, July 4, 1788* . . . (Philadelphia, 1788), 14; and see the *Boston Gazette,* Oct. 29, 1787, in Kaminski and Saladino, eds., *The Documentary History of the Ratification of the Constitution.* Volume 13, *Commentaries on the Constitution: Public and Private,* 1 (1981), 511–12.

25. Schwartz, ed., *Roots of the Bill of Rights,* 4:748–49.

26. Kaminski and Saladino, eds., *The Documentary History of the Ratification of the Constitution,* 13:331, 418. See also ibid., 14:286–87, 307–8, 400.

27. Jan. 30, 1788, Kaminski and Saladino, eds., *The Documentary History of the Ratification of the Constitution.* Volume 15, *Commentaries on the Constitution: Public and Private,* 3 (1984), 509.

I do not believe that this Federalist pamphleteer indulged in writing "fiction" any more than "A Farmer," one of the most theoretical of the Anti-Federalist advocates, who published in several Philadelphia newspapers during April 1788. Sovereignty, he wrote,

> consists in the understanding and will of the political society, and this understanding and will is originally and inherently in the people; the society having rested it where and in what manner it pleases, he or they to whom it is delegated is the sovereign and is thus vested with the political understanding and will of the people for their good and advantage solely.
>
> The power of making rules or laws to govern or protect the society is the essence of sovereignty, for by this the executive and judicial powers are directed and controuled, to this every ministerial agent is subservient, and to this all corporate or privileged bodies are subordinate: this power not only regulates the conduct, but disposes of the wealth and commands the force of the nation. To keep this sovereign power therefore in due bounds hath fundamental laws, which we call constitutions and bills of rights, been made and declared.[28]

Curiously enough, this writer's emphasis upon the sequence by which the people entrust power to their chosen officials is not very different from the schematization sketched by George Washington to his nephew late in 1787:

> The power under the Constitution will always be in the People. It is entrusted for certain defined purposes, and for a certain limited period, to representatives of their own chusing; and whenever it is executed contrary to their Interest, or not agreeable to their wishes, their Servants can, and undoubtedly will be, recalled.[29]

I do not believe that Washington subscribed to political fictions either.

His statement did reflect, however, a more conservative perception of popular sovereignty that emerged and attracted many moderates during 1787–88: namely, power may be derived from the people; but once

28. April 16 and 23, 1788, in Storing, ed., *The Complete Anti-Federalist,* 3:182–83.

29. Washington to Bushrod Washington, Nov. 10, 1787, in Kaminski and Saladino, eds., *The Documentary History of the Ratification of the Constitution,* 14:86.

they elect officials, the power is transmitted; and the people may not resume it unless magistrates abuse their authority. Benjamin Rush so argued early in 1787. Edmund Pendleton of Virginia re-emphasized this point eight months later in a letter to James Madison:

> A Republic was inevitably the American form, and its Natural danger Pop Tumults & Convulsions. With these in view I read over the Constitution accurately; do not find a Trait of any Violation of the great Principles of the form, all Power being derived mediately or immediately from the People. . . . The People, the Origin of Power, cannot act personally, & can only exercise their Power by representation.[30]

Among other observers a genuine mistrust of democratic excesses, noticed ever since 1781, provoked calls, both quiet and explicit, for reasonable constraints to be placed upon popular sovereignty in 1787.[31] No individual followed this fine line more thoughtfully (though not without some vacillation) than James Madison. In so far as he promoted popular sovereignty during 1787–88, Madison did so primarily in order to restrain the excesses of state sovereignty, which he considered "the

30. Benjamin Rush, "Address to the People of the United States," Feb. 1, 1787, ibid., 13:47–49; Pendleton to Madison, Oct. 8, 1787, ibid., 354–55. See also three remarkably symptomatic statements. (1) Benjamin Rush in 1787: "The people of America have mistaken the meaning of the word sovereignty. . . . It is often said that 'the sovereign and all other power is seated *in* the people.' This idea is unhappily expressed. It should be—'all power is derived *from* the people.' They possess it only on the days of their elections. After this, it is the property of their rulers, nor can they exercise it or resume it, unless it is abused." (2) Judge Alexander Hanson of Maryland in 1787: "All power indeed flows from the people; but the doctrine that the power, actually, at all times, resides in the people, is subversive of all government and law." (3) This exchange of views between John and Samuel Adams in 1790: "Whenever I use the word 'republic' with approbation," John explained, "I mean a government in which the people have . . . an essential share in the sovereignty." His cousin responded with a question: "Is not the *whole* sovereignty, my friend, essentially in the people?" Samuel's mind-set hadn't changed since 1776; but John's had. Rush and Hanson are quoted in Wood, *Creation of the American Republic,* 373–74 and 370 respectively. For Noah Webster in the same vein (1788), see ibid., 376–78. The Adams exchange is quoted in Lance Banning, *The Jeffersonian Persuasion: Evolution of a Party Ideology* (Ithaca, N.Y., 1978), 96.

31. See George Mason to George Mason, Jr., June 1, 1787, in Rutland, ed., *Papers of George Mason,* 3:892; Morris, *Forging of the Union,* 285; Kaminski and Saladino, eds., *The Documentary History of the Ratification of the Constitution,* 13:396; Wood, *Creation of the American Republic,* 445–46.

mortal diseases of the existing constitution" (i.e., government under the Confederation). Nevertheless, by advocating an increase in power for the national government, and somewhat less for the states, Madison simultaneously took a step back from the strong commitment to "people power" that had characterized the mood of the 1770s.[32]

The reasonable balance that he hoped to achieve between republican populism and national stability is most clearly elaborated in *Federalist* number 37:

> The genius of Republican liberty, seems to demand on one side, not only that all power should be derived from the people; but, that those entrusted with it should be kept in dependence on the people, by a short duration of their appointments; and, that, even during this short period, the trust should be placed not in a few, but in a number of hands. Stability, on the contrary, requires, that the hands, in which power is lodged, should continue for a length of time, the same. A frequent change of men will result from a frequent return of electors, and a frequent change of measures, from a frequent change of men: whilst energy in Government requires not only a certain duration of power, but the execution of it by a single hand.[33]

Late in 1788 Madison confided to Philip Mazzei his anxiety about achieving a proper equilibrium between liberty, on the one hand, and social order under sound government on the other: "It is of infinite importance to the cause of liberty to ascertain the degree of it which will consist with the purposes of Society. An error on one side may be as fatal as on the other. Hitherto the error in the U.S. has lain in the excess."[34]

---

32. See Madison to Jefferson, March 19, 1787, in Robert A. Rutland et al., eds., *The Papers of James Madison,* 9 (Chicago, 1975), 318–19; Charles F. Hobson, "The Negative on State Laws: James Madison and the Crisis of Republican Government," *William and Mary Quarterly* 36 (April 1979): 217–18.

33. Cooke, ed., *The Federalist,* 234. See also ibid., 128–29, 250. For an excellent summary of Madison's wish to distribute sovereignty, and the arrangements that he envisioned for doing so, see Lance Banning, "The Practicable Sphere of a Republic: James Madison, the Constitutional Convention, and the Emergence of Revolutionary Federalism," in Richard Beeman et al., eds., *Beyond Confederation: Origins of the Constitution and American National Identity* (Chapel Hill, N.C., 1987), 187.

34. Madison to Mazzei, Dec. 10, 1788, in Rutland et al., eds., *Papers of James Madison,* 11 (Charlottesville, Va., 1977), 389.

Madison, along with a number of his contemporaries, continued to use, in 1787–88, the metaphor for popular sovereignty that had been pervasive ever since 1776: "the people are the fountain of power."[35] So too, on occasion, did James Wilson of Pennsylvania. But Wilson's distinctive contribution was the articulation of an alternative metaphor more appropriate to the new political realism that prevailed during the Constitutional Convention and subsequent contests over ratification. His crispest elaboration of that metaphor came on December 11, 1787, in Pennsylvania's convention.

> A free government has often been compared to a pyramid. This allusion is made with peculiar propriety in the system before you; it is laid on the broad basis of the people; its powers gradually rise, while they are confined, in proportion as they ascend, until they end in that most permanent of all forms. When you examine all its parts, they will invariably be found to preserve that essential mark of free governments — a chain of connection with the people.[36]

During June, even as the Grand Convention met, an anonymous piece appeared in a Philadelphia newspaper (possibly written by Wilson) which seemed so compelling that it was reprinted twenty-three times in ten colonies within three weeks. A lengthy extract appears on the epigraph page that precedes the Introduction to this book. The lines most pertinent to my discussion, however, are in the exhortation: "May this building rise like a pyramid upon the broad basis of the people! and may they have wisdom to see that if they delegate a little more power to their Rulers, the more liberty they will possess themselves. . . ."[37]

A fountain of power is active, energizing, perhaps even volatile, but

35. See Morris, *Forging of the Union*, 117 (for Pittsfield, Mass., in 1776); Adams, *The First American Constitutions*, 126 (for Stoughton, Mass., in 1779); Kaminski and Saladino, eds., *The Documentary History of the Ratification of the Constitution*, 13:432 (for Tench Coxe in 1787); and Jensen, ed., *The Documentary History of the Ratification of the Constitution*. Volume 3, *Ratification of the Constitution by the States: Delaware, New Jersey, Georgia, Connecticut* (1978), 569 (for Samuel Holden Parsons of Middletown, Conn., in 1788).

36. Jonathan Elliot, comp., *The Debates in the Several State Conventions on the Adoption of the Federal Constitution . . . (2d ed.; Philadelphia, 1891), 2:524. See also Morris, *Forging of the Union*, 279; Wood, *Creation of the American Republic*, 530.

37. From the *Philadelphia Independent Gazetteer*, June 27, 1787, in Kaminski and Saladino, eds., *The Documentary History of the Ratification of the Constitution*, 13:148.

above all continuous (barring a drought at the source). A pyramid of power seems more passive, stable, undergirding, and supportive of a much smaller concentration of mass at the apex. This transition in imagery tells much about the nuances of American political thought between 1776 and 1787. In the years following 1787 the pyramid achieved popularity among those who wished to convey other images as well: as part of the national iconography (represented on the dollar bill), and as a visual embodiment of the states as a solid collective entity. Here, for example, is a poem, written in 1792 by Philip Freneau, titled "The Pyramid of the Fifteen American States."

> No more let barbarous Memphis boast
>   Huge structures reared by servile hands —
> A nation on the Atlantic coast
>   Fettered no more in foreign bands,
> A nobler Pyramid displays
> Than Egypt's tyranny could raise.
>
> Columbia's sons, to extend the fame
>   Of their exploits to future years,
> No marble from the quarry claim,
>   But, soaring to the starry spheres,
> Materials seek in Jove's blue sky
> To endure when brass and marble die!
>
> Arrived among the shining host,
>   Fearless, the proud invaders spoil
> From countless gems, in æther lost,
>   These Stars, to crown their mighty toil:
> To heaven a Pyramid they rear
> And point the summit with a star.
>
> Old wasteful Time! though still you gain
>   Dominion o'er the brazen tower,
> On This your teeth will gnaw in vain,
>   Finding its strength beyond their power:
> While kindred stars in æther glow,
> This Pyramid will shine below![38]

38. Fred Lewis Pattee, ed., *The Poems of Philip Freneau: Poet of the American Revolution*, 3 (Princeton, N.J., 1907), 83.

IV

"Despite the celebration of popular sovereignty in America," Joyce Appleby has observed, "the sovereign people were restrained once the Constitution was ratified." I believe that Appleby is right, though partly, perhaps, for the wrong reasons. It was not so much the result of the difficult amending process, which she considers anti-populistic.[39] To emphasize procedural or structural impediments to democracy in the Constitution is to transmute effects into fundamental causes. The Constitution did not produce a contraction of democratic potential in American life. Rather, its very nature was itself a product of diminished faith in the capacity of ordinary folk to be a fully sovereign people.

Abundant evidence informs us that fears of a "democratical despotism" were widespread in 1787 — not merely within social elites, but even among optimistic Whigs who had expressed glowing enthusiasm for the political potential of common men back in the spirited mood of the 1770s. Growing signs of cynicism concerning human nature appeared in the press during those years of destiny, 1787–88. Sometimes the skeptical outlook was directed at rulers, sometimes at the ruled, and sometimes at both. As one young North Carolinian put it in a private letter: "if we expect a constitution the principles of which *cannot* be violated, we had better, instead of amending that proposed, amend the hearts of men."[40]

By over-emphasizing rather than simply acknowledging the existence of this awakened cynicism (or realism, if you will), we risk a genuine danger of distortion — one whose lineage dates back to the early years of this century when Progressive scholars, such as Charles Beard and J. Allen Smith, regarded the composition and promulgation of the United States Constitution as a conservative counter-revolution, a betrayal of the egalitarian principles of 1776.

In the following chapter I shall look more closely at 1776 as a point of departure, a basis for comparison with 1787. But in order to avoid

39. Appleby, "The American Heritage: The Heirs and the Disinherited," *Journal of American History* 74 (December 1987): 804.

40. David Witherspoon to James Iredell, April 3, 1788, in Griffith J. McRee, *Life and Correspondence of James Iredell*, 2 (New York, 1858), 222. See also Archibald Maclaine to Iredell, ibid., 219; Kaminski and Saladino, eds., *The Documentary History of the Ratification of the Constitution*, 13:131, 188.

the fallacy of Beard's over-reaction, it may be useful to make some historical comparisons. The same James Wilson who preferred the pyramid metaphor to the fountain nevertheless did *not* perceive popular sovereignty as a political fiction. Moreover, he believed in American distinctiveness — especially as revealed by comparative constitutionalism. Here is a key extract from Wilson's *Lectures on Law,* delivered at Philadelphia in 1790.

> Surely I am justified in saying, that the principles of the constitutions and governments and laws of the United States, and the republicks, of which they are formed, are materially different from the principles of the constitution and government and laws of England; for that is the only country, from the principles of whose constitution and government and laws, it will be contended, that the elements of a law education ought to be drawn. I presume to go further: the principles of our constitutions and governments and laws are materially *better* than the principles of the constitution and government and laws of England.
>
> Permit me to mention one great principle, the *vital* principle I may well call it, which diffuses animation and vigour through all the others. The principle I mean is this, that the supreme or sovereign power of the society resides in the citizens at large; and that, therefore, they always retain the right of abolishing, altering, or amending their constitution, at whatever time, and in whatever manner, they shall deem it expedient.[41]

Wilson had repeatedly insisted upon the connection between American distinctiveness and popular sovereignty. He formulated the relationship this way in his major address to the Pennsylvania ratifying convention:

> To control the power and conduct of the legislature by an overruling constitution, was an improvement in the science and practice of government reserved to the American States. Perhaps some politician, who has not considered, with sufficient accuracy, our political systems, would answer, that, in our governments, the supreme power was vested in the constitutions. This opinion approaches a step nearer to the truth, but does not reach it. The truth is, that, in our governments, the supreme, absolute, and uncontrollable power remains in the people.

41. Robert G. McCloskey, ed., *The Works of James Wilson* (Cambridge, Mass., 1967), 1:77.

As our constitutions are superiour to our legislatures; so the people
are superiour to our constitutions.[42]

Modern authorities on European constitutionalism in general, and
on British in particular, are basically in accord with Wilson's formulation. Robert R. Palmer has noted numerous similarities in constitutional developments throughout the Western world during the final
quarter of the eighteenth century. But in the United States, he contends, the constitutional convention "embodied the sovereignty of the
people. The people chose it for a specific purpose, not to govern, but
to set up institutions of government. . . . Such was the theory, and it
was a distinctively American one. European thinkers, in all their discussion of a political or social contract, of government by consent and of
sovereignty of the people, had not clearly imagined the people as actually contriving a constitution and creating the organs of government.
They lacked the idea of the people as a constituent power."[43]

In Great Britain, throughout the 1780s and '90s, perceptions of the
British constitution remained in disarray. Edmund Burke tried to reconcile parliamentary sovereignty with sensible concessions to the opinions
and feelings of political reformers; but he failed. Nothing even close
to a consensus emerged from diverse views concerning the nature of
mixed and balanced government; or the legitimacy of opposition; or
the proper role of political influence; or the function of public opinion
in constitutional matters.[44] A characteristic statement, articulated in 1792
by the Earl of Stair, is simply unimaginable in the American context.

Our *Constitution*, although it may not be an *excellent* one, is truely,
in its execution, an *happy* one, because *Corruptions*, of various kinds,
are so fortunately blended, as, in great measure, to correct each de-
fect; and the whole is subject to the *controul* of *Publick Opinion*: This,
although no part of the nominal Constitution is paramount to all![45]

42. Ibid., 770. See also 304, 309–33, and 405.

43. Palmer, *The Age of the Democratic Revolution: A Political History of Europe and America,
1760–1800*. Volume I, *The Challenge* (Princeton, N.J., 1959), 214–15.

44. H. T. Dickinson, *Liberty and Property: Political Ideology in Eighteenth-Century Britain*
(New York, 1977), 215; J. A. W. Gunn, "Influence, Parties and the Constitution: Changing
Attitudes, 1783–1832," *The Historical Journal* 17 (June 1974): 301–28.

45. John Dalrymple, Earl of Stair, *Parliamentary Reform, as it is called, Improper in the Present*

Moreover, public opinion in Great Britain did not influence constitutionalism there so swiftly as it did in the United States, where popular sovereignty as fiction *and* as reality would become far more determinative.[46]

Unfortunately, public opinion does not necessarily translate into public understanding; and John Adams conveyed the limitations of popular sovereignty—owing to the limits of popular knowledge—in a letter that he sent to Thomas Jefferson in 1821: "I think a free Government is necessarily a complicated Piece of Machinery," Adams wrote, "the nice and exact Adjustment of whose springs, wheels and weights are not yet well comprehended by the Artists of the Age and still less by the People."[47]

Adams may have been pessimistic, but not excessively so. The paradox of popular sovereignty, regardless of its form as a fountain or a pyramid, is that all too often it has not been well-grounded in public information concerning the Constitution.[48]

One character in an American political cartoon from 1790 declares: "It is bad to have a gouty Constitution."[49] So true; but where popular sovereignty is supposed to reign supreme, yet remains ill-informed, even a constitution that is *not* gouty is likely to limp along rather lamely.

State of This Country (London, 1792), 15; J. A. W. Gunn, *Beyond Liberty and Property: The Process of Self-Recognition in Eighteenth-Century Political Thought* (Kingston and Montreal, 1983), 289–90.

46. See chapter four below and Norman H. Clark, *Deliver Us from Evil: An Interpretation of American Prohibition* (New York, 1976), 107.

47. Adams to Jefferson, May 19, 1821, in Lester J. Cappon, ed., *The Adams-Jefferson Letters* (Chapel Hill, N.C., 1959), 2:573.

48. See Michael Kammen, *A Machine That Would Go of Itself: The Constitution in American Culture* (New York, 1986), esp. chs. 1–3; and Giuseppe Buttà, *Sovranità: Diritto di Voto e Rappresentanza in Massachusetts e South Carolina, 1776–1860* (Milan, 1988).

49. See Michael Kammen, "'The Promised Sunshine of the Future': Reflections on Economic Growth and Social Change in Post-Revolutionary New York," in Manfred Jonas and Robert V. Wells, eds., *New Opportunities in a New Nation: The Development of New York After the Revolution* (Schenectady, N.Y., 1982), 119.

This essay was honed and revised following its presentation as a paper at four seminars during the autumn of 1987. The host institutions that provided congenial environments for discussion were Washington and Lee University in Lexington, Virginia; Southeastern Massachusetts University in North Dartmouth, Massachusetts; Towson State University in Towson, Maryland; and the National Conference of State Humanities Councils, held in Chicago.

1. "Triumph of Liberty," an engraving by Peter C. Verger after John Francis Renault (1796). The allegorical figure at the center, "Genius of America," is attended by Liberty, Justice, Peace, and Plenty. (Print Collection, Miriam and Ira D. Wallach Division of Art, Prints & Photographs, The New York Public Library, Astor, Lenox and Tilden Foundations.)

2. "William Pitt" by Charles Willson Peale (1768). Commissioned by a group
of gentlemen in Westmoreland County, Virginia, this painting originally hung
in the home of Richard Henry Lee; then in the state capitol of Richmond;
then in the county court house; and now in the county museum. Pictured
as a republican Roman consul, Pitt is speaking in defense of the American
colonies. His left hand holds a copy of Magna Carta, and his right points to
a statue of "British Liberty" that is trampling on New York's petition concerning the Stamp Act. The allegorical busts supporting the altar on which
the flame of liberty burns represent John Hampden and Algernon Sydney. A
popular mezzotint based upon this painting bore the legend: "Worthy of Liberty, Mr. Pitt Scorns to invade the Liberties of other People." (Westmoreland
34   County Museum, Montross, Va.)

3. Furnace (or "warming machine") made in London in 1770 and sent to Williamsburg, where it was used by the Virginia House of Burgesses until 1782. Note the scroll depicting Magna Carta beneath the figure of Justice. (Wallace Gallery, Colonial Williamsburg Foundation.)

4. John Locke desk and bookcase (ca. 1760s), Chew Estate, Germantown, Pennsylvania. Although the desk itself was made by Benjamin Randolph, the bust of John Locke may have been carved by Hercules Courtenay, an Irish immigrant to Philadelphia. (Courtesy of Cliveden of the National Trust for Historic Preservation.)

5. Desk and bookcase made in 1765 by Benjamin Randolph of Philadelphia for the Poulson family. The bust at the top represents John Locke. (Collection of the Diplomatic Reception Rooms, United States Department of State.)

6. Fireback from Virginia (made in York County, South Carolina, at the Aera Furnace in 1778), with the motto "Liberty or Death." (Collection of the Museum of Early Southern Decorative Arts, Winston-Salem, N.C.)

7. The Newmarket (Shenandoah County), Virginia, silk regimental battleflag (1799), with the motto "Liberty or Death." (Collection of the Museum of Early Southern Decorative Arts, Winston-Salem, N.C.)

8. "Samuel Vaughan" by Robert Edge Pine (ca. 1787). Vaughan, an English friend of Benjamin Franklin who visited the United States during the mid-1780s, sat for this portrait in Philadelphia holding a copy of the new Constitution. The volume beneath it says "Locke" on its spine. (American Philosophical Society, Philadelphia.)

9. "Thomas McKean and His Son, Thomas Jr.," by Charles Willson Peale (1787). McKean served as chief justice of Pennsylvania, 1777–99, and as governor, 1799–1809. (Philadelphia Museum of Art. Bequest of Phebe Warren McKean Downs.)

10. "George Washington," a painted wood sculpture by William Rush (1814). The scroll in Washington's right hand is presumably the Constitution; the document beneath his right foot most likely represents the Articles of Confederation. The statue was displayed at Independence Hall for Lafayette's visit in 1824. The City of Philadelphia purchased it in 1831. (Independence National Historical Park Collection, Philadelphia.)

Two

"We Began the Dance"

The Reel of Revolutions and Constitutions in American Culture, 1775–1788

HOW CAN WE best comprehend the relationship between American political discourse in 1787–88, when the federal Constitution was written and ratified, and in 1775–76, when independence was broached and the first state constitutions started to emerge? Although that question has not been entirely neglected — indeed, it has provided the stimulus for some superb scholarship — it still stands as a major challenge to our full understanding of the genesis of the United States as a nation and of values that have guided the conduct of public affairs over the past two centuries.

Since so much has already been written that pertains to these issues in one way or another, I feel obliged to begin by raising another question: why after two hundred years do we not yet know the answer to such a question? Because my response is going to be a complex one, I will open with a schematization of obstacles to comprehension as I see them. They can be regarded in three categories: enduring historiographical cul-de-sacs; unintended as well as deliberate obfuscation in the very language of politics; and ideological or intellectual agendas, both liberal and conservative, that have caused observers to see only the part of the story that suited their predisposition or the nation's mood at a given moment in time.

After a brief discussion of those matters, I want to shift (through a series of sections) to an inquiry into the meaning of three concepts in the minds of Americans who were active in public life between, let us say, 1775 and 1788. The components of my triptych are sovereignty, liberty, and equality. I would like to examine each concept in terms of two paramount considerations: first, to what degree did it change or remain constant between 1775 and 1788? And second, to what extent was its perceived meaning affected by American attitudes toward human nature?

Time and temperament — or perhaps I should say, the passage of time and the variability of temperaments — seem to me in retrospect to have been profoundly influential. The revolutionaries' reading of human nature and political possibilities (a highly *responsive* reading during those thirteen years of grave uncertainty) powerfully reshaped the meanings that they ascribed to sovereignty, liberty, and equality. Inevitably, then, their attitudes also shaped the federal Constitution created two hundred years ago.

I

Historiography. Was the "climate of opinion" in 1787–88 conservative by contrast to the more radical or egalitarian mood of 1776? Did a reactionary counter-revolution help to precipitate and set the tone for the framers who gathered at the Grand Convention in Philadelphia? Did that illustrious group produce an instrument of government that basically betrayed the humane and hopeful principles so eloquently articulated by Thomas Jefferson in the Declaration of Independence? And finally, is the period 1775–88 therefore most striking on account of its ideological discontinuities?[1]

From time to time, ever since the days of the most disaffected Anti-Federalists, an affirmative answer to those queries has been heard from

1. For the historiographical evolution of these issues, see Benjamin Fletcher Wright, *Consensus and Continuity, 1776–1787* (Boston, 1958), esp. ch. 3, "Was the Constitution Reactionary?"; Merrill Jensen, *The American Revolution within America* (New York, 1974), esp. ch. 4, "The Revolution of 1787"; and Earl Latham, ed., *The Declaration of Independence and the Constitution* (rev. ed.; Boston, 1956).

labor leaders, abolitionists, social critics active during the Progressive era of the early twentieth century, and some modern scholars who remain persuaded that Charles A. Beard, J. Allen Smith, Vernon L. Parrington, and other Progressive analysts were fundamentally right even though their evidence may have been selectively arranged or manipulated in an unseemly way.[2]

Even so, a contrary case can be made (a perspective that has been *at least* equally pervasive) that most of the moderate abolitionists, such as James G. Birney, saw no inconsistency between the Declaration of Independence and the Constitution with regard to slavery. Some of them, in fact, even insisted that the fundamental principles of the Declaration had been incorporated into the Constitution.[3] Careful scrutiny by modern scholars, moreover, suggests that a strong argument can be made for fundamental ideological continuities between 1776 and 1787.[4]

The point that has been largely neglected, however, and one that I must insist upon, is that continuity (combined with consistency) epitomizes the dominant view held by most Americans even remotely interested in these issues during the last two centuries. The fact that they constitute a majority—and are therefore indicative of the mainstream perspective, as it were—does not mean that they are altogether correct. It merely means that we must take seriously the evidence and arguments that sustained their view. In the nineteenth century, for example, John Quincy Adams, John C. Calhoun, Edward Everett, and

2. See, for example, Alpheus T. Mason, ed., *The States Rights Debate: Antifederalism and the Constitution* (Englewood Cliffs, N.J., 1964); Jackson Turner Main, *The Antifederalists: Critics of the Constitution, 1781–1788* (Chapel Hill, N.C., 1961); Horace Greeley, *The American Conflict: A History of the Great Rebellion . . .* , 1 (Hartford, Conn., 1864), 53; Henry Wilson, *History of the Rise and Fall of the Slave Power in America* (Boston, 1872), esp. ch. 4, "Compromises of the Constitution," and 54–56, 115–17; Ronald G. Walters, *The Antislavery Appeal: American Abolitionism after 1830* (Baltimore, Md., 1976), 137; and H. Arnold Bennett, *The Constitution in School and College* (New York, 1935), 77–78.

3. See Aileen S. Kraditor, *Means and Ends in American Abolitionism: Garrison and His Critics on Strategy and Tactics, 1834–1850* (New York, 1969), 190; Judith A. Baer, *Equality Under the Constitution: Reclaiming the Fourteenth Amendment* (Ithaca, N.Y., 1983), 61–62.

4. See Ralph Lerner, "The Constitution of the Thinking Revolutionary," and Gordon S. Wood, "Interests and Disinterestedness in the Making of the Constitution," in Richard Beeman et al., eds., *Beyond Confederation: Origins of the Constitution and American National Identity* (Chapel Hill, N.C., 1987), 67, 81, 109.

Supreme Court Justice Joseph Story shared a firm belief that the great charter produced in 1787 embodied a fulfillment of the spirit of 1776.[5]

A century later, during the 1920s and '30s, that assumption still predominated in American thought.[6] Its roots may be found in James Madison's private correspondence with Jefferson in 1787, and in Madison's public explication of the Constitution during 1787–88. As he wrote in *Federalist* number 39 (January 16, 1788): "The first question that offers itself is, whether the general form and aspect of the government be strictly republican? It is evident that no other form would be reconcileable with the genius of the people of America; [and] with the fundamental principles of the revolution. . . ."[7]

The language of politics. Early in the nineteenth century, following his retirement from a long career in public affairs throughout the Revolutionary era, Edmund Randolph of Virginia wrote an essay in which he commented upon the distinctive characteristics of written and unwritten constitutions. He offered this noteworthy observation in passing: "It should not be forgotten that the spirit of a people will in construction frequently bend words seemingly inflexible, and derange the organization of power."[8] The most obvious example of his point may be found among the nationalists of 1787 who grabbed for themselves the inappropriate label of "Federalists," thereby leaving their opponents with the awkwardly negative name "Anti-Federalists." A less familiar aspect of the same phenomenon will be found in the Federalist pretense that they had brilliantly concocted the concept of federalism *de novo* as

5. See Pauline R. Maier, "The Road Not Taken: Nullification, John C. Calhoun, and the Revolutionary Tradition in South Carolina," *South Carolina Historical Magazine* 82 (January 1981): 17; R. Kent Newmyer, *Supreme Court Justice Joseph Story: Statesman of the Old Republic* (Chapel Hill, N.C., 1985), 189.

6. See *New York Times*, Feb. 15, 1929, p. 24.

7. Madison to Jefferson, March 19, 1787, in Robert A. Rutland et al., eds., *The Papers of James Madison*, 9 (Chicago, 1975), 318; Jacob E. Cooke, ed., *The Federalist* (Middletown, Conn., 1961), 250; Lance Banning, "The Practicable Sphere of a Republic: James Madison, the Constitutional Convention, and the Emergence of Revolutionary Federalism," in Beeman et al., eds., *Beyond Confederation*, 182, 187.

8. Randolph, "Essay on the Revolutionary History of Virginia," in Bernard Schwartz, ed., *The Roots of the Bill of Rights* (2d ed.; New York, 1980), 2:248.

a response to newly recognized American political needs in 1787. In reality, of course, the concept of federalism had its roots in the Anglo-American colonial relationship; and the very word "federalism" was frequently used during the years from 1776 until 1787.[9]

The phrase "popular sovereignty" offers an equally instructive example, as we have seen. Although the Anti-Federalists were fundamentally more sympathetic to that concept's quintessential meaning, it appears only twice in the corpus of Anti-Federalist literature (1787–88). On the first of these occasions, "Cato," writing in the *New York Journal*, asserted the following:

> In democratic republics the people collectively are considered as the sovereign—all legislative, judicial, and executive power, is inherent in and derived from them. As a people, your power and authority have sanctioned and established the present government—your executive, legislative, and judicial acknowledge it by their public acts—you are again solicited to sanction and establish the future one—yet this Caesar mocks your dignity and laughs at the majesty of the people.[10]

"Caesar" and the sardonic Federalists enjoyed the last laugh, however, by frequently and persuasively invoking popular sovereignty in rather superficial (even insincere) ways and thereby affecting the illusion that they were the true heirs and bearers of this basic principle that had emerged so resoundingly in 1776.[11]

Similarly, when one reads Hamilton in *Federalist* number 32 one cannot help feeling that sham had crept into (or perhaps even permeated) political discourse: "As the plan of the Convention aims only at a partial Union or consolidation, the State Governments would clearly retain all the rights of Sovereignty which they before had and which were not by that act *exclusively* delegated to the United States." In his heart of

9. See Don Higginbotham, "James Iredell and the Origins of American Federalism," in George G. Suggs, Jr., ed., *Perspectives on the American Revolution* (Carbondale, Ill., 1977), 107, 112, 114; Catherine Drinker Bowen, *Miracle at Philadelphia: The Story of the Constitutional Convention, May to September 1787* (Boston, 1966), 62, 85, 102, 104, 139, 198, 238, 281, 283.

10. Herbert J. Storing, ed., *The Complete Anti-Federalist* (Chicago, 1981), 2:107. See also ibid., 138–39 (the "Letters of Centinel," prepared in Philadelphia by the most prolific Anti-Federalist writer).

11. See Jensen, *American Revolution within America*, 214–15.

hearts, Hamilton wanted a truly national government built upon sub-
ordinate states. His words, quoted above, were meant to cajole—perhaps
even to deceive. Although Madison genuinely believed that the government created in 1787 would be "partly national, partly federal," he explicitly echoed Hamilton in writing *Federalist* papers 40 and 62.[12]

If the language of politics that was deployed to vindicate the Constitution puzzles *us* at times, consider how ordinary citizens and delegates to the state ratifying conventions must have felt. How were they
to interpret the more ambiguous provisions of the Constitution, never
mind the framers' intent? Rarely in the history of American public life
has essential language been misused with such caprice.

Ideology and selective use of evidence. Just as radical and liberal ideologues
have followed the lead of Beard and others in emphasizing discontinuity
and the development of a reactionary counter-revolution in 1787, so conservative scholars have gone too far in the opposite direction by need-
lessly and naively insisting upon continuity and wondrous fulfillment
from 1776 through 1787. The following illustration from an important
essay by the late Martin Diamond is characteristic.

> Far from its being retrograde with respect to democracy, it was in
> the Constitution that the American people finally made the commit-
> ment to the democratic form of government. It was in the Consti-
> tution that they chose the democratic form as the means by which
> to secure the Declaration's equal liberty for themselves and their
> posterity.[13]

Although Diamond makes several quite valuable points in that essay,
to which I shall return, he insists upon continuity and the realization
in 1787 of particular principles established in 1776—but at the peril of
flagrantly ignoring evidence that undermines his argument.

It is my belief that single-minded emphases upon either continuity or
discontinuity are misguided. Some scholars have been led to overesti-
mate the alterations that occurred between 1776 and 1787 by utilizing

---

12. Cooke, ed., *The Federalist,* 199–200, 262, 417.
13. Diamond, "The American Idea of Equality: The View from the Founding," *Review
of Politics* 38 (July 1976): 315–16.

a transformational model that traces a shift from egalitarianism as an ideal to "social control." Many of the scholars disposed in this radical direction acknowledge the existence of domestic constitutional conflict in 1787, but not in 1776. The problem with their reductive comparison, however, is that Whigs and Tories in 1776 are not the proper analogue to Federalists and Anti-Federalists. A closer parallel may be found in the conflict that occurred in 1775–76 between Radical and Moderate Whigs. Therein lies the basis for more meaningful comparisons between 1776 and 1787.

There has been a curious tendency to neglect some other significant continuities as well. It is the conventional wisdom to assume, for example, that Shays' Rebellion provoked an unprecedented scare among the respectable strata of society in 1786–87; that it evoked, in fact, a determination to quell disorder and to introduce stabilizing institutions that would be capable of controlling those elements in the populace with levelling (or worse, anarchistic) tendencies.[14] Too easily overlooked, somehow, is the Whig apprehension of anarchy in 1775–76, when in diverse localities the "canaille" rose up and closed county courts, created locally elected "people's courts" and "people's militias." Shays' Rebellion had its roots in comparable events that terrified high-toned Whigs a decade earlier.[15]

Similarly, we seem to remember that most Anti-Federalists, and even many Federalists, felt apprehensive in 1787–88 because the newly minted Constitution lacked a bill of rights. Nevertheless we somehow manage to forget the passion for state bills of rights that prevailed between 1776 and 1780. Counties in North Carolina, for instance, instructed their delegates to the 1776 provincial congress that there must be a bill of rights "containing the rights of the people and individuals which shall never be infringed in any future time by the lawmaking power or other derived powers in the state."[16]

14. See Don Higginbotham, *The War of American Independence: Military Attitudes, Policies, and Practice, 1763–1789* (New York, 1971), 447–49; Edmund S. Morgan, *The Birth of the Republic, 1763–1789* (Chicago, 1956), 128; H. James Henderson, *Party Politics in the Continental Congress* (New York, 1974), 400–404.

15. See Jensen, *American Revolution within America,* 51–52, 65, 74; Robert J. Taylor, *Western Massachusetts in the Revolution* (Providence, R.I., 1954).

16. Nov. 1, 1776, in William L. Saunders, ed., *The Colonial Records of North Carolina,* 10 (Raleigh, N.C., 1890), 870 a–d.

What provided George Mason of Virginia with greater pride (though less subsequent recognition) than drafting Virginia's Declaration of Rights between May 20 and June 12, 1776? What seemed most immediately incumbent upon John Adams when he composed the highly successful Massachusetts constitution of 1780 (the oldest written constitution still in continuous existence anywhere in the world)? Answer: not Part Two, "The Frame of Government," but Part One, "A Declaration of the Rights of the Inhabitants of the Commonwealth of Massachusetts," specified in no less than thirty articles.[17]

If we have underestimated some of the basic continuities, however, we have also paid too little attention to some of the profoundly important shifts that took place. Whereas the most resounding rhetorical note to be heard in 1775–76 was *liberty*, it would be partly supplanted during the later 1780s by *sovereignty*. This assertion requires prudent qualification as well as precision. One word-concept did not simply displace the other; but at each critical "moment" in time one appears to have been key while the other seems secondary albeit still meaningful. Two sentences that appeared in a Philadelphia newspaper early in September 1787 convey the very essence of this transition. "The year 1776 is celebrated (says a correspondent) for a revolution in favor of *Liberty*. The year 1787, it is expected, will be celebrated with equal joy, for a revolution in favor of *Government*."[18]

It is imperative for us to notice that the writer used the word "revolution" in describing both 1776 *and* 1787. Contemporaries recognized them as different yet necessary and complementary transformations. Both of these revolutions looked to republicanism in government as being fundamental. No continuity was more rudimentary than that. But the revolution of 1776 was made, above all, in the sacred name of liberty,[19]

---

17. Robert A. Rutland, ed., *The Papers of George Mason, 1725–1792* (Chapel Hill, N.C., 1970), 1:274–91; Ronald M. Peters, Jr., *The Massachusetts Constitution of 1780: A Social Compact* (Amherst, Mass., 1978), 196–201.

18. *Pennsylvania Gazette*, Sept. 5, 1787, p. 3.

19. See Nathan O. Hatch, *The Sacred Cause of Liberty: Republican Thought and the Millennium in Revolutionary New England* (New Haven, Conn., 1977); and carefully peruse the titles of the pamphlets and broadsides, chronologically arranged in Peters, *The Massachusetts Constitution of 1780*, 227–37.

whereas the one that took place almost a dozen years later was made, as we well know, to promote energy and stability in government.[20]

Less obvious, though equally important, was the American quest for security in 1787–88. Polemicists such as "Cato III" would quote from Montesquieu in their newspaper squibs: "Political liberty consists in security, or at least in the opinion we have of security." When Hugh Williamson appealed to the voters of North Carolina on behalf of ratification, he emphasized "those parts of the new system which are of the greatest import — those which respect the general question of liberty and safety. . . ."[21]

The word "security" appears in the *Federalist* papers no fewer than 116 times. Hamilton would contend in *Federalist* number 1, for instance, that "the vigour of government is essential to the security of liberty." In *Federalist* number 45, James Madison connected the revolutions of 1776 and 1787 by linking liberty with security (in a manner foreign to the literature of 1776):

> Was then the American revolution effected, was the American confederacy formed, was the precious blood of thousands spilt, and the hard earned substance of millions lavished, not that the people of America should enjoy peace, liberty and safety; but that the Governments of the individual States, that particular municipal establishments, might enjoy a certain extent of power, and be arrayed with certain dignities and attributes of sovereignty?[22]

The unacceptable alternative suggested at the close of that passage calls to our attention yet another major shift in American political thought

20. The word "energy" appears twenty-five times in *The Federalist,* for example, and "energetic" five times. The word "stability" appears twenty-three times. See Thomas S. Engeman et al., eds., *The Federalist Concordance* (Middletown, Conn., 1980).

21. Cato III, published in the *New York Journal* on October 25, 1787, appears in John P. Kaminski and Gaspare J. Saladino, eds., *The Documentary History of the Ratification of the Constitution.* Volume 13, *Commentaries on the Constitution: Public and Private,* 1 (Madison, Wis., 1981), 475; Williamson, "Remarks on the New Plan of Government printed in the *State Gazette* of North Carolina" [1788], in Paul Leicester Ford, ed., *Essays on the Constitution of the United States Published During Its Discussion by the People, 1787–1788* (Brooklyn, N.Y., 1892), 404–5.

22. Cooke, ed., *The Federalist,* 5, 309.

between 1775–76 and 1787–88: a redefinition of the most viable meaning of sovereignty. More on that redefinition in a moment.

Meanwhile, it seems appropriate for us to recognize that a precarious equilibrium between liberty and security has remained central in
American public life and discourse ever since James Madison's day. As
Justice William O. Douglas wrote in 1958, after a decade of high anxiety about the prospect of domestic Communist conspiracies: "In recent
years as we have denounced the loss of liberty abroad we have witnessed
its decline here. We have, indeed, been retreating from our democratic
ideals at home. We have compromised them for security reasons."[23] A
decade later Americans were willing, indeed eager, to diminish the civil
liberties protected by their Bill of Rights in order to achieve enhanced
security against alleged criminals in what suddenly seemed to be a very
disorderly domestic scene.[24]

II

In 1943, when Chief Justice Harlan Fiske Stone drafted an opinion for
one of the Japanese internment cases, he referred to Americans as a "free
people whose institutions are founded upon the doctrine of equality."
Fourteen years earlier, however, Henry W. Taft, member of a prestigious
law firm and the brother of Chief Justice William Howard Taft, had insisted in an essay written for the *New York Times* that the most representative political philosophers of the 1770s and '80s were never "deluded"
into thinking that all men are created equal. That had been a naive dogma
that Thomas Jefferson smuggled in from France.[25] Which of the two
views, Stone's or Taft's, most closely approximated historical reality?

Generalizations are always risky, but particularly so in this instance

23. Douglas, *The Right of the People* (Garden City, N.Y., 1958), 12.

24. See Richard C. Cortner, *The Supreme Court and the Second Bill of Rights: The Fourteenth Amendment and the Nationalization of Civil Liberties* (Madison, Wis., 1981), 263–64; Allen J.
Matusow, *The Unraveling of America: A History of Liberalism in the 1960s* (New York, 1984),
chs. 7 and 14; Paul L. Murphy, *The Constitution in Crisis Times, 1918–1969* (New York, 1972),
427–57.

25. Stone is quoted in Peter Irons, *Justice at War: The Story of the Japanese-American Internment Cases* (New York, 1983), 236; *New York Times*, Feb. 15, 1929, p. 24.

because source materials survive that support both positions. Where, then, will the *preponderant* weight of existing evidence be found? Unfortunately the evidence cannot be calibrated and measured. Unquestionably, voices arose from time to time that echoed the insistence heard in western Pennsylvania (in 1764) upon "our natural privileges of freedom and equality."[26] Although comparable claims emerged in several cities and in western Massachusetts after 1776, two prominent authorities on American ideology in this period think that outright egalitarianism was the minority position.[27] I believe that they are correct. Occasional murmurs arose in 1787 that the real purpose of the American Revolution had been to secure "the rights of equality." Late in June, however, when Charles Pinckney of South Carolina argued that America had already become an egalitarian society, James Madison and Alexander Hamilton both scoffed at the notion.[28]

It is my contention that they scoffed because they found the assertion implausible, either as prospect or as reality, even in a society that cherished republicanism. The great majority of American Whigs perceived an inescapable tension between equality and liberty, and opted for the latter when confronted with a choice. They assumed that social inequality arose from an unavoidably uneven distribution of ability and property. Ordinarily, Alexander Hamilton was *not* a representative American thinker; but when he spoke in the Constitutional Convention on June 26, he articulated a widely shared view:

> Nothing like an equality of property existed. . . . An inequality would exist as long as liberty existed, and that it would unavoidably result from that very liberty itself. This inequality of property constituted the great & fundamental distinction in society.[29]

26. Jensen, *American Revolution within America,* 96.

27. Willi Paul Adams, *The First American Constitutions: Republican Ideology and the Making of the State Constitutions in the Revolutionary Era* (Chapel Hill, N.C., 1980), 148; Gerald Stourzh, *Fundamental Laws and Individual Rights in the 18th-Century Constitution* (Claremont, Calif. [Bicentennial Essay Number 5], 1984), 8–9.

28. Jensen, *American Revolution within America,* 82–84, 118. See also Willmoore Kendall and George W. Carey, *The Basic Symbols of the American Political Tradition* (Baton Rouge, La., 1970), ch. 5.

29. Max Farrand, ed., *The Records of the Federal Convention of 1787* (2d ed.; New Haven,

Although Hamilton's two sentences had *implications* for equality of persons, which is what ordinarily comes to mind when we discuss equality, his explicit concern was equality of property. I find occasional references to "equal representation," though not without controversy.[30] I also encounter this sort of statement, made in 1776: "Few opportunities have ever been offered to mankind of framing an entire constitution of government upon equitable principles."[31]

It seems especially symptomatic that during this period we find fewer references to the abstract noun "equality" than to modifiers related to it. The most frequent use of "equal" as an adjective occurred, interestingly enough, in conjunction with liberty. Just as significant, perhaps, it seems to have been utilized by Whigs of every persuasion in 1776, and by Federalists as well as Anti-Federalists in 1787–88. John Adams liked the phrase "equal liberty and public virtue"; it appears often in his writings. In 1776 he favored making "the acquisition of land easy to every member of society" in order to achieve equal liberty and public virtue. Nevertheless, he opposed social levelling and expressed anxiety at the prospect of "an equal voice" for all in politics. Equal liberty did not mean social or full political equality in the mind of John Adams.[32]

Even so, their commitment to equal liberty contributed to the founders' belief in American exceptionalism. Like many other American Whigs, Adams felt certain that the enhancement of freedom was an essential aspect of America's destiny. As he wrote to Patrick Henry in June 1776: "The decree is gone forth, and it cannot be recalled, that a more equal liberty than has prevailed in other parts of the earth, must

---

1937), 1:424. Hamilton's observation was a revisionist elaboration upon a statement made by David Hume in his essay titled "Idea of a Perfect Commonwealth" (1752): "The natural equality of property favors liberty." Quoted in Douglass Adair, "'That Politics May Be Reduced to a Science': David Hume, James Madison, and the Tenth Federalist," in Trevor Colbourn, ed., *Fame and the Founding Fathers: Essays by Douglass Adair* (New York, 1974), 99.

30. See "An Act Providing for a More Equal Representation in the General Court," May 4, 1776, in Oscar and Mary Handlin, eds., *The Popular Sources of Political Authority: Documents on the Massachusetts Constitution of 1780* (Cambridge, Mass., 1966), 78; Jensen, *American Revolution within America*, 66, 95–96, 105.

31. From the *Pennsylvania Journal*, quoted in Jensen, *American Revolution within America*, 54.

32. Adams to James Sullivan, May 26, 1776, in Charles Francis Adams, ed., *The Works of John Adams*, 9 (Boston, 1854), 376–78.

be established in America." Just two weeks earlier Virginia's Revolutionary Convention had called for the preparation of a Declaration of Rights and the kind of constitution "as will be most likely to . . . secure substantial and equal liberty to the people."[33]

During the ensuing twelve years, that phrase recurred in New England and in the South, among radicals as well as moderates. What, exactly, did they mean by it? It is not easy to say with assurance; but so far as I can tell they did not have in mind a redistribution of property, or social equality, or equal moral worth. Nevertheless, morality of a particular sort mattered very much — namely, civic virtue — because they rarely mention equal liberty without including virtue in the same breath. Here is Gilbert Livingston, for example, speaking at New York's ratifying convention in June of 1788. He looks back upon the last dozen years.

> Our present Congress cannot serve longer than three years in six: they are at any time subject to recall. These and other checks were considered as necessary at a period which I choose to honor with the name of *virtuous*. Sir, I venerate the spirit with which every thing was done at the trying time in which the Confederation was formed. America had then a sufficiency of this virtue to resolve to resist perhaps the first nation in the universe, even unto bloodshed. What was her aim? Equal liberty and safety. What ideas had she of this equal liberty? Read them in her Articles of Confederation.[34]

It is my impression that "equal liberty," a ubiquitous phrase in those days, essentially meant that all persons should be protected against repressive behavior by government at any level. If civil liberty meant the protection by government of one's person and property against encroachment by a private individual, or a group, or the polity itself, if political

33. Adams to Henry, June 3, 1776, ibid., 387; Journal of the Virginia Convention, May 18, 1776, in Schwartz, ed., *Roots of the Bill of Rights*, 2:237. For the ambiguity of equality (as a theory) on account of slavery (as a reality), see the important material cited in Richard B. Morris, *The Forging of the Union, 1781–1789* (New York, 1987), 182–83.

34. June 24, 1788, in Jonathan Elliot, comp., *The Debates in the Several State Conventions on the Adoption of the Federal Constitution* . . . (2d ed.; Philadelphia, 1891), 2:287. For context, see Rowland Berthoff, "Peasants and Artisans, Puritans and Republicans: Personal Liberty and Communal Equality in American History," *Journal of American History* 69 (December 1982): 584.

liberty meant the right to participate in public affairs (vote, hold office, serve on a jury, etc.),[35] and if personal liberty meant freedom of conscience and of physical movement,[36] then "equal liberty" meant approximately what Justice William O. Douglas had in mind when he frequently cited the "right to be let alone" during the 1950s and '60s.[37] All persons were equally entitled to immunity from unwarranted governmental intervention in their lives.[38]

Equality then, like democracy, is a word-concept whose meaning and value were perceived more narrowly two hundred years ago than they are today. Equality under the law (or equal treatment by those who administer the law), and "equal protection of the laws" as specified in Section One of the Fourteenth Amendment, are values that we have come to cherish.[39] We cannot assume, however, that they enjoyed the same systematic salience back in the days when we began the dance.

III

By comparison, the centrality of *liberty* in American thought at that time is overwhelming. As Samuel Adams succinctly wrote to Elbridge Gerry in 1785: "our government at present has liberty for its object."[40]

---

35. See Michael Kammen, *Spheres of Liberty: Changing Perceptions of Liberty in American Culture* (Madison, Wis., 1986), 17–18, 33–36.

36. See "Personal Liberty and American Constitutionalism," chapter three below.

37. Douglas, *Right of the People*, Lecture II, "The Right to Be Let Alone."

38. For the later 1770s, see Peters, *The Massachusetts Constitution of 1780*, 72–73. For James Monroe, *Some Observations on the Constitution* (1788), see Storing, ed., *The Complete Anti-Federalist*, 5:281. For the period 1776–89 in its entirety, see Stourzh, *Fundamental Laws and Individual Rights*, 20–22.

39. See Carl B. Swisher, *Stephen J. Field: Craftsman of the Law* (Washington, D.C., 1930), 414; Richard Kluger, *Simple Justice: The History of Brown v. Board of Education and Black America's Struggle for Equality* (New York, 1975), 630. Cf. Kenneth L. Karst, "Equality as a Central Principle in the First Amendment," *University of Chicago Law Review* 43 (Fall 1975): 20–68.

40. Quoted in Jensen, *American Revolution within America*, 152. See Patrick Henry's remark to the Virginia state ratifying convention on June 5, 1788: "You are not to inquire how your trade may be increased, nor how you are to become a great and powerful people, but how your liberties can be secured; for liberty ought to be the direct end of your government." Elliot, comp., *Debates in the Several State Conventions*, 3:44–45. Later, in the same long speech, he added: "The most valuable end of government is the liberty of the inhabitants" (62).

Invocations of liberty, in one form or another, flourished from 1765 onward and became an endless incantation after 1774. Some writers linked liberty with the "protection of property," whereas others tied it to the "pursuit of happiness." Still others took a position that linked populism with accusations of agnosticism. Here is an anonymous extract from the Bridgeton, New Jersey, *Plain Dealer* early in 1776: "I believe many people who Bellow very loud about Liberty neither know, nor care anything about it, farther than it serves their own private interest."[41]

It should come as no surprise that Americans living through that era would have more to say about liberty than about equality. The concept of liberty had a much longer lineage in Western political thought, and especially in British discourse ever since the seventeenth century. In 1791 Edmund Burke could persuasively invoke "the pedigree of our liberties"; and a few years later Edward Gibbon would retrospectively label his lifetime an "age of light and liberty."[42] By contrast, the political concept of equality was in its infancy in 1776, and perhaps only entered adolescence during the age of the French Revolution.[43]

A critical question for purposes of this essay, however, might very well be phrased as follows: the nature of liberty when "we began the dance" — change or continuity? There is, to be sure, abundant evidence to support the latter. First, an endless parade of political pamphlets with metaphorical or militant titles: *A Chariot of Liberty* (1774), *The Meridian of Liberty* (1774), *In Defence of Liberty* (1777), and *The Struggle for Liberty* (1779).[44] Second, assertions by proud patriots that they lived in an era in which "the great principles of liberty are better understood" (1779).[45] And third, the on-going appearance of objects in American

41. Elliot, comp., *Debates in the Several State Conventions,* 3:71; "The Political Creed of Shary O'Brion," [Bridgeton, N.J.] *Plain Dealer,* Jan. 22, 1776, in Larry R. Gerlach, ed., *New Jersey in the American Revolution, 1763–1783: A Documentary History* (Trenton, N.J., 1975), 176–77.

42. See J. G. A. Pocock, *The Ancient Constitution and the Feudal Law: A Study of English Historical Thought in the Seventeenth Century* (Cambridge, 1957), 16–17, 189, 211, 218, 221, 231, 232, 241; Christopher Hill, "The Norman Yoke," in Hill, *Puritanism and Revolution* (London, 1964), 57, 60, 62, 65–67, 71, 74, 76, 83, 86, 88, 94, 100; Dero A. Saunders, ed., *The Autobiography of Edward Gibbon* (New York, 1961), 175.

43. See J. R. Pole, *The Pursuit of Equality in American History* (Berkeley, Calif., 1978), 38–58.

44. See Peters, *The Massachusetts Constitution of 1780*, 227–36.

45. Samuel Stillman, *A Sermon Preached before the Honorable Council and House of Repre-*

material culture that indicate a steady commitment to the notion of America as liberty's true and predestined home.[46] (See the frontispiece and figures 1, 6, 7, 14, and 15.)

There is equally abundant evidence, however, to suggest that significantly substantive changes occurred that were all too apparent in the eyes of beholders. Documentation is readily found in the pressures that arose during the 1780s to revise the first state constitutions. Republicans in Pennsylvania, for instance, urged that popular sovereignty be divided and distributed more widely in order to prevent "the danger to liberty from an aristocracy."[47] (A bit of sophistry on their part, to be sure.)

Federalists and Anti-Federalists alike seemed to agree in 1788 that the meaning of liberty in American life had altered. They disagreed sharply, however, concerning the nature of the change. Speaking against the Constitution with great passion at Virginia's ratifying convention, Patrick Henry compared the glorious days of 1765–76 (as he remembered them) with the lamentable deterioration of American values by 1787–88. "When the American spirit was in its youth, the language of America was different: liberty, sir, was then the primary object." Speaking the next month in New York's ratifying convention—a situation that called for considerable politesse—Alexander Hamilton offered a retrospective view of what had gone wrong since the dance began: "The zeal for liberty became predominant and excessive. In forming our Confederation, this passion alone seemed to actuate us."[48]

---

sentatives of the State of Massachusetts-Bay, at Boston, May 26, 1779 (Boston, 1779), 8. On February 21, 1783, James Madison rose in Congress and gave a speech in which he defended general revenues as being consistent with "the principles of liberty and the spirit of the constitution." Quoted in Lance Banning, "James Madison and the Nationalists, 1780–1783," *William and Mary Quarterly* 40 (April 1983): 245. I find it fascinating that Madison seems to have felt (and communicated) the sense of a national constitution at least five years before the "genuine article" came into being.

46. See Kammen, *Spheres of Liberty,* 54–64, 117–23.

47. See Gordon S. Wood, *The Creation of the American Republic, 1776–1787* (Chapel Hill, N.C., 1969), 445–46. See also Robert F. Williams, "The Influence of Pennsylvania's 1776 Constitution on American Constitutionalism During the Founding Decade" *Pennsylvania Magazine of History and Biography* 112 (January 1988), 25–48.

48. Elliot, comp., *Debates in the Several State Conventions,* 3:53–54; 2:301.

James Madison characterized the altered sense of liberty most carefully as both a blessing and a problem; and he said so publicly as well as in confidence. Writing in *Federalist* number 63 (March 1, 1788), he noted that "liberty may be endangered by the abuses of liberty, as well as by the abuses of power." That became a recurrent refrain for Madison; and in October of 1788, when he ruminated upon Jefferson's draft of a constitution for Virginia, Madison speculated that "the experience of every state in the Union proves that the real danger to liberty lurks in a mistaken zeal for too much liberty."[49]

Between 1783 and 1787 especially, those interested in the so-called "new science of politics" increasingly recognized that adjustments were needed in the delicate relationship between liberty and government. Despite the comment made by Edmund Pendleton of Virginia, a Federalist, that "there is no quarrel between government and liberty," the growing sense of tension between the two required a fundamental redefinition of sovereignty in 1787 that proceeded at two levels.[50]

One of those levels, at which a redistribution of sovereignty between the states and a more potent national government took place, has been treated quite thoroughly by scholars.[51] It required a redefinition of sovereignty in geopolitical terms that was exceedingly controversial in 1787–88, remained intermittently so until the later 1860s, and perpetuates polemics concerning the nature of federalism even today.

IV

When the Articles of Confederation were stitched together late in the 1770s, no consensus existed concerning the proper configuration of sovereignty. A small minority of nationalists, like Hamilton, wanted

49. Cooke, ed., *The Federalist*, 428; Observations on the "Draught of a Constitution for Virginia," in Rutland et al., eds., *Papers of James Madison*, 11 (Charlottesville, Va., 1977), 294, n. 1.

50. Elliot, comp., *Debates in the Several State Conventions*, 3:36–37; [Noah Webster], *Examination into the Leading Principles of the Federal Constitution Proposed by the Late Convention* . . . (Philadelphia: Prichard & Hall, 1787), 40–41.

51. In addition to references cited in the notes that follow, see Jensen, *American Revolution within America*, 138, 140–41; Adams, *The First American Constitutions*, 144–47; Wood, *Creation of the American Republic*, 544–45.

the new government to have "complete sovereignty." But the likes of North Carolina's Thomas Burke, much more in tune with the majority, managed to incorporate the principle of state sovereignty into the Articles of Confederation.[52]

The framers of the Constitution, however, regarded that conceptualization as being fundamentally flawed. Several of them said so during the Convention, and Madison conveyed the point concisely in *Federalist* number 42: the Articles had "inconsiderately endeavored to accomplish impossibilities; to reconcile a partial sovereignty in the Union, with compleat sovereignty in the States."[53]

Anti-Federalists, needless to say, expressed just the opposite view. Sam Adams resented the new Constitution because "the idea of sovereignty in these states must [inevitably] be lost." George Mason, speaking in the Virginia ratifying convention on June 16, 1788, flatly feared "the annihilation of the state governments."[54] One year earlier, active at the Convention in Philadelphia, Mason had insisted that the people at large, rather than state legislatures, should ratify the new instrument of government.[55] Mason urged that course of action because he had a genuinely populistic tendency; but his insistence brings to our attention once again the *other* aspect of sovereignty that was subtly changing between 1775–76 and 1787–88: the concept of popular sovereignty.

Its trajectory is the most difficult to trace among our three concepts (equality, liberty, and sovereignty) because the Federalists, in their public utterances, continued to reiterate an enthusiastic commitment to popular sovereignty. James Wilson of Pennsylvania did, for example; and Edmund Randolph, the wishy-washy Governor of Virginia, made an uncharacteristically decisive declaration that the new Constitution

---

52. Hamilton to James Duane, Sept. 3, 1780, in Harold C. Syrett, ed., *The Papers of Alexander Hamilton*, 2 (New York, 1961), 401; Jack N. Rakove, *The Beginnings of National Politics: An Interpretive History of the Continental Congress* (New York, 1979), 172, 176.

53. Farrand, ed., *Records of the Federal Convention*, 1:466; Cooke, ed., *The Federalist*, 284–85. See also Frederick R. Black, "The American Revolution as 'Yardstick' in the Debates on the Constitution, 1787–1788," *Proceedings of the American Philosophical Society* 117 (June 1973): 174, 182.

54. Adams to Richard Henry Lee, Dec. 3, 1787, quoted in Jensen, *American Revolution within America*, 212–13; Rutland, ed., *Papers of George Mason*, 3:1053. See also Mason to George Mason, Jr., May 20, 1787, ibid., 880.

55. See Rutland, ed., *Papers of George Mason*, 3:929–30, 949–50, 957.

"is more a government of the people, than the present Congress ever was," and consequently the new charter was "more in favour of liberty."[56] The Constitution does, after all, begin with those euphonious words, "We the People."

In 1776 citizens commonly read or listened to variations on this theme: "the people are the fountain of power."[57] A dozen years later Americans still heard popular sovereignty being invoked and applied in diverse ways, though often hedged about or qualified. John Adams raised the core question as early as 1776: "It is certain, in theory, that the only moral foundation of government is, the consent of the people. But to what an extent shall we carry this principle?"[58] With the passage of time, doubts and doubters proliferated. In 1784, for instance, a clergyman in New Hampshire conceded that government originates from the people, but then revealed a pervasive mood that some might call cynicism, but others realism: "let the people be taught . . . that they are not able to govern themselves."[59]

For us to recognize that such sentiments could be openly expressed amidst the gospel of republicanism in 1784 makes it easier to comprehend the candor with which Roger Sherman of Connecticut spoke in the Convention of 1787: "The people immediately should have as little to do as may be about the Government. They want information and are constantly liable to be misled."[60]

Salus populi suprema lex esto. "Let the good of the people be the supreme law." That phrase would be invoked in 1764, by James Otis, for example, with increasing popularity in 1775–76, and even in 1787–88. What seems most revealing, however, is that the source of its validation shifted, and so did the nuances with which it was used. Otis, a radical patriot, derived the principle from natural law. Federalists, by contrast, who literally appropriated the phrase from their foes, derived it from the political theory of republicanism.[61] Upon re-reading the ten

56. Wood, *Creation of the American Republic,* 534–35, 599.
57. Jensen, *American Revolution within America,* 65, 78, 92, 102. And see chapter one above.
58. Adams to James Sullivan, May 26, 1776, in Adams, ed., *Works of John Adams,* 9:375.
59. Quoted in Jensen, *American Revolution within America,* 155.
60. Farrand, ed., *Records of the Federal Convention,* 1:48 (May 31, 1787).
61. Otis, *The Rights of the British Colonies Asserted and Proved* (1764), in Bernard Bailyn,

words of the translation, however, we should notice that they lend themselves to divergent strains of republicanism ranging from the most radical assertion of popular sovereignty to the most elitist belief that the
better sort were intended to rule in the interests of the people, who
lacked both the knowledge and the self-restraint to govern themselves
wisely. What might explain this degree of interpretive deviance? The
inescapable answer will be found in varied views of human nature.

V

There has been a simplistic and misleading tendency to assume that
most Americans shared a fundamentally positive view of human nature
in 1776, but subsequently retreated to a negative or skeptical one by
1787. Although there is ultimately some validity to that generalization,
what actually happened is considerably more complex. Yes, it is true
that in 1776 John Adams declared that the achievement of liberty was
contingent upon society's exemplifying virtue, and that in 1787 he believed that virtue lay beyond reach. "It is the insatiability of human
passions," he wrote the next year, "that is the foundation of all government. Men are not only ambitious, but their ambition is unbounded:
they are not only avaricious, but their avarice is insatiable. . . . This fact
being allowed, it will follow that it is necessary to place checks upon
them all."[62]

There has been an unfortunate propensity to seize upon bold but
uncomplicated or ambiguous pronouncements, such as this one by the
New Jersey Assembly in 1775: "The true foundation of American liberty is in human nature. . . ."[63] I am persuaded that throughout the
Revolutionary era large numbers of Americans mistrusted the intentions or the integrity of those who held, or aspired to hold, political
power, yet glorified the good will and virtue of ordinary "chaps." Such

ed., *Pamphlets of the American Revolution, 1750–1776* (Cambridge, Mass., 1965), 1:424 and 719
n. 3; Wood, *Creation of the American Republic*, 532–36.

62. Lerner, "The Constitution of the Thinking Revolutionary," 59–60; Adams to Thomas
Brand-Hollis, April 5, 1788, in Adrienne Koch, ed., *The American Enlightenment: The Shaping
of the American Experiment and a Free Society* (New York, 1965), 195.

63. Quoted in Jensen, *American Revolution within America*, 33.

a distinction helped to make *and keep* popular sovereignty a viable basis for their political philosophy.[64] Most Anti-Federalists, moreover, continued to emphasize that dichotomy during the heated debates of 1787–88.[65]

Some, however, admitted apprehension in their private correspondence. The Federalists, by comparison, expressed their doubts in statements designed to persuade others that the new Constitution warranted approval, as well as in letters that derided the "dignity of human nature" in general and scoffed at farmers and mechanics who possessed "too little virtue to govern themselves."[66] David Witherspoon's comment in his letter to James Iredell of North Carolina can be noted as representative of such views: "if we expect a constitution the principles of which *cannot* be violated, we had better, instead of amending that proposed, amend the hearts of men."[67]

Some of the most prominent Federalist polemicists, such as Hamilton, were arrogant snobs who regarded the "ordinary depravity of human nature" as normative among the ill-born and uneducated. Other advocates of constitutional reform in 1787 were more tentative, and acknowledged the existence of disagreement. "Is it not time," one asked, "for politicians to begin to consider mankind *as they are* and not *what they ought to be?*—If I mistake not, this is the rock upon which many of our best writers on government have split."[68]

James Madison meticulously considered mankind as it had been his-

---

64. For illustrations, see ibid., 40, 43, 47, 54, 67; George Mason's address to the Virginia ratifying convention, June 4, 1788, in Rutland, ed., *Papers of George Mason,* 3:1052.

65. See, e.g., Monroe, *Some Observations on the Constitution* (1788), in Storing, ed., *The Complete Anti-Federalist,* 5:281.

66. See Richard Henry Lee to George Mason, May 15, 1787, in Rutland, ed., *Papers of George Mason,* 3:877–78; [Webster], *Examination into the Leading Principles of the Federal Constitution,* 47; and the revealing letters quoted in Jensen, *American Revolution within America,* 156, 164–65.

67. Witherspoon to Iredell, April 3, 1788, in Griffith J. McRee, *Life and Correspondence of James Iredell,* 2 (New York, 1858), 222. See also George Washington to John Jay, Aug. 1, 1786: "We have errors to correct; we have probably had too good an opinion of human nature in forming our confederation. Experience has taught us, that men will not adopt and carry into execution measures the best calculated for their own good, without the intervention of a coercive power." In John C. Fitzpatrick, ed., *The Writings of George Washington,* 28 (Washington, D.C., 1938), 502.

68. Hamilton, *Federalist* number 78, in Cooke, ed., *The Federalist,* 529–30; Extract of a

torically, but more particularly Americans as they had behaved in the intense partisanship of republican politics ever since 1775. He did not differentiate between officeholders and ordinary folks because he harbored skepticism regarding human nature in both. Officeholders had to be reined in because they were motivated by ambition and personal interest. Simultaneously, however, Madison feared the "common passion" of a majority. Hence that most memorable passage in *Federalist* number 51, no less remarkable because it is now so familiar: "What is government itself but the greatest of all reflections on human nature? If men were angels, no government would be necessary. If angels were to govern men, neither external nor internal controuls on government would be necessary."[69]

VI

It is all too easy to read through the proceedings of the Constitutional Convention, plus the printed debates and accounts of the state ratifying conventions that ensued, and discern a configuration of statements critical of three overlapping aspects of contemporary politics: an excess of democracy (i.e., "mixed government" in disequilibrium); malfunctioning state constitutions; and, as one North Carolina delegate wrote home from Philadelphia in 1787, legislative bodies that seemed out of control.[70] One way to interpret the framers' response is to call the Constitution they produced a reactionary document, and the government they created counter-revolutionary.

---

letter from a gentleman in Washington county to his friend in Albany, *Albany Gazette,* June 21, 1787, in Kaminski and Saladino, eds., *The Documentary History of the Ratification of the Constitution,* 13:143.

69. Cooke, ed., *The Federalist,* 349. See also ibid., 343; Jensen, *American Revolution within America,* 115–16.

70. Jensen, *American Revolution within America,* 169 (Edmund Randolph of Virginia); Farrand, ed., *Records of the Federal Convention,* 1:134–35 (Madison on June 6, 1787); Kaminski and Saladino, eds., *The Documentary History of the Ratification of the Constitution,* 13:144; Richard Dobbs Spaight to James Iredell, Aug. 12, 1787, in McRee, *Life and Correspondence of Iredell,* 2:168–70; Schwartz, ed., *Roots of the Bill of Rights,* 4:948 (Archibald Maclaine in the North Carolina ratifying convention, July 29, 1788).

Most contemporaries did not see it that way, however. Nor did those who looked back a generation later with the benefit of hindsight. Nor should we today. In order to understand why, we might fruitfully reflect upon two retrospective passages that were alluded to earlier in this essay. The first is that remarkably positive judgment written by the normally negative John Adams.

> The last twenty-five years of the last century, and the first fifteen years of this, may be called the age of revolutions and constitutions. We began the dance, and have produced eighteen or twenty models of constitutions. . . . they are, no doubt, the best for us that we could contrive and agree to adopt.[71]

The second is that pithy comparison that appeared in the *Pennsylvania Gazette*: "The year 1776 is celebrated . . . for a revolution in favor of *Liberty*. The year 1787 . . . will be celebrated . . . for a revolution in favor of *Government*."[72]

One conclusion, at the very least, seems inescapable: what the framers did at Philadelphia was ultimately a revolutionary act. Both Federalists as well as Anti-Federalists said so, even though they placed very different value judgments upon the outcome and its necessity.[73] With the passage of time, however, the United States Constitution swiftly achieved legitimacy, and that would make it possible for an American president, such as Martin Van Buren, to look back upon the founders' mode of proceeding as "an heroic though perhaps a lawless act."[74]

A second conclusion seems equally inescapable. People who witnessed the events of the years from 1776 to 1787, and then participated in the "grand republic" that ensued, did not question for a minute the notion

71. Adams to James Lloyd, March 29, 1815, in Koch, ed., *American Enlightenment*, 223.

72. *Pennsylvania Gazette*, Sept. 5, 1787, p. 3.

73. See "Letters of Centinel" (Nov. 8, 1787), in Storing, ed., *The Complete Anti-Federalist*, 2:156–57; Patrick Henry in the Virginia convention (June 5, 1788), in Elliot, comp., *Debates in the Several State Conventions*, 3:44; Hugh Williamson, "Address to the freemen of Edenton and the County of Chowan . . . ," in Ford, ed., *Essays on the Constitution of the United States*, 404. See also Rakove, *The Beginning of National Politics*, 390–91.

74. Van Buren, *Inquiry into the Origin and Course of Political Parties in the United States* (New York, 1867), 50.

of American exceptionalism. They referred endlessly to the "genius" of America, and more particularly to the "political genius" of Americans. This was true of Federalists and Anti-Federalists alike.[75]

American exceptionalism, as they understood it, was not so much rooted in the American character, which remained inchoate in 1787, but rather in American government, which had been republican since 1776.[76] Were the American constitutions really different from that of Great Britain? James Wilson of Pennsylvania answered with a resounding "yes."[77] (William R. Davie, one of North Carolina's delegates to the Convention in Philadelphia, kept urging James Iredell to read John Adams' *Defence of the Constitutions of Government of the United States of America* despite the fact that Adams' work was "one continued encomium on the British constitution."[78])

And finally, did the United States Constitution cause Americans to have a distinctive political system? The only conceivable response to that question would be resoundingly affirmative. The framers regarded the system they had designed as a unique hybrid. Oliver Ellsworth of Connecticut called it "partly national; partly federal," and James Madison deliberately parroted that satisfying phrase. He also called their creation a compound republic.[79]

With too little opportunity to achieve a detached perspective, Anti-Federalists in 1788 wondered whether such a "consolidated" compound could possibly endure. By 1805, even critical partisanship dared not re-

75. See Archibald Maclaine to James Iredell, March 4, 1788, in McRee, *Life and Correspondence of Iredell,* 2:219; Luther Martin, "Information to the General Assembly of the State of Maryland," March 30, 1788, in Storing, ed., *The Complete Anti-Federalist,* 2:48; Patrick Henry in the Virginia ratifying convention, June 9, 1788, in Elliot, comp., *Debates in the Several State Conventions,* 3:162.

76. See "Essays by a Farmer," [Baltimore] *Maryland Gazette,* April 8, 1788, in Storing, ed., *The Complete Anti-Federalist,* 5:59–60; Charles Pinckney in the South Carolina ratifying convention, May 14, 1788, in Schwartz, ed., *Roots of the Bill of Rights,* 4:748.

77. Wilson, *Lectures on Law* (1790), in Robert G. McCloskey, ed., *The Works of James Wilson* (Cambridge, Mass., 1967), 1:77, 309–33; Wilson, "Speech Delivered on 26th November, 1787, in the Convention of Pennsylvania," ibid., 2:777.

78. Davie to Iredell, June 19 and Aug. 6, 1787, in McRee, *Life and Correspondence of Iredell,* 2:161, 168.

79. Farrand, ed., *Records of the Federal Convention,* 1:468; 2:8; Banning, "Practicable Sphere of a Republic," 169, 177, 187.

press a more optimistic response. "Notwithstanding the apprehensions which have pervaded the minds of many," wrote Mercy Otis Warren, "America will probably long retain a greater share of freedom than can perhaps be found in any other part of the civilized world."[80] She said that in her *History.* In this instance, an apprehensive reading of history contained the seed of sound prophecy.

80. "Observations Leading to a Fair Examination of the System of Government Proposed by the Late Convention . . . in a Number of Letters from the Federal Farmer" (no. 8, Jan. 3, 1788), in Storing, ed., *The Complete Anti-Federalist,* 2:273; Warren, *History of the Rise, Progress and Termination of the American Revolutuion* (1805), ibid., 6:216.

This essay was commissioned for presentation in Winston-Salem, North Carolina, on March 19, 1987, as part of the Tocqueville Forum of Wake Forest University.

I wish to thank Professor Robert L. Utley, Jr., Director of the Forum, President James Ralph Scales, Mrs. Patsy Gray, and Professor Cyclone Covey for making my stay at Wake Forest so pleasant.

Three

Personal Liberty and American Constitutionalism

THE HISTORY of liberty in American thought and culture is endlessly enigmatic yet intriguing. Part of the fascination lies in the fact that liberty has meant different things to different people, depending upon the period and its circumstances. In 1985 I developed a schematization for comprehending the history of liberty in American life. It emphasized the distinctive way that we have tended to conceptualize liberty at any given time in relation to other essential attributes or qualities in our political culture. Consequently I stressed the tension between liberty and authority in the age of colonization; liberty and property during the eighteenth century; the dialectic of liberty and order for the nineteenth; and liberty and justice in our own era. I concluded that liberty and equality—a linkage that has long been problematic and precarious—might very well become the determinative nexus for liberty in the years ahead.[1]

Throughout my research I encountered various particular applications of the concept of liberty, such as natural liberty, civil liberty, political liberty, and liberty of conscience. Defining each of those phrases

---

1. Kammen, *Spheres of Liberty: Changing Perceptions of Liberty in American Culture* (Madison, Wis., 1986).

presented no problem because the writers who employed them were usually quite explicit. And wherever authors failed to define their terms fully, a careful look at context would solve the problem. One variation eluded me, however, because its usage seemed so protean and vague. At any given moment, even, different people meant different things when they invoked the notion of "personal liberty." Nevertheless, the concept turns up with such frequency from the age of the founders to our own time that for me it became a special challenge and a personal agenda, as it were, to trace and identify what appeared to be the most elusive single facet of the history of liberty in American constitutional thought: the notion of personal liberty.

My mission in this essay, therefore, is an attempt to fill a fairly curious gap in our constitutional and cultural history. The reader will find that the meaning of personal liberty has evolved historically—which should hardly surprise anyone. We also learn that, at any given time, the notion of personal liberty has been appealed to by radicals, moderates, and conservatives—even though customarily each group attached its own particular meaning or interpretation to the phrase.

Finally, I find that in a very real sense personal liberty was a concept that had not one, but two, fairly concrete connotations during the age of the American Revolution. Subsequently it has become a curious catch-all. Without anyone's quite intending it to happen, "personal liberty" came to be used very casually and carried quite disparate meanings. (It could also be invoked in ways that were utterly meaningless.) During the past thirty-five years, however, from the era when Communist witch-hunts were commonplace, through the sexual revolution (with an increasing premium being placed upon the "right" of privacy), personal liberty has been transformed from a sometimes vapid *omnium gatherum* to a meaningful aspect of discourse about values that many Americans hold dear. Personal liberty no longer means what it did in 1787. The vagaries of its transformation reveal much about the history of American thought during the past two centuries.

I

It seems appropriate to begin with the vexing idiosyncracies of the concept. There has been a tendency for public figures, when obliged to deliver addresses on ceremonial or commemorative occasions, or even in politically controversial situations, to refer to personal liberty without defining it or providing a sufficient texture that might clarify its meaning in the instance at hand. That was the case when Charles Evans Hughes addressed the annual meeting of the American Bar Association in 1925 ("our cherished traditions of personal liberty"); when Franklin Delano Roosevelt delivered a fireside chat on the radio right after the announcement of his "Court-packing" plan in 1937 ("the present attempt by those opposed to progress to play upon the fears of danger to personal liberty"); and when Lewis F. Powell, president of the American Bar Association in 1965, spoke at Runnymede in ceremonies honoring the 750th anniversary of Magna Carta.[2]

Even serious works by modern students of American culture and constitutionalism are more likely to use the phrase casually than precisely.[3] Contemporary journalism rarely bothers to define the term. Thus *The Nation's* lead editorial in June 1986 expressed concern because the Supreme Court seemed to be moving in a conservative direction: "Its rulings on personal liberty and equality reach into every corner of our national life, from abortion to affirmative action."[4] And throughout the nineteenth century writers were likely to use such phrases as "individual liberty" and "personal freedom" in a manner that seemed synonymous with personal liberty.[5]

Americans engaged by constitutional issues during the later 1780s

2. Hughes, "Liberty and Law," *Report of the 48th Annual Meeting of the American Bar Association* (Baltimore, Md., 1925), 187; Roosevelt on March 9, 1937, in Samuel I. Rosenman, comp., *The Public Papers and Addresses of Franklin D. Roosevelt*, 6 (New York, 1941), 132; *New York Times*, June 16, 1965, p. 8. See also William J. Brennan, Jr., "Landmarks of Legal Liberty," in Bernard Schwartz, ed., *The Fourteenth Amendment: Centennial Volume* (New York, 1970), 2.

3. See Peter Clecak, *America's Quest for the Ideal Self: Dissent and Fulfillment in the 60s and 70s* (New York, 1983), 12; Laurence H. Tribe, *God Save This Honorable Court: How the Choice of Supreme Court Justices Shapes Our History* (New York, 1985), 11–12, 35; Richard Kluger, *Simple Justice: The History of Brown v. Board of Education and Black America's Struggle for Equality* (New York, 1975), 36, 241. On pp. 88 and 118 Kluger at least offers a brief definition: "the right of the citizen to free association in his private dealings."

4. "The Court's Right Turn," *The Nation* 242 (June 28, 1986): 1. See also Eleanor Blau, "Personal Freedoms: Topic of Liberty Weekend Sessions," *New York Times*, June 22, 1986, p. A26.

5. See George Bancroft to Mrs. J. C. B. Davis, Oct. 3, 1870, in Mark De Wolfe Howe, *The Life and Letters of George Bancroft* (New York, 1908), 2:243; Charles Francis Adams, "The

might on occasion refer to "public liberty," which implied the existence of a complementary type that could be designated as personal liberty.[6] In *Federalist* number 10, James Madison did provide a separation between "public and personal liberty." Whereas the former apparently referred to the right to vote, hold office, and assemble peacefully, the latter (also referred to as "private rights") seems to have subsumed freedom of worship, expression, and physical movement. Later in the same paper, Madison also condemned pure democracies as being incompatible with "personal security, or the rights of property."[7]

In those few, brief phrases he came closest to revealing what the founders meant by personal liberty. Using a classic dichotomy of political philosophy, they differentiated between positive and negative liberty. For purposes of our inquiry, that meant understanding public liberty as *freedom to* do something and personal liberty as *freedom from* some act of intervention or encroachment, particularly by government.[8] Only on occasion, however, did subsequent writers sustain this distinction between public and private (or personal) liberty during the nineteenth century.[9]

Progress of Liberty," an address given at Taunton, Massachusetts, on July 4, 1876, published as an "Extra" pamphlet by the *New-York Tribune*, 32–33.

6. See the Anti-Federalist who wrote as "Brutus" (Nov. 29, 1787), and Thomas Jefferson to James Madison, March 15, 1789, both in Michael Kammen, ed., *The Origins of the American Constitution: A Documentary History* (New York, 1986), 327, 377.

7. Jacob E. Cooke, ed., *The Federalist* (Middletown, Conn., 1961), 57, 61.

8. Both James Otis (1764) and Martin Howard (1765) distinguished between political and personal rights ("life, liberty, and estate"). Howard contended that personal rights were secured by the common law tradition. Similarly, the *Encyclopaedia Britannica* (first published 1778–83), differentiated in the entry for "Liberty" between political and personal liberty. Under "personal immunities" it included the rights of personal security, personal liberty, and private property. See Bernard Bailyn, ed., *Pamphlets of the American Revolution, 1750–1776* (Cambridge, Mass., 1965), 1:535, 538; Gaetano Salvemini, "The Concepts of Democracy and Liberty in the Eighteenth Century," in Conyers Read, ed., *The Constitution Reconsidered* (2d ed.; New York, 1968), 113.

9. See, for example, A. Lawrence Lowell, *Essays on Government* (Boston, 1889), 60, 62. See also Edward S. Corwin to A. A. Hamblen, Jan. 9, 1940, Corwin Papers, box 2, Seeley G. Mudd Manuscript Library, Princeton University: "Have you ever given consideration to the idea that the term 'liberty' as used in legal philosophy has two different meanings; 1. civil liberty which is that liberty that we enjoy in consequence of the restraints which the ordinary law imposes upon our neighbors; 2. constitutional liberty or the liberty which comes when

The dissent written by Justice Joseph P. Bradley in the famous *Slaughter-House Cases* (1873), however, is noteworthy for our purposes because he traced all the way back to Magna Carta the right of habeas corpus, "or the right of having any invasion of personal liberty judicially examined into, at once, by a competent judicial magistrate. Blackstone classifies these fundamental rights under three heads, as the absolute rights of individuals, to wit: the right of personal security, the right of personal liberty, and the right of private property."[10] Bradley thereby leads us quite appropriately back to the British origins of the quarry that we seek.

II

Blackstone is, indeed, the most relevant British writer. In his *Commentaries on the Laws of England* (1765–69) he ranked personal security among "the absolute rights of individuals"; but when he referred to personal liberty *per se,* he simply meant "the power of locomotion, of changing situation." Precisely because *we* now take for granted freedom of the person from physical restraint, an act of historical imagination is required in order to understand that in medieval and early modern times such a right could not be taken for granted at all. Although it was protected, in theory, by the Thirty-ninth Article of Magna Carta, by statutes passed during the reign of King Edward III, and by common law, subjects recognized its vulnerability.[11]

Blackstone is also important as the primary agent in the intellectual transmission of this concept to the world of the framers. When James

---

one is entitled to appeal against the restrictions which government and the ordinary law imposes upon our own actions. I think a little reflection will convince you that the former is much the more important, and that the latter—which we have so much emphasized in this country—while important, is distinctly of less importance than civil liberty."

10. 16 Wallace 115 (1873).

11. See Edward S. Corwin, *Liberty Against Government: The Rise, Flowering and Decline of a Famous Juridical Concept* (Baton Rouge, La., 1948), 140; Charles E. Shattuck, "The True Meaning of the Term 'Liberty' in Those Clauses in the Federal and State Constitutions Which Protect 'Life, Liberty, and Property'," *Harvard Law Review* 4 (March 1891): 369, 373–77; and Bernard Bailyn, *Voyagers to the West: A Passage in the Peopling of America on the Eve of the Revolution* (New York, 1986), 53.

Wilson of Pennsylvania touched upon personal liberty in his *Lectures on Law* (1790), he cited Blackstone as his authority. The same is true of Timothy Dwight of Connecticut, who in 1794 distinguished repeatedly between the right of private property, the right of personal security (against physical harm), and the right of personal liberty (physical mobility); he, too, cited Blackstone as his authority. It is noteworthy, however, that whereas Blackstone designated all of these as "civil liberties," Americans preferred to regard them as natural rights.[12] That emphasis would reappear in language used by Justice William O. Douglas during the 1950s and '60s.

Before we turn our attention exclusively to American interpretations, however, we should notice two other (pre-Blackstone) elements in the British background to our story. The first is secular, and the second might be termed ecclesiastical.

Concerning the first: Infringements of personal liberty (physical restraint) provided the principal complaint lodged in the Petition of Right of 1627. Those deep hostilities that deteriorated into tragic civil war during the 1640s elicited some public polemics involving personal liberty—though ultimately a total impasse developed between Royalists and Roundheads. Parliament passed the Habeas Corpus Act of 1679 solely to protect personal liberty against Crown usurpation.[13] The most important legacy to the colonists from seventeenth-century England, however, came from John Locke; and it came to them as an assertion that a man's personal freedom could be constrained only if due process of law had been observed.[14] (See figures 4, 5, and 8.)

Concerning the second: During the middle decades of the seven-

---

12. Robert G. McCloskey, ed., *The Works of James Wilson* (Cambridge, Mass., 1967), 2:588–89; Dwight, in Charles S. Hyneman and Donald S. Lutz, eds., *American Political Writing during the Founding Era, 1760–1805* (Indianapolis, Ind., 1983), 2:888–89.

13. Shattuck, "The True Meaning of the Term 'Liberty'," 376; Charles H. McIlwain, *Constitutionalism: Ancient and Modern* (Ithaca, N.Y., 1947), 127.

14. H. T. Dickinson, *Liberty and Property: Political Ideology in Eighteenth-Century Britain* (New York, 1977), 68; A. J. Carlyle, *Political Liberty: A History of the Conception in the Middle Ages and Modern Times* (Oxford, 1941), ch. 1. The Brookline Historical Society in Brookline, Massachusetts, owns a portrait of the Reverend Ebenezer Devotion (1714–71), painted by Winthrop Chandler in 1770. Two volumes on the clergyman's bookshelf, prominent at the extreme right in the picture, have lettered on their spines: "Lock Work."

teenth century, when the English civil war engendered so much fer-
ment in customary political thought, the Puritan cause nourished a new
concern for what its advocates called Christian liberty. The immediate
implication was a belief in the equality of all believers. But John Milton
anticipated its long-term impact by placing the concept of Christian
liberty at the very core of his rationale for religious toleration. Although
the Presbyterians and Independents differed over nuances, they both believed in freedom of conscience as the birthright of a Christian. Eventually the doctrine of Christian liberty would be used to sustain campaigns for religious freedom.[15] Young John Locke, writing his first
philosophical treatises in 1660–61, elaborated that outlook, and it subsequently came to fruition in 1689 in the Act of Toleration.[16]

Those Puritans who emigrated to New England carried with them
John Milton's concept of Christian liberty. They had not yet read Milton, nor did they really need to; for their views were formed in the
very same crucible of experience that shaped Milton's. John Winthrop
reflected upon Christian "libertie" before he ever left England; and the
concept would be formalized in 1641 when the Massachusetts Bay Colony promulgated its Body of Liberties.[17]

John Wise, a Puritan clergyman who lived in Ipswich, Massachusetts,
published a defense of congregational church government in 1717 in which
he insisted that man's "Personal Liberty and Equality [are] to be cherished, and preserved to the highest degree." Twenty-seven years later
Elisha Williams published in Boston *The essential Rights and Liberties
of Protestants,* an appeal for liberty of conscience that ran in direct line
of descent from John Milton's assertions a century earlier. Williams described Christian liberty as "the most valuable of all our rights," and
connected it to the privilege of private judgment.[18]

Elisha Williams (1694–1755) cannot be described as a typical writer

---

15. A. S. P. Woodhouse, ed., *Puritanism and Liberty: Being the Army Debates (1647–9)*
. . . (Chicago, 1951), 59–60, 65–67, 80.

16. Locke, *Two Tracts on Government,* ed. by Philip Abrams (Cambridge, 1967), 129, 142.

17. Edmund S. Morgan, *The Puritan Dilemma: The Story of John Winthrop* (Boston, 1958),
10; Oscar and Mary Handlin, *The Dimensions of Liberty* (Cambridge, Mass., 1961), 58, 71.

18. Lengthy extracts from Wise and Williams will be found in Edmund S. Morgan, ed.,
Puritan Political Ideas, 1558–1794 (Indianapolis, Ind., 1965), 257, 269, 285–87.

of his age. He spoke for a vocal minority during the first half of the eighteenth century, however—an articulate group highly aware that their avant-garde ideas derived some legitimacy from Milton and Locke. During the 1770s and '80s, though, their legacy entered the mainstream of American thought, with the result that the Revolutionary generation was most likely to identify personal liberty as freedom of conscience. They took care to differentiate between "civil liberties and those of religion"; and it is clear from their language that civil liberties were essentially political (freedom to) whereas "ecclesiastical liberties" were essentially personal (freedom from).[19]

Coming upon the American scene during the 1830s, Tocqueville listened to accounts of those distinctions—by then blurred in a society swept by evangelical impulses—and misunderstood the language of liberty as it had been used by the Revolutionary generation: "For the Americans the ideas of Christianity and liberty are so completely mingled that it is almost impossible to get them to conceive of the one without the other." Tocqueville's generalization *did* convey the "climate of opinion" during the 1830s, however, and thereby serves as a measure of American drift toward total imprecision in the use of liberty as a cultural concept.[20]

III

When we shift from the Anglo-American ideal of Christian liberty—which clearly developed into the doctrine of liberty of conscience (one of the major connotations of personal liberty in the eighteenth century)—to more secular aspects of American political culture during the Revolutionary generation, we encounter a growing concern that emerged

19. See Anon., "Four Letters on Interesting Subjects" (Philadelphia, 1776) in Hyneman and Lutz, eds., *American Political Writing during the Founding Era*, 1:381; Levi Hart, *Liberty Described and Recommended; in a sermon, preached to the Corporation of Freemen in Farmington . . . Sept. 20, 1774* (Hartford, Conn., 1775), 14, 22; Melvin B. Endy, Jr., "Just War, Holy War, and Millenialism in Revolutionary America," *William and Mary Quarterly* 42 (January 1985): 12.

20. Alexis de Tocqueville, *Democracy in America*, ed. by J. P. Mayer (Garden City, N.Y., 1969), 293. Cf. William G. McLoughlin, "The Role of Religion in the Revolution: Liberty of Conscience and Cultural Cohesion in the New Nation," in Stephen G. Kurtz and James H. Hutson, eds., *Essays on the American Revolution* (Chapel Hill, N.C., 1973), 197–255.

after the 1750s. In 1775, for example, the author of a letter written to a Massachusetts newspaper declared that "personal liberty, personal security and private property are the only motives" that explain why people abandon a state of nature and willingly place themselves under government.[21]

"Property" in this instance means just what it says, individual or family ownership of land and goods; and "security" refers to safety from possible physical harm and to the protection of one's home. "Personal liberty," as usual, is not entirely clear. It *could* refer to freedom of conscience; but comparable statements from the period suggest either a Blackstonian sense of freedom from restraint, or else the right to be a "free" person in the commonly understood Lockean sense of that day,[22] or even an embryonic form of what Justice Douglas would call, almost two centuries later, the right to be let alone and to have that right respected as well as protected by the government.

In 1787–88, however, Americans not only mentioned personal liberty with greater frequency, but they also began to use the phrase with increasing specificity. No one would deny that Montesquieu was the most persistently cited political philosopher when the federal Constitution came to be written and ratified. Although he alluded to "liberty of the subject" in *The Spirit of the Laws,* however, Montesquieu's emphasis was upon political liberty and physical security.[23]

By contrast, when Gouverneur Morris spoke critically in the Constitutional Convention of abuses by state legislatures during the 1780s, he specified "excesses agst. personal liberty, private property, & personal safety."[24] James Wilson would reinforce that sort of tripartite differen-

21. See *Pennsylvania Journal and Weekly Advertiser,* Feb. 23, 1758, quoted in Lawrence Leder, *Liberty and Authority: Early American Political Ideology, 1689–1763* (Chicago, 1968), 121; and Benjamin F. Wright, *Consensus and Continuity, 1776–1787* (New York, 1967), 13.

22. See John Locke, *Two Treatises of Government,* ed. by Peter Laslett (Cambridge, 1960), ch. 4, "Of Slavery," 301–3.

23. Montesquieu, *The Spirit of Laws* [sic], ed. by David Wallace Carrithers (Berkeley, Calif., 1977), 215–17. For the French philosopher Jean Louis De Lolme, see Salvemini, "The Concepts of Democracy and Liberty," 113.

24. Max Farrand, ed., *The Records of the Federal Convention of 1787* (2d ed.; New Haven, Conn., 1937), 1:512 (Morris spoke on July 2). See also William Grayson's remarks in the Confederation Congress on Sept. 27, 1787, in Merrill Jensen, ed., *The Documentary History of the*

tiation;[25] but, perhaps predictably, it would be James Madison (in a neglected passage from *Federalist* number 10) who commented upon a growing concern for "public and personal liberty," and then noted the "prevailing and increasing distrust of public engagements, and alarm for private rights, which are echoed from one end of the continent to the other."[26]

How nice it would be if we could know just what James Madison meant by the phrases "personal liberty" and "private rights." I do not claim to know for certain; but there are two essential clues. The first comes in Madison's own words, spoken at the Convention, when he declared that "a man has property in his opinions and the free communication of them, he has property in the free use of his faculties, in the safety and liberty of his person."[27]

The second clue is deductive. In 1789 Madison prepared for the first United States Congress the Bill of Rights that so many persons, Federalists as well as Anti-Federalists, had pleaded for in 1787–88. There is reason to believe that bills of attainder and *ex post facto* laws (already prohibited by Article I, section 9, of the Constitution) and other such abhorrent legal actions were viewed as unwarranted violations of personal liberty. Hence the expansive supplementary protections provided by Amendments One through Eight.[28]

How nice it would be, as well, if we could conclude that by 1787–89 some sort of consensus had been achieved concerning the meaning of personal liberty. That did not happen, however, and various sorts of incantations were uttered. Although each is symptomatic and unexceptionable in its own way, they do not cohere into a pattern. Samuel Chase, the prominent Anti-Federalist from Maryland, opposed "the pro-

---

Ratification of the Constitution. Volume 1, *Constitutional Documents and Records, 1776–1787* (Madison, Wis., 1976), 331.

25. See McCloskey, ed., *Works of James Wilson*, 2:648–49; Brennan, "Landmarks of Legal Liberty," 8.

26. Cooke, ed., *The Federalist*, 57.

27. Quoted in Catherine Drinker Bowen, *Miracle at Philadelphia: The Story of the Constitutional Convention, May to September 1787* (Boston, 1966), 71.

28. See Robert C. Palmer, *Liberties as Constitutional Provisions, 1776–1791* (Williamsburg, Va., 1987), esp. n. 255.

posed national government, because it *immediately* takes away the power from our *state* legislature to protect the *personal* liberty of the citizen."[29]

Late in 1788 Thomas Jefferson wrote to George Washington from Paris that Lafayette had fallen "out of favor with the court, but [is] high in favor with the nation. I once feared for his personal liberty. But I hope him on safe ground at present." Finally, it is believed that the title preferred by Washington was "His High Mightiness, the President of the United States and Protector of their Liberties."[30] It is unclear whether the liberties he had in mind were those of the states or those of individuals. Perhaps the ambiguity was not accidental, but rather a means of mollifying the fears of men like Samuel Chase.

In any case, as the eighteenth century drew to a close, James Wilson would make the most acute summary judgment: "In some respects, private liberty is still the orphan neglected."[31]

IV

The decades from 1790 until 1865 — from the end of the Revolutionary era until the close of the Civil War — did very little to refine or clarify American conceptions of personal liberty. Complaints voiced by artisans and small shopkeepers indicated that Wilson's lament remained valid. As one vexed individual wrote in New York City: "If a man seeks credit, he does not pledge his *personal* liberty for payment."[32] That grievance, uttered in 1811, would not be resolved until another generation had passed. Imprisonment for debt became an exceedingly controversial issue among reformers during the Jacksonian era.

So far as the United States Supreme Court and state supreme courts were concerned, personal liberty received scant illumination. When it

---

29. James A. Haw, ed., "Samuel Chase's 'Objections to the Federal Government'," *Maryland Historical Magazine* 76 (September 1981): 277. The italics are Chase's.

30. Jefferson to Washington, [Dec. 4,] 1788, in Julian P. Boyd, ed., *The Papers of Thomas Jefferson*, 14 (Princeton, N.J., 1958), 332; Max Farrand, *The Framing of the Constitution of the United States* (New Haven, Conn., 1913), 163.

31. Wilson, *Lectures on Law* (1790), in McCloskey, ed., *Works of James Wilson*, 2:648.

32. Quoted in Sean Wilentz, *Chants Democratic: New York City and the Rise of the American Working Class, 1788–1850* (New York, 1984), 44.

was referred to at all, the concept seemed to reflect its most conventional implication: freedom from physical restraint.[33] Presidential messages to Congress and inaugural addresses occasionally included the phrase; but it meant somewhat different things in different situations—when it meant anything at all. In 1825 John Quincy Adams seemed to use it as a euphemism for economic individualism and opportunity. William Henry Harrison conveyed no clear sense of the concept; and John Tyler, after reassuring Southerners that the Constitution would be upheld, promised with meaningless vagueness that personal liberty would be "placed beyond hazard or jeopardy."[34]

Because Tyler was decidedly unsympathetic to the anti-slavery movement, his incantation may seem oddly inappropriate. We too easily forget the casuistry and half-truths that characterized American discourse concerning slavery between the Revolution and Civil War. Here, for instance, is David Ramsay, the Philadelphian transplanted to South Carolina, offering a platitudinous paradox in 1789: "All masters of slaves who enjoy personal liberty will be both proud and jealous of their freedom."[35]

The most important development during this period, for the concept that we have under consideration, involved the passage by Northern states of personal liberty laws designed to challenge and undermine the Fugitive Slave Laws of 1793 and 1850. Although the history of that movement has been carefully analyzed,[36] we should at least note that pamphleteers were responsible for a new wrinkle that set them apart from the Revolutionary generation. They tended to conflate, rather than differentiate between, civil and personal liberty. As Noah Porter, the president of Yale, put it in 1856: "Civil liberty implies firm guarantees of personal liberty." The guarantees provided by our form of govern-

33. For Justice Joseph Story in 1829, for example, see Corwin, *Liberty Against Government*, 67. For a highly representative decision made by the Supreme Court of Vermont in 1855, see Charles Warren, "The New 'Liberty' Under the Fourteenth Amendment," *Harvard Law Review* 39 (February 1926): 443–44.

34. See James D. Richardson, comp., *A Compilation of the Messages and Papers of the Presidents, 1789–1897* (Washington, D.C., 1896–99), 2:303; 4:7, 336.

35. Ramsay, "Poverty," [Charleston, S.C.] *City Gazette and Daily Advertiser*, Dec. 8, 1789, in Hyneman and Lutz, eds., *American Political Writing during the Founding Era*, 2:723.

36. See Thomas D. Morris, *Free Men All: The Personal Liberty Laws of the North, 1780–1861* (Baltimore, Md., 1974).

ment, he continued, were threefold: the principle that a man's home is his castle; the constitutional protection against general warrants; and the privilege of habeas corpus.[37]

Once the Civil War got under way and emergency war powers took effect, the primary locus of meaning for personal liberty shifted from legal protection for fugitive slaves and free blacks to the problem of habeas corpus and President Lincoln's perceived abuse of that time-honored protection.[38]

V

From the onset of Reconstruction until the end of World War I, the history of personal liberty performed like a compass moving through the Bermuda Triangle: it whirled and pointed every which way. Even though the words became more commonplace in American culture than ever before, they carried markedly different meanings for diverse segments of society. While some of these meanings were regressive, others were far ahead of their time. In no other phase of our history did the phrase resound more, yet mean less. The best that we can do is note the predominant directions of that gyrating compass.

First and most obvious, passage of the Thirteenth Amendment in 1865 seemed (and in fact was) a stunning step forward for advocates of personal liberty. When Justice Samuel F. Miller delivered the Court's opinion in the *Slaughter-House Cases* (1873), he even incorporated the text of that Amendment and praised "this grand yet simple declaration of the personal freedom of all the human race within the jurisdiction of this government."[39]

Second, and more important though much less obvious, passage of the Fourteenth Amendment in 1866, and ratification two years after

37. Noah Porter, *Civil Liberty: A Sermon Preached in Farmington, Connecticut, July 13, 1856* (New York, 1856), 6; James Barnett, *Personal Liberty for All Men* (Albany, N.Y., 1860).

38. See Edward Ingersoll, *Personal Liberty and Martial Law: A review of some pamphlets of the day* (Philadelphia, 1862); Carl B. Swisher, *Stephen J. Field: Craftsman of the Law* (Washington, D.C., 1930), 136.

39. See Stanley I. Kutler, ed., *The Supreme Court and the Constitution: Readings in American Constitutional History* (2d ed.; New York, 1977), 227. See also Miller's use of "personal rights" in *Davidson v. New Orleans*, 96 U.S. 97 (1878), at 101–2.

that, surely must have expanded the meaning of personal liberty even more. Senator Jacob M. Howard of Michigan, discussing the Amendment in 1866, referred to "the personal rights guaranteed" by the first eight amendments in the Bill of Rights. More than a century later, in *Roe v. Wade,* the Supreme Court's controversial decision upholding a woman's right to have an abortion, Justice Potter Stewart concurred "that the right asserted by Jane Roe is embraced within the personal liberty protected by the Due Process Clause" of the Fourteenth Amendment. Justice Powell proposed a similar rationale.[40]

Although "liberty" is mentioned with some frequency in the justices' opinions concerning abortion, the text of the Fourteenth Amendment never mentions personal liberty. Nor does the Constitution itself. Nevertheless, Supreme Court decisions that developed in the wake of *Roe v. Wade* candidly built upon precedents that carried a greater weight of fairness and ethical concern for the pregnant female than of constitutional solidity. A 1977 decision, for example, written by Justice William J. Brennan, absorbed much of the language of *Roe v. Wade,* acknowledging that "although 'the Constitution does not explicitly mention any right of privacy,' the Court has recognized that one aspect of the 'liberty' protected by the Due Process Clause of the Fourteenth Amendment is 'a right of personal privacy, or a guarantee of certain areas or zones of privacy'."[41] The wonderfully elastic Fourteenth Amendment has come to be regarded by jurists as a major milestone in the history of a concept about which it is essentially mute.

A third trend that is pertinent in this period involved a far more tortured use of the Fourteenth Amendment to uphold a doctrine labelled liberty to contract. Various pieces of protective, pro-labor legislation from the states, for instance, were declared unconstitutional be-

40. Richard C. Cortner, *The Supreme Court and the Second Bill of Rights: The Fourteenth Amendment and the Nationalization of Civil Liberties* (Madison, Wis., 1981), 5; *Roe v. Wade,* 410 U.S. 113 (1973), esp. at 129, 153, 170.

41. *Carey v. Population Services International,* 431 U.S. 678 (1977), at 684; Judith A. Baer, *Equality Under the Constitution: Reclaiming the Fourteenth Amendment* (Ithaca, N.Y., 1983), 234. See also Charles Evans Hughes, *The Supreme Court of the United States: Its Foundation, Methods and Achievements* (New York, 1928), 166, where he included freedom of speech and of the press "among the fundamental personal rights and liberties" protected by the Due Process Clause of the Fourteenth Amendment.

cause they deprived someone of the "personal liberty" of working unusually long hours under unhealthy conditions. This was not only the
essence of Justice Rufus Peckham's opinion for the Court in the notorious
case of *Lochner v. New York* (1905),[42] but of Justice John Marshall Harlan
in *Adair v. United States* (1908), a decision that upheld "yellow-dog con-
tracts" (by invalidating a statute that protected labor union membership) on grounds that the law exceeded Congress's power to regulate
interstate commerce and violated the freedom of contract guaranteed
by the Fifth Amendment. Harlan's language and reasoning are so representative of the era that a lengthy extract may be instructive.

> It is not within the power of Congress to make it a criminal offense
> against the United States for a carrier engaged in interstate commerce,
> or an agent or officer thereof, to discharge an employé simply because
> of his membership in a labor organization; and the provision to that
> effect . . . concerning interstate carriers is an invasion of personal lib-
> erty, as well as of the right of property. . . . It was the defendant
> Adair's right—and that right inhered in his personal liberty, and was
> also a right of property. . . . Is this a fair, reasonable and appropriate
> exercise of the police power of the State, or is it an unreasonable,
> unnecessary and arbitrary interference with the right of the individual
> to his personal liberty or to enter into those contracts in relation to
> labor which may seem to him appropriate or necessary for the sup-
> port of himself and his family?[43]

Justice Oliver Wendell Holmes dissented, just as he had in *Lochner*;
but this time, given Harlan's emphatic yet (to Holmes) perverse use
of "personal liberty," Holmes briefly articulated his understanding of
that concept: namely, "the paramount individual rights, secured by the
Fifth Amendment."[44] A year later Roscoe Pound reinforced Holmes's
position with a resounding essay that put reverse spin on the history
of our concept. "Personal liberty is always subject to restraint," wrote

42. For Peckham's use of personal liberty in this opinion, see Kutler, ed., *The Supreme
Court and the Constitution*, 283–84.

43. *Adair v. United States*, 208 U.S. 161 (1908), at 161, 172, 174. For a very similar case,
in which Justice Mahlon Pitney's opinion for the Court also invoked personal liberty several
times, see *Coppage v. State of Kansas*, 236 U.S. 1 (1915), esp. at 2.

44. *Adair v. United States*, 208 U.S. 161.

Pound, drawing upon a recent decision by the Court of Appeals of New York, "when its exercise affects the safety, health or moral and general welfare of the public, but subject to such restraint, an employer and employee may make and enforce such contract relating to labor as they may agree on."[45]

What should happen if personal liberty conflicted directly with interests of the State? The answer, in any given situation, depended upon ideology, circumstances, and whether or not the State's interest was "compelling." In 1907 for example, the Supreme Court decided (8 to 1) that private individuals had "unlawfully exposed to public view, sold . . . and had in their possession for sale a bottle of beer, upon which, for purposes of advertisement, was printed and painted a representation of the flag of the United States." The defendants had pleaded not guilty, insisting that the Nebraska law under which they were prosecuted was null and void "as infringing their personal liberty" guaranteed by the Fourteenth Amendment. The state of Illinois had already held such a statute unconstitutional on several grounds, among them "infringing the personal liberty" guaranteed by the state and federal constitutions.[46]

In the High Court's opinion, however, the State's desire to cultivate feelings of patriotism constituted a legitimate basis for constraining personal liberty. Justice Harlan elucidated the Court's ban upon beer bottles that desecrated Old Glory.

> We cannot hold that any privilege of American citizenship or that any right of personal liberty is violated by a state enactment forbidding the flag to be used as an advertisement on a bottle of beer. The privileges of citizenship and the rights inhering in personal liberty are subject, in their enjoyment, to such reasonable restraints as may be required for the general good.[47]

45. Pound, "Liberty of Contract," *Yale Law Journal* 18 (May 1909): 481. The opinion cited by Pound is *People v. Marcus,* 85 N.Y. 255 (1906).

46. *Halter v. Nebraska,* 205 U.S. 34 (1907), at 38–40.

47. Ibid., 42. In Pittsburgh, Pennsylvania, during the later 1880s a Personal Liberty League was organized by retail liquor dealers in order to combat a law-and-order crusade led by temperance partisans. See Francis G. Couvares, "The Triumph of Commerce: Class Culture and Mass Culture in Pittsburgh," in Michael H. Frisch and Daniel J. Walkowitz, eds., *Working-Class America: Essays on Labor, Community, and American Society* (Urbana, Ill., 1983), 127.

Justice Harlan had not consistently taken an anti-libertarian position, however. Writing one of the great dissents in Supreme Court history, he opposed the doctrine of "separate but equal" in *Plessy v. Ferguson*. That case involved racial segregation in railroad cars, enjoined by the state of Louisiana. Harlan opposed his brethren on the explicit basis of Blackstone's concern for freedom of movement. "The fundamental objection . . . to the statute," Harlan wrote, "is that it interferes with the personal freedom of citizens. 'Personal liberty,' it has been well said, 'consists in the power of locomotion, of changing situation, or removing one's person to whatsoever place one's own inclination may direct, without imprisonment or restraint, unless by due course of law'." Straight from Blackstone's *Commentaries*. Six pages later Harlan concluded in his own words: "I am of opinion that the statute of Louisiana is inconsistent with the personal liberty of citizens, white and black, in the State, and hostile to both the spirit and letter of the Constitution of the United States."[48]

Few other voices were effectively raised on behalf of personal liberty during these years. One might hear the phrase mentioned in the hortatory urgings of Eugene V. Debs, or encounter it in the writings of men so diverse as Brooks Adams and Upton Sinclair.[49] One could even find it in the work of America's most influential legal theorist during the later nineteenth and early twentieth century, Thomas M. Cooley. His book called *Constitutional Limitations* (1868) does mention "jury trials and other safeguards to personal liberty"; and in *A Treatise on the Law of Torts* (1879) Cooley anticipates the language of Justices Louis D. Bran-

---

48. *Plessy v. Ferguson*, 163 U.S. 537 (1896), at 557 and 563. Harlan was not alone among his contemporaries in remembering Blackstone. Four years later Chief Justice Melville Fuller wrote: "Undoubtedly the right of locomotion, the right to remove from one place to another, according to inclination is an attribute of personal liberty." *Williams v. Fears*, 179 U.S. 270 (1900), at 274. Georgia had passed, in a general revenue act, a tax upon numerous occupations, including that of "emigrant agent," meaning a person engaged in hiring laborers to be employed beyond the limits of the state. Fuller's opinion asserted that personal liberty (as locomotion) was protected by the Fourteenth Amendment.

49. See Nick Salvatore, *Eugene V. Debs: Citizen and Socialist* (Urbana, Ill., 1982), 153–54, 174–75, 191–92; Warren I. Susman, *Culture as History: The Transformation of American Society in the Twentieth Century* (New York, 1984), 46; Michael Kammen, *A Machine That Would Go of Itself: The Constitution in American Culture* (New York, 1986), xvi.

deis and William O. Douglas. *"Personal immunity,"* as defined by Cooley, meant that "the right of one's person may be said to be a right of complete immunity; the right to be let alone."[50]

Cooley's treatises lent themselves in various ways to conservative interpretations, however, which may help to explain his remarkably broad appeal at that time. Be that as it may, the messages of presidents like Benjamin Harrison, and the jurisprudence of justices like Stephen J. Field and Stanley Matthews, were likely to be sprinkled with references to personal liberty, yet equally likely to sustain the needs of corporate interests or the State as against the rights of individuals.[51]

VI

From World War I until the mid-twentieth century our concept continued to be utilized in contradictory ways, though the range of possibilities narrowed; and there were fewer instances (as with Cooley, Field, and Matthews) of libertarian language being put to conservative purposes. In retrospect, at least, men's motives as well as their discourse seem less convoluted. People who opposed Prohibition, for example, insisted that their personal liberty was being violated. Conservatives like Chief Justice William Howard Taft and David Jayne Hill declared candidly that excessive application or expansion of the "democratic principle" threatened the freedom of action (meaning dominance) and personal liberty of those best situated to understand what the founders had intended in 1787.[52]

A symptomatic public lecture that Taft presented in 1922 resounded

50. See Corwin, *Liberty Against Government,* 117; Cooley, *A Treatise on the Law of Torts* (Chicago, 1879), 29.

51. Harrison, Third Annual Message to Congress, Dec. 9, 1891, in Richardson, comp., *Messages and Papers of the Presidents,* 9:197; Swisher, *Stephen J. Field,* 264; Matthews' opinion in *Hurtado v. California,* 110 U.S. 516 (1884), at 529, 530, 537.

52. For Hill, see "A Defense of the Constitution," *The North American Review* 205 (March 1917): 389–91, 395–96. For Charles Evans Hughes ("democracy has its own capacity for tyranny"), see "Liberty and the Law" (1925), 187. See also George Bryan Logan, Jr., *Liberty in the Modern World* (Chapel Hill, N.C., 1928), 48, 67, who saw no inherent conflict between personal liberty and social control, and who urged that personal liberties be protected against the intolerance of popular government.

with familiar chords from Alexander Hamilton, Gouverneur Morris, and other Whigs most protective of private property 135 years earlier. "The Federal Constitution today," Taft intoned, "guards a man in the enjoyment of his personal liberty, his property and his pursuit of happiness, whether violated by the Federal or State Government." Over and over again, Taft sang the same refrains:

- Our Constitution has been called too individualistic. It rests on personal liberty and the right of property. In the last analysis, personal liberty includes the right of property as it includes the right of contract and the right of labor.

- To be useful, democracy and liberty must be regulated.

- The rights of personal liberty and of property as protected by the courts are not obstructive to any reasonable qualification of these rights in the interest of the community.[53]

Were these the last gasps of "personal liberty" as a shibboleth on behalf of the status quo and resistance to compassionate social progress? Not quite. In Governor Franklin D. Roosevelt's final message to the New York State Assembly (1932), and in Herbert Hoover's ideological manifesto, *The Challenge to Liberty* (1934), personal liberty remained nearly synonymous with unfettered economic opportunity for the enterprising individual.[54]

Even so, significant signs of change could be spotted from the mid-1920s onward—shifts that would herald new meanings for personal liberty from the mid-1950s until the present. The shift began, unremarkably, with increased *thoughtfulness* about civil liberties even when

53. Taft, *Liberty Under Law: An Interpretation of the Principles of Our Constitutional Government* (New Haven, Conn., 1922), 14, 25–26, 40, 51.

54. Rosenman, comp., *Public Papers and Addresses of Roosevelt,* 1 (1938), 112; Hoover, *The Challenge to Liberty* (New York, 1934), 130, 163. Rowland Berthoff, "Peasants and Artisans, Puritans and Republicans: Personal Liberty and Communal Equality in American History," *Journal of American History* 69 (December 1982), 582, 588, 594, 596, and 598, contends that achieving a balance between personal liberty and communal equality has been at the very core of the "American dream." Berthoff conflates personal liberty, however, with equal economic opportunity (esp. at 588). I insist that personal liberty has meant considerably more in American culture than merely bourgeois individualism.

those in authority persisted in repressing civil liberties. In its landmark decision involving the case of *Gitlow v. New York* (1925), the Supreme Court declared that freedom of speech and of the press "are among the fundamental personal rights and 'liberties'" protected by the Due Process Clause of the Fourteenth Amendment.[55]

A number of additional cases that came before the Court during the period 1931–38 elicited appeals on behalf of personal liberty that urged greater concern for the rights of petition and assembly; expanded concern for speech and press; and, by 1938, the Court's opinion in *Missouri ex. rel. Gaines v. Canada,* written by Chief Justice Charles Evans Hughes, considered the right to attend a law school in the state of one's residence a personal liberty.[56]

Meanwhile, various state-based civil liberties committees emerged and began fund-raising as well as public consciousness-raising activities. In 1936 moreover, the American Academy of Political and Social Science invited several individuals, selected for their diverse backgrounds, to prepare essays explicitly devoted to the theme of personal liberty. Congressman John W. McCormack, then a Representative from Massachusetts, Chairman of the Special House Committee Investigating Nazi and Un-American Activities, and subsequently Speaker of the House (1962–71), provided a fairly pedestrian article that primarily defined personal liberty in terms of the Bill of Rights. I suspect that his response may have been representative of the American mainstream at that time.[57]

A different sort of contribution came from Roger N. Baldwin, who had served as director of the American Civil Liberties Union in New York City since 1920. Baldwin's response was more realistic, complex, and prescient. Baldwin too acknowledged the "personal liberties set forth in the Bill of Rights"; but he insisted that they had been "adopted not

55. *Gitlow v. New York,* 268 U.S. 652 (1925), at 666.

56. Cortner, *The Supreme Court and the Second Bill of Rights,* 80, 81, 84, 94, 96–97; Herbert Wechsler, *Principles, Politics, and Fundamental Law: Selected Essays* (Cambridge, Mass., 1961), 88; Kluger, *Simple Justice,* 213.

57. Harold Rotzel (Executive Secretary of the Civil Liberties Committee of Massachusetts) to Arthur M. Schlesinger, Oct. 23, 1929, Schlesinger Papers, box 5, Harvard University Archives, Pusey Library, Cambridge, Mass.; John W. McCormack, "Personal Liberty," *Annals of the American Academy of Political and Social Science* 185 (May 1936): 154–61.

by the founding fathers but by the pressure of the people themselves," and added that they "rest on two sets of guarantees — those protecting freedom of agitation, and those protecting defendants on trial." He recognized the complex implications of Roosevelt's New Deal reforms for traditional American perceptions of personal freedom, and called attention to these emerging tensions in his opening paragraph.

> "Personal liberty" at once arouses the concept of freedom from restraint in habits of living. Its most vivid recent application involved the attempted philosophy which justified violating the prohibition amendment. Its loudest immediate application concerns the rights of private property in the conflict between rugged individualism and state control. Less vocal but more in the American tradition are the genuine libertarians whose political thinking, running back to the founding fathers and beyond, regards liberty as the priceless possession of free men to agitate, to alter governments, to remold economic systems.[58]

In recognizing that big government, regardless of which party controlled it, could pose a threat to personal liberty, Baldwin offered a cautionary note that has become more meaningful, rather than less, in the half-century since.

The 1939–40 term of the United States Supreme Court marked the beginning of a new day in the Court's preoccupation with issues involving one or another aspect of personal liberty. In the volume of *U.S. Reports* for that term (number 310), the index entry for "Constitutional Law, Fourteenth Amendment, Due Process Clause," includes eighteen cases — an unprecedented number. The volume for 1943 (number 319) is the first to have a separate index sub-entry for "personal liberty" under Constitutional Law.

Needless to say, this hardly meant that the apogee of personal liberty had been achieved. In 1943, after all, the Court decided *Hirabayashi v. United States,* and the following year *Korematsu v. United States,* two of the cases that sanctioned war-time internment for more than 110,000 Japanese-Americans living on the Pacific Coast. It does seem notewor-

---

58. Roger N. Baldwin, "Personal Liberty," *Annals of the American Academy of Political and Social Science* 185 (May 1936): 162–69.

thy, however, that Edward J. Ennis, director of the Justice Department's Alien Enemy Control Unit, who fought valiantly on behalf of the Japanese-Americans, framed his queries for the Supreme Court in terms of "traditional standards of personal liberty" in the United States.[59] Perhaps one might say that the tragedy occurred, in part, because those standards were not "traditional" enough, or were not sufficiently engrained to protect personal liberties when racism became virulent.

Willful large-scale violations of the rights of Japanese-Americans constituted yet another unattractive example of what can happen when the quest for security (or else the relentless apprehension of insecurity) causes Americans to violate their vaunted traditions of liberty. A variation on that theme, sparked by hysterical anxiety over communism, led to the unattractive episode in our political culture that is encapsulated in a single word: McCarthyism. The damage done to personal liberty during that fevered phase—ranging from reputation to employment—has now been thoroughly documented.[60]

Even while such a bizarre melodrama was being played out, other episodes led to steady yet unspectacular victories for an expansion of the meaning of personal liberty in America. Many of these victories involved First Amendment freedoms—more particularly the issue of school prayer[61]—and caused those freedoms to be called, during the 1940s and '50s, "preferred freedoms," which meant that in case of conflict they should enjoy a higher status than subsequent amendments in the Bill of Rights.[62]

There are diverse ways to discern and particularize the great transformation that personal liberty underwent between the early 1940s and the 1970s in the United States. One way would utilize the constitu-

---

59. Peter Irons, *Justice at War: The Story of the Japanese-American Internment Cases* (New York, 1983), 183, 190. For a most ironic (and truly droll) aspect of Gordon K. Hirabayashi's quest for personal liberty, see 251.

60. See Alan Rogers, "Passports and Politics: The Courts and the Cold War," *The Historian* 47 (1985): 497–511; Leonard Boudin, "The Constitutional Right to Travel," *Columbia Law Review* 56 (1956): 47–75; *Kent v. Dulles,* 357 U.S. 116 (1958); Ellen W. Schrecker, *No Ivory Tower: McCarthyism and the Universities* (New York, 1986).

61. See Vashti Cromwell McCollum, *One Woman's Fight* (Boston, 1952), esp. 119.

62. It may be a minor irony of American constitutionalism that the best succinct history of the "preferred freedom doctrine" appears in a critical opinion by Justice Felix Frankfurter in 1949 for the case of *Kovacs v. Cooper,* 336 U.S. 77 (1949), at 89–97.

tional treatment of obscene language and freedom of expression. In the case of *Chaplinsky v. New Hampshire* (1942), Justice Frank Murphy, one of the Supreme Court's most liberal members, upheld Chaplinsky's conviction for uttering "fighting words" to a policeman. Murphy developed his definitional test in this passage.

> There are certain well-defined and narrowly limited classes of speech, the prevention and punishment of which have never been thought to raise any Constitutional problem. These include the lewd and obscene, the profane, the libelous, and the insulting or "fighting" words—those which by their very utterance inflict injury or tend to incite an immediate breach of the peace.[63]

In 1971 the case of *Cohen v. California* came before the Supreme Court. It concerned the prosecution of a man who engaged in a protest against the Vietnam War at a Los Angeles courthouse by wearing a jacket with the words "Fuck the Draft" emblazoned across the back. This time Justice John Marshall Harlan, one of the most conservative members of the Court, wrote its decision.

> While the particular four-letter word being litigated here is perhaps more distasteful than most others of its genre, it is nevertheless often true that one man's vulgarity is another's lyric. Indeed, we think it is largely because governmental officials cannot make principled distinctions in this area that the Constitution leaves matters of taste and style so largely to the individual.[64]

American decorum may have deteriorated; but perhaps it can be said that the notion of personal liberty expanded, at the very least, and perhaps even progressed between 1942 and 1971.[65]

VII

During the past few decades, in my view, more genuinely new dimensions have been added to the notion of personal liberty than at any other

63. *Chaplinsky v. New Hampshire*, 315 U.S. 568 (1942), at 571–72.
64. *Cohen v. California*, 403 U.S. 15 (1971), at 25.
65. For a thoughtful overview and case study, see Donald Alexander Downs, *Nazis in Skokie: Freedom, Community, and the First Amendment* (Notre Dame, Ind., 1985). See also Justice Wiley B. Rutledge concurring in the case of *In re Oliver*, 333 U.S. 257 (1948), at 280.

time in our entire history. The concept has achieved levels of complexity, richness, and controversy previously unimagined. In part these developments resulted from technological revolutions which had implications ranging from silent governmental surveillance of the individual to matters involving sexual intimacy and means of dealing with unwanted consequences of such intimacy. Above all, however, these developments are linked to the concept of a right to privacy, a right perceived as extra-constitutional when first proposed by Louis D. Brandeis and Samuel D. Warren in 1890, yet one that gradually has become "constitutionalized" since 1965.

Although the cultural and legal history of a "right to privacy" would require a separate volume,[66] we can at least look at some of the ways in which it has made the concept of personal liberty more meaningful (and more palpable) than ever before. That explication by Brandeis and Warren was stimulated by the increasing intrusiveness of low-level journalism upon American life in general and its impact upon personal reputation in particular—what the two lawyers designated with an ungainly yet memorable phrase as the "newspaperization" of private life. The authors believed that government was already constrained to respect an individual's right to privacy; they urged that comparable constraints be placed upon newspapers and similar sources of gossip-mongering. But they contended that a right to privacy was implicit in the common law, "as a part of the more general right to the immunity of the person —the right to one's personality." The right to privacy, therefore, was a torts concept rather than a constitutional right.[67]

In 1928, twelve years after he had been named to the United States Supreme Court, Brandeis confronted a case that caused him to feel less sanguine about the normatively benign role of government. The issue involved wiretapping and the government's use of evidence obtained illegally. Brandeis's brethren approved; but his trenchant dissent would

66. See, for the moment, a valuable anthology developed for classroom use: P. Allan Dionisopoulos and Craig R. Ducat, eds., *The Right to Privacy: Essays and Cases* (St. Paul, Minn., 1976).

67. Warren and Brandeis, "The Right to Privacy," *Harvard Law Review* 4 (December 1890): 207; Dorothy J. Glancy, "The Invention of the Right to Privacy," *Arizona Law Review* 21 (1979): 1–39.

be an exceedingly important harbinger of new directions in American constitutionalism more than a generation later. Brandeis used a lengthy extract from an 1886 case in order to review the historical background of the Fourth and Fifth Amendments, more particularly government invasion of the sanctities of a man's home and the private aspects of his life. What had become unacceptable in the Anglo-American tradition was "the invasion of [a person's] indefeasible right of personal security, personal liberty and private property, where that right has never been forfeited by his conviction of some public offence." Four pages later Brandeis boldly sounded a phrase that has acquired considerable resonance in our own time — a phrase that connects, as no other could, the right to privacy with personal liberty.

> The makers of our Constitution . . . conferred, as against the Government, the right to be let alone — the most comprehensive of rights and the right most valued by civilized men. To protect that right, every unjustifiable intrusion by the Government upon the privacy of the individual, whatever the means employed, must be deemed a violation of the Fourth Amendment.[68]

Despite that eloquent dissent, the Supreme Court remained very muddled on this matter through the 1950s, and spoke with varied voices concerning the question of when illegally obtained evidence was admissible. Not when brutality, physical assault, or coercion had been used, apparently, yet acceptable when trespass, burglary, or the planting of microphones by police had been authorized. What rationale legitimized these distinctions is not clear; but the fact remains that until the decision in *Mapp v. Ohio* (1961), the Fourth Amendment did not apply to the states. Writing the Court's opinion in that case, Justice Tom C. Clark acknowledged the existence of "consitutional documentation of the right of privacy free from unreasonable state intrusion."[69]

In 1960, meanwhile, quite a different aspect of personal liberty and the right to privacy received the Court's imprimatur. The question that arose involved whether or not compulsory disclosure of membership

---

68. *Olmstead v. United States,* 277 U.S. 438 (1928), at 474, 478. See also Brandeis concurring in *St. Josephs Stock Yards Co. v. United States,* 298 U.S. 77 (1936).

69. Cortner, *The Supreme Court and the Second Bill of Rights,* 169–71, 185–86.

lists of local branches of the National Association for the Advancement of Colored People would interfere with the freedom of association of members. Justice Potter Stewart defined the issue in this manner: had the cities, as instrumentalities of the State, demonstrated so cogent a public interest in obtaining and making public membership lists as to justify the substantial abridgment of associational freedom? Stewart responded with caution and prudence. "Where there is a significant encroachment upon personal liberty," he wrote, "the State may prevail only upon showing a subordinating interest which is compelling."[70]

Justice William O. Douglas helped to prepare the way for these decisions during the 1950s by building upon the two concepts that Louis D. Brandeis had introduced in 1890 and 1928. A case came before the High Court in 1952 because the Washington, D.C., transit system decided to enhance its revenues by installing continuous radio broadcasting on its buses. Although the Court approved, Douglas dissented because he objected to any form of coerced listening. His language is stirring, but also important because it anticipated major developments in constitutional doctrine that occurred during the 1960s and '70s. Douglas grounded his argument as much in natural right, or in constitutional implications, as he did in the Constitution itself.

> Liberty in the constitutional sense must mean more than freedom from unlawful governmental restraint; it must include privacy as well, if it is to be a repository of freedom. The right to be let alone is indeed the beginning of all freedom. . . . The right of privacy should include the right to pick and choose from competing entertainments, competing propaganda, competing political philosophies. If people are let alone in those choices, the right of privacy will pay dividends in character and integrity.[71]

Less than six years later Douglas expanded upon this theme in reaching a wider audience. The longest section in a published collection

---

70. *Bates v. Little Rock,* 361 U.S. 516 (1960), at 524. See also *McLaughlin v. Florida,* 379 U.S. 184 (1964).

71. *Public Utilities Commission of the District of Columbia v. Pollak,* 343 U.S. 451 (1952), at 467–69. See also Dorothy J. Glancy, "Getting Government Off the Backs of People: The Right of Privacy and Freedom of Expression in the Opinions of Justice William O. Douglas," *Santa Clara Law Review* 21 (1981): 1047–67.

of lectures first given at Franklin and Marshall College was entitled "The Right to Be Let Alone"; and the first installment of that section Douglas called "The Right of Privacy." Having linked economic opportunity with personal freedom in the 1940s, he moved during the '50s toward positions that some others would come to share in the next decade — yet remain controversial among jurists and scholars to this day. Referring to personal liberty and privacy as "natural rights," he insisted in 1958 that some of these rights had been "written explicitly into the Constitution. Others are to be implied. The penumbra of the Bill of Rights reflects human rights which, though not explicit, are implied from the very nature of man as a child of God."[72]

Quite early in his career on the Court, Douglas staunchly opposed intervention by the State in the intimate relationships or reproductive rights of an individual. In 1942, for example, he wrote the High Court's opinion reversing a judgment by the Supreme Court of Oklahoma that the State could legally sterilize a man who was a habitual criminal. In 1961, when the United States Supreme Court refused to overturn Connecticut's law prohibiting the sale of contraceptives, Douglas supplied a resounding dissent.[73]

Thereafter others on the Court became willing to follow the path that Douglas had marked out for years. The decision in 1965 to overturn Connecticut's ban on contraceptives is too familiar to require extended commentary. The point most pertinent to this essay is that Justices Arthur J. Goldberg and Byron R. White quoted Potter Stewart's assertion in *Bates v. Little Rock* (1960): "Where there is a significant encroachment upon personal liberty, the State may prevail only upon showing a subordinating interest which is compelling." White characterized reproductive decisions as being within the "sensitive areas of liberty" protected by the Court; and Goldberg proscribed governmental invasion of marital privacy.[74]

Seven years later Justice Brennan wrote the Court's opinion that extended the implications of *Griswold* to unmarried persons. "If the right

---

72. Douglas, *The Right of the People* (Garden City, N.Y., 1958), esp. 85–94, the quotation at 89; James F. Simon, *Independent Journey: The Life of William O. Douglas* (New York, 1981), 251.

73. *Skinner v. Oklahoma*, 316 U.S. 535 (1942); *Poe v. Ullman*, 367 U.S. 497 (1961), at 517.

74. *Griswold v. Connecticut*, 381 U.S. 479 (1965) at 496–97, 503–4.

to privacy means anything," he declared, "it is the right of the *individual,* married or single, to be free from unwarranted governmental intrusion into matters so fundamentally affecting a person as the decision whether to bear or beget a child."[75] In a major expansion of the widely questioned basis for the 1965 decision, the Supreme Court now recognized that a right to privacy unfolded from the right to personal liberty in a general sense, rather than emerging from murky penumbras created by various articles in the Bill of Rights.

In retrospect it seems almost inevitable that Justice Harry A. Blackmun's opinion in *Roe v. Wade* would derive a woman's right to terminate her pregnancy from "the concept of personal 'liberty' embodied" in the Due Process Clause of the Fourteenth Amendment. Justice Stewart's concurrence used language that was technically more correct in acknowledging the act of judicial interpretation: "The right asserted by Jane Roe is embraced within the personal liberty protected" by the Due Process Clause.[76]

VIII

There is considerably more to the story of personal liberty and the right to privacy—a relationship that has become particularly interesting and complex during the past quarter-century. Since 1965 the Supreme Court has tended to protect "personal privacy" on the grounds that it is inherent in the term "liberty." Lest the preceding section convey an impression of emerging consensus and steady progress, however, it seems prudent to conclude by noting some patterns of inconsistency.

Two cases that came to the High Court from Georgia are indicative of ups and downs if not outright inconsistency. In 1969 the Court ruled that persons may possess and view obscene films in the privacy of their

---

75. *Eisenstadt, Sheriff, v. Baird,* 405 U.S. 438 (1972), at 453.

76. *Roe v. Wade,* 410 U.S. 113 (1973), at 129, 152–53, 170. For a complex case involving a woman facing criminal charges concerning her allegedly irresponsible conduct during pregnancy, see *New York Times,* Oct. 9, 1986, p. A22. The woman's child died (as a result of her behavior) soon after its birth. The director of the American Civil Liberties Union's reproductive freedom project, which is serving as the woman's co-counsel, has insisted that "a woman's right to privacy means the state is restricted from having any interest in her pregnancy."

homes. As Justice Thurgood Marshall explained on behalf of the majority, "mere categorization of these films as 'obscene' is insufficient justification for such a drastic invasion of personal liberties guaranteed by the First and Fourteenth Amendments." In 1986, however, the Court ruled (by a sharply contested vote of 5 to 4) that a Georgia law prohibiting sodomy could stand. Twenty-three other states also have such laws. As the *New York Times* summarized the situation: "The Constitution does not protect homosexual relations between consenting adults, even in the privacy of their own homes."[77]

Why does the concept of a right to privacy, protected by the Fourteenth Amendment, justify the sale of contraceptives (even to unmarried minors), a woman's decision to have an abortion, and the privilege of watching any sort of film in one's home, but not homosexual acts performed by consenting adults in private? It may be quite some time before the inconsistency is clarified or rectified.

President Reagan has seemed to have a low regard for the right of privacy. In September 1986 he directed the heads of federal agencies to establish programs designed to test drug abuse (through urinalysis) among a broad range of government employees. Three days after the President's mandate appeared, a judge at the Federal District Court in Newark, New Jersey, declared it an unconstitutional invasion of privacy. By the end of 1986, law suits had successfully stopped thirteen out of seventeen programs for random drug-testing on the grounds that such tests violate the Fourth Amendment protection against unreasonable search and seizure.[78] Where certain sorts of issues were concerned, the Reagan administration has appeared to follow the policy that a person is guilty until proven innocent.

Although it is possible, and even historically sensible, to say that notions of personal liberty have come a long way in American thought

77. *Stanley v. Georgia,* 394 U.S. 557 (1969), at 565; *Bowers v. Hardwick,* 106 S. Ct. 2841 (1986), reported in *New York Times,* July 1, 1986, p. 1.

78. See *New York Times,* Sept. 19, 1986, p. 1, Nov. 13, 1986, p. D27, and Dec. 11, 1986, p. 1. For a citizen's damage suit involving privacy (illegal wiretapping and harassment) brought against federal agents by black and Vietnam peace activists, pending since 1976 and still being fought by the Justice Department, see *New York Times,* Sept. 28, 1986, p. 35.

and culture, a sampling of statements made by prominent opinion-shapers in 1986–87 suggests that resistance to change remains strong. The mainstream apparently prefers moderate balancing. Justice Hugo Black's belief in absolute governmental guarantees of those freedoms protected by the Constitution is not currently fashionable. On the eve of Liberty Weekend in 1986, the widely respected James Reston had this to say:

> In the civil life of the nation, personal liberty has a lovely sound but often means license to break the law, traffick in drugs, abandon families and put personal or special interests ahead of the general good. . . . The modern nation-state, operating for the first time in a complicated world economy, has to find practical ways of reconciling personal liberty with the general welfare if it is to compete successfully with other industrial nations. . . .[79]

Quite frankly, it never occurred to me — nor do I believe it occurred to the framers — that personal rights protected by the United States Constitution would ever have to be subordinated to the exigencies of international economic competition. Adam Smith does not yet rank above John Milton, Roger Williams, Thomas Jefferson, Frederick Douglass, or Louis D. Brandeis in my pantheon of heroes or hierarchy of values.

In 1984 the United States Bishops' "Ad Hoc Committee on Catholic Social Teaching and the U.S. Economy" produced a pastoral letter that urged the government to adopt more compassionate economic policies in order to achieve a "just economic order," particularly for the "poor and deprived members of the human community." That might require some governmental intervention in the marketplace; but, once again, it seems fair to point out that Adam Smith has been dead since 1790.[80]

Not to the Lay Commission on Catholic Social Teaching and the U.S. Economy, however. That conservative group wrote a rebuttal to the bishops that tendentiously condemned "radical individualism." It also called for necessary counterweights to personal liberty:

79. Reston, "Liberty and Authority," *New York Times*, June 29, 1986, p. E23.

80. "First Draft — Bishops' Pastoral: Catholic Social Teaching and the U.S. Economy," *Origins: N.C. Documentary Service* 14 (22/23): 337–38.

> Every human society must strike a proper balance between individual liberty and common action. The American experiment has entailed a keen struggle to find that balance. On the one side is the unique commitment of our people to personal liberty, as enshrined in and animating the federal Constitution. On the other is the central presupposition of that historical document: that our vigorous familial and communal life continue healthy and strong, a common unity. Strong families and strong communities teach those personal virtues without which the Constitution cannot be preserved, and provide care for those who are in need of help and guidance.[81]

If the concept of personal liberty has not only grown but changed over time, there is little wisdom in the assumption that it should change no more. What is curious about the Lay Commission's letter, however, is that it represents a reactionary return to the Calvinist value system of Massachusetts Bay. There is much to admire in that value system; but we must not lose sight of the fact that the socio-economic circumstances of a seventeenth-century colony are several hundred light years removed from our own.

We should also keep in mind that the meaning of personal liberty has repeatedly altered over time, in part, because the concept is not explicitly mentioned in the United States Constitution. It is not frozen into a singular form by virtue of inclusion in a sacred text. In so far as it has variously meant liberty of conscience; opposition to chattel slavery; freedom from physical restraint; freedom of political association; freedom from surveillance where no threat to the State is involved; and a right to privacy that includes control over one's body, it has drawn upon both of the great traditions of liberty: negative as well as positive freedom, "freedom from" and "freedom to."

As Justices Brandeis and Douglas so eloquently explained, the concept of personal liberty is considerably older than our Constitution.[82]

---

81. *Toward the Future: Catholic Social Thought and the U.S. Economy: A Lay Letter* (New York, 1984), xi–xii.

82. The comparative history of personal liberty lies beyond the scope of this essay. For leads in the direction of such comparisons, however, I would suggest the following: Edward Muir, *Civic Ritual in Renaissance Venice* (Princeton, N.J., 1981), 17; Frederic May Holland, *Liberty in the Nineteenth Century* (New York, 1899), 159–63, 202–6, 210–32; *Federal Constitution*

The latter *began* to catch up with the former in 1789, with passage of the Bill of Rights. It gained additional ground in 1868, with ratification of the Fourteenth Amendment. It achieved a significant degree of re-conceptualization between 1928 and 1965; and since then the notion of a constitutional right to privacy has infused personal liberty with palpable new meaning.

In historical terms, I cannot conceive of a more significant phenome-non in our culture than the spasmodic adjustment of American con-stitutionalism to the process whereby we discover new imperatives in those two simple words, personal liberty. In contemporary terms, I can-not imagine a more significant social and political agenda than the on-going clarification of what we mean by personal liberty in response to our growing concern for human happiness, dignity, and autonomy.

of Malaysia (Kuala Lumpur, 1986), 3–4 ("Liberty of the Person"); The Constitution of India, Part III ("Fundamental Rights"), article 21, in Amos J. Peaslee, ed., *Constitutions of Nations* (3d ed.; The Hague, 1966), 2:314; [United Nations], "The [Universal] Declaration of Human Rights" (1948), esp. articles 3, 6, 12, and 13, in Robert E. Sherwood, ed., *Peace on Earth* (New York, 1949), 225–31.

This essay was initially presented on March 12, 1987, as a Walter Prescott Webb Memorial Lecture at the University of Texas at Arlington. I wish to thank my hosts on that occasion for their gracious hospitality: Professors Sandra L. Myres, David E. Narrett, Stanley H. Palmer, and Dr. Charles B. Lowry, Director of Libraries at "UTA." I am also indebted to the Texas A&M University Press for permission to reprint the essay in this collection, and to Professor Joyce S. Goldberg for her editorial precision.

I subsequently offered a briefer version on May 28, 1987, at an International Congress, "The Constitution and What It Means Today," held at the University of Bologna's Palazzo Hercolani, in Bologna, Italy, on the occasion of the 900th anniversary of the University's found-ing. My deepest appreciation goes to Professor Tiziano Bonazzi and to Luisa Pece Pasquino for their marvelous handling of so many complex logistical matters.

Four

The United States Constitution, Public Opinion, and the Question of American Exceptionalism

---

HOW DISTINCTIVE is the American constitutional system? Although that question has not been altogether neglected, rarely has it been responded to in cultural rather than structural terms. It has traditionally been answered, in fact, by contrasting the operational relationships among governmental institutions or branches in the United States and in Great Britain. Frequently the analyst then carries the comparison a step further by indicating a preference for one system rather than the other, or else by arguing that one's own arrangement would be improved by incorporating certain essential attributes of the other.[1]

I would like to explore the issue along cultural lines by looking historically at the role of public opinion in our constitutional set-up. More specifically, I am interested in American attitudes toward the function or proper place of public opinion in a governmental system that aspires to be democratic while having an independent (and largely unelected) judiciary at its upper echelons.

---

1. See Michael Kammen, *A Machine That Would Go of Itself: The Constitution in American Culture* (New York, 1986), ch. 6; Donald L. Robinson, ed., *Reforming American Government: The Bicentennial Papers of the Committee on the Constitutional System* (Boulder, Colo., 1985), esp. 11–29, 50–58, 131–54, 191–208, 299–306.

It is necessary to acknowledge at the outset that we cannot comfortably generalize about public opinion in a singular way, either in a diachronic or in a synchronic sense. Why? Because we find either ambivalence or an absence of consensus at any given moment in time (whether it be the 1830s, the 1870s, or the 1980s), but also because there have been fundamental changes over time in American feelings about the proper role of public opinion in constitutional matters. More on these shifts in a moment. First I should clarify what I mean by "exceptionalism," especially in the context of constitutional affairs.

For nearly a decade now we have been sensitized to the importance of comparative analysis in order to avoid the parochialism that has caused too many historians of the United States to make contestable claims for the uniqueness or autonomy of American history.[2] It is particularly noteworthy, however, that increased attention to comparisons has caused many observers, American as well as foreign, to be more impressed by differences than by similarities. Reports that American exceptionalism is dead seem to have been premature, to say the least. If anything, that phenomenon or perspective has been rather solidly bolstered by new bodies of impressive evidence.[3]

If we look at constitutionalism in the United States through the lens of American exceptionalism, we should not be surprised to find multiple patterns arranged around a complex core of kaleidoscopic changes. James Madison, for example, along with most members of his generation, subscribed to the belief that the American people possessed their own peculiar "genius," particularly in politics, and that the federal Constitution of 1787 *had* to be both a product of that genius and also

2. For the most succinct assessments, see Laurence Veysey, "The Autonomy of American History Reconsidered," *American Quarterly* 31 (Fall 1979): 455–77; and Carl N. Degler, "In Pursuit of an American History," *American Historical Review* 92 (February 1987): 1–12.

3. See, for example, Alfred D. Chandler, Jr., *The Visible Hand: The Managerial Revolution in American Business* (Cambridge, Mass., 1977), 64, 93, 205; Wyn Wachhorst, *Thomas Alva Edison: An American Myth* (Cambridge, Mass., 1981), 120; Sean Wilentz, *Chants Democratic: New York City and the Rise of the American Working Class, 1788–1850* (New York, 1984), 141–42, 156–57, 238; Kenneth T. Jackson, *Crabgrass Frontier: The Suburbanization of the United States* (New York, 1985); Bernard Bailyn, *The Peopling of British North America* (New York, 1986), 60, 68, 85, 112, 114, 120; Bailyn, *Voyagers to the West: A Passage in the Peopling of America on the Eve of the Revolution* (New York, 1986), 4; and Rebecca Scott, "Comparing Emancipations: A Review Essay," *Journal of Social History* 20 (Spring 1987): 565–83, esp. 574, 576.

remain consistent with it. As Madison wrote in his essay on "Charters," published in *The National Gazette* early in 1792: "In Europe, charters of liberty [i.e., constitutions] have been granted by power. America has set the example . . . of charters of power granted by liberty. . . . The citizens of the United States have peculiar [i.e., distinctive] motives to support the energy of their constitutional charters."[4]

Less than a century later, however, serious students of American constitutionalism would acknowledge that in significant respects our system shared common origins with the British, and, moreover, had become more like it with the passage of time.[5] By the middle of the twentieth century, when Perry Miller became immersed in his work on *The Legal Mind in America, from Independence to the Civil War* (1962), he sought guidance from authorities at Harvard's Law School. This extract from a long advisory letter written by Professor Henry M. Hart is indicative of a cosmopolitan and spreading skepticism concerning American exceptionalism:

> It seems to me important to make clear that the controversy over codification was raging at the same time in Europe [the 1840s and '50s] and with comparable intensity. I do not mean to say that this fact invalidates your thesis that the codification movement here was an expression of a significant strain in American culture. But codification was not an American conception. The idea simply found hospitable soil here.[6]

Judicial review, by way of contrast, has frequently been touted as the most distinctive American contribution to the entire history of Western constitutionalism; and its origins are traditionally located between 1796 (*Hylton v. United States*), when the Supreme Court upheld an act of Congress, and 1803 (*Marbury v. Madison*), when the Court invalidated one section of the Federal Judiciary Act of 1789.

Invariably overlooked, however, is the American propensity—visible

---

4. Madison, "Charters," *The National Gazette*, Jan. 19, 1792, in Gaillard Hunt, ed., *The Writings of James Madison*, 6 (New York, 1906), 83–85; Joyce Appleby, *Capitalism and a New Social Order: The Republican Vision of the 1790s* (New York, 1984), 80.

5. Kammen, *Machine That Would Go of Itself*, 166–70.

6. Hart to Miller, Hart Papers, box 5, fol. 6, Harvard Law School Library, Langdell Hall, Cambridge, Mass.

even before state constitutions first appeared in 1776 — to declare unacceptable policies or actions by a government unconstitutional. Assertions of that sort were common in 1774–75, and provide one of the earliest as well as one of the most striking instances of constitutionalism firmly rooted in popular opinion at the grassroots level. In 1774, for example, the standing Committee of Correspondence in Gloucester County, Virginia, resolved "That it is the opinion of this meeting, that taxation and representation are inseparable. . . . Every attempt of [Parliament] to impose internal taxes on *America,* is arbitrary, unconstitutional, and oppressive." Echoes of that resolve could be heard in Kent County, Delaware, and Hackensack, New Jersey.[7]

Populist patriots discoursed on matters *un*constitutional even before they learned and contributed to the language of constitutionalism (see figure 2). From the eve of the American Revolution onward, public opinion and constitutionalism powerfully reinforced one another. They made a potent combination. Except for a brief and unsuccessful flurry in Britain during the 1780s and '90s, they had no counterpart as a tandem anywhere else in the world. It seems fair to assert, then, that an incipient notion of popular constitutionalism preceded and helped to provide an impetus for our most creative phase of formal constitution-making, 1776–87.

That truly remarkable era would stamp American constitutionalism as a distinctive phenomenon for a long time to come. Constitutions that are written, succinct, and new cannot serve as "mythical charters," which is what one finds through most of recorded history up until that time, and even well into the nineteenth century. The heroic epics of ancient Greece, transmitted by means of oral tradition, served as mythical charters, just as the discolored skull of a venerable chieftain, wrapped in cloth strips taken from the robes of all his successors, fulfilled the same role for certain "primitive" or pre-industrial peoples.[8] Such "charters" were simultaneously mystical yet suffused with sacred stories, and

7. Peter Force, comp., *American Archives: Consisting of a Collection of Authentick Records, State Papers, Debates, and Letters and Other Notices of Publick Affairs* . . . (Washington, D.C., 1837–53), series 4, 1:539, 665; 2:130–31.

8. See M. I. Finley, *The Use and Abuse of History* (New York, 1975), 26; Bronislaw Malinowski, *Magic, Science and Religion and Other Essays* (Garden City, N.Y., 1954), 117; Jan Vansina,

hence with human interest, in a way that the American constitutions of 1776–87 could not be. However much the latter enjoyed the imprimatur and legitimacy of popular sovereignty, they could not and would not embody the broad appeal of popular myths meant to explain the origin of a people or the founding of a state.

Other sorts of contrasts emerge if we examine the constitution of Renaissance Venice, which was literally displayed in the traditional ducal procession. As Edward Muir has explained:

> Besides illustrating the symbiosis of the religious and political organs of authority, the origins of Venetian independence, and the harmony of Venetian society, the [ducal] procession created a paradigmatic arrangement of the Venetian constitution and social structure. . . . More than merely reinforcing the ideology of Venice, the ducal processions helped create that ideology by serving as a conscious, visible synthesis of the parts of society: each symbol or person in the procession corresponded to a specific principle or institution; placed together and set in motion, they were the narrative outline for the myth of Venetian republicanism.[9]

Unlike the American constitutions, which combined a degree of popular sovereignty with domination by accessible elites, the Venetian constitution wrapped patrician domination in a myth of social harmony and the legitimacy of historic origins. That myth provided the Venetians with more than a modicum of constitutional flexibility. As Muir puts it: "What could be more delightful than a political paragon that was kaleidoscopic? Turned slightly this way or that, the Venetian constitution could become almost anything one wanted or needed it to be." Note well, however, that "one" refers to patrician leaders, not to popular opinion. The constitution and political culture of republican Venice were vastly different from those in republican America.[10]

"History in the Field," in D. G. Jongmans and P. C. W. Gutkind, eds., *Anthropologists in the Field* (Assen, 1967), 107.

9. Muir, *Civic Ritual in Renaissance Venice* (Princeton, N.J., 1981), 211. See also Felix Gilbert, "The Venetian Constitution in Florentine Political Thought," in Gilbert, *History: Choice and Commitment* (Cambridge, Mass., 1977), 179–214.

10. Muir, *Civic Ritual in Renaissance Venice*, 49, 189–90. For the promulgation of a re-

Similarly, the Constitution of Epidaurus that launched modern Greek independence in 1822, and the long-standing British notion of an "ancient constitution," and the symbol-laden constitution that the British bestowed upon India in Victorian times, were all susceptible to manipulation in various ways—but did not lend themselves to being applied or revised through the filters of public opinion.[11] By contrast, the new American constitutions were, on paper, more fixed and less flexible; yet the force of public opinion could and did result in periodic revisions— and even replacements. One of the most remarkable (yet unremarked) differences between most early modern constitutions and our own is that ours were not mythical charters. They were real, written, and consequently less malleable in any immediate way. With the passage of time, however, that would change.

II

Although scholars have not been indifferent to the role of public opinion in American life, the historical attention devoted to it has been somewhat random, episodic, and hortatory, rather than systematic and substantive.[12] We know that a journal called *Public Opinion* appeared in the 1890s, for instance; and that in time of war, especially, public opinion has been used as coercive pressure in order to mobilize support. During World War I, for example, a widely distributed poster displayed a woman (presumably a compound of Columbia and Miss Liberty) in classical drapery, with her right fist clenched and her left hand raised

---

markably comparable constitution in 1889, see Carol Gluck, *Japan's Modern Myths: Ideology in the Late Meiji Period* (Princeton, N.J., 1985), 42–49.

11. See Michael Herzfeld, *Ours Once More: Folklore, Ideology, and the Making of Modern Greece* (Austin, Tex., 1982), 6; J. G. A. Pocock, *Politics, Language and Time: Essays on Political Thought and History* (New York, 1971), 209; Bernard S. Cohn, "Representing Authority in Victorian India," in Eric Hobsbawm and Terence Ranger, eds., *The Invention of Tradition* (Cambridge, 1983) 179–83, 190, 197–98.

12. See Melvin Small, ed., *Public Opinion and Historians: Interdisciplinary Perspectives* (Detroit, 1970); Lee Benson, "An Approach to the Scientific Study of Past Public Opinion," in Benson, *Toward the Scientific Study of History: Selected Essays* (Philadelphia, 1972), 105–59; Joseph R. Strayer, "The Historian's Concept of Public Opinion," in Mirra Komarovsky, ed., *Common Frontiers of the Social Sciences* (Glencoe, Ill., 1957), 263–68.

in a gesture that seems to suggest the imminence of a citizen's arrest. Above her head, in very bold letters, four words appear:

I AM PUBLIC OPINION

followed by this admonition.

> All men fear me!
>
> I declare that Uncle Sam shall not go to his knees to beg you to buy his bonds. That is no position for a fighting man. But if you have the money to buy and do not buy, I will make this No Man's Land for you!
>
> I will judge you not by an allegiance expressed in mere words.
>
> I will judge you not by your mad cheers as our boys march away to whatever fate may have in store for them.
>
> I will judge you not by the warmth of the tears you shed over the lists of the dead and the injured that come to us from time to time.
>
> I will judge you not by your uncovered head and solemn mien as our maimed in battle return to our shores for loving care.
>
> But, as wise as I am just, I will judge you by the material aid you give to the fighting men who are facing death that you may live and move and have your being in a world made safe.
>
> I warn you—don't talk patriotism over here unless your money is talking victory over there.
>
> *I AM PUBLIC OPINION!*
>
> *AS I JUDGE, ALL MEN STAND OR FALL!*

Directly below those stanzas the poster advised:

> Buy U.S. Gov't. Bonds Fourth Liberty Loan[13]

By the early 1920s, Walter Lippmann and Edward L. Bernays alerted the country, as never before, to the potential force of popular opinion

---

13. Stephen Vaughn, *Holding Fast the Inner Lines: Democracy, Nationalism, and the Committee on Public Information* (Chapel Hill, N.C., 1980), 164.

in business and advertising as well as public affairs.[14] Within a decade scholars had made the scientific study of public opinion an innovative sub-discipline. Public opinion polling developed rapidly during the later 1930s and has proliferated for various purposes ever since.[15] Indeed, it is one of the more precise areas of activity within the social sciences.

To what extent, then, did the framers of the United States Constitution anticipate that public opinion would swiftly emerge as a prominent force in American politics? The customary response to such a query has ranged somewhere between "not at all" and "barely." I would like to suggest that they were not so naive. On the one hand, they recognized that public opinion is an exceedingly elusive phenomenon; but on the other, they believed that republicanism and popular sovereignty, by their very nature, permitted public opinion to play a more influential role than it had in any other governmental system ever known.

There is abundant evidence that public opinion began to be taken into account as an inescapable factor by the boldest expounders of political thought in Great Britain during the last decades of the eighteenth century.[16] Their writings circulated in North America and confirmed what many inhabitants there already knew: namely, that the Stamp Act crisis of 1765–66 had aroused widespread political consciousness and activity. One of the most telling legacies of that crisis, in fact, may very well have been an insatiable hunger for political news—a direct result of the recognition that such news could affect behavior as well as attitudes. In 1795, for example, when St. George Tucker of Virginia asked Jeremy Belknap how Massachusetts had managed to abolish Negro slav-

14. Lippmann, *Public Opinion* (New York, 1922); Bernays, *Crystallizing Public Opinion* (New York, 1923). See also A. Lawrence Lowell, *Public Opinion and Popular Government* (New York, 1914).

15. See *The Gallup Poll: Public Opinion, 1935–1971* (New York, 1972), 3 vols.; Hans Speier, "Historical Development of Public Opinion," *American Journal of Sociology* 55 (January 1950): 376–88.

16. J. A. W. Gunn, *Beyond Liberty and Property: The Process of Self-Recognition in Eighteenth-Century Political Thought* (Kingston and Montreal, 1983), ch. 7, "Public Spirit to Public Opinion"; H. T. Dickinson, *Liberty and Property: Political Ideology in Eighteenth-Century Britain* (New York, 1977), 188–92, 195, 209–15, 219–21. See also Paul A. Palmer, "The Concept of Public Opinion in Political Theory," in *Essays in Historical and Political Theory in Honor of Charles Howard McIlwain* (Cambridge, Mass., 1936), 230–57.

ery, Belknap replied with the following sentence: "The general answer is, that slavery hath been abolished here by *public opinion*; which began to be established about thirty years ago."[17]

Among the delegates to the Constitutional Convention in 1787 there certainly was no "representative" position concerning the most appropriate or ideal role of public opinion in the governmental system they hoped to establish. Nevertheless, remarks made by William Paterson of New Jersey on June 9 seem to have been a reasonable summation of the sentiments shared by many. According to Paterson (as reported by James Madison):

> The idea of a national Govt. as contradistinguished from a federal one, never entered into the mind of any of them [i.e., the state legislatures], and to the public mind we must accommodate ourselves. We have no power to go beyond the federal scheme, and if we had the people are not ripe for any other. We must follow the people; the people will not follow us.[18]

From Paterson's perspective, the nature of the new government ought to be responsive to the "public mind," not merely in an expedient sense, but as a matter of republican political ethics.

On June 18 Alexander Hamilton delivered a very long address to the Convention, a schematization of his ideal constitution that is said to have lasted for more than five hours. Half a century later, at the time of the Constitution's Golden Jubilee, John Quincy Adams found a copy of Hamilton's speech in the papers of James Madison. Although Adams admired many particular aspects of Hamilton's plan, he conceded that it would have placed too much power in the new national government and that it bore too many similarities to the British constitution. Consequently its tendencies were such "as the public opinion of that day never would have tolerated."[19]

17. *Collections of the Massachusetts Historical Society for the Year 1795*, first series, Volume 4 (Boston, 1795), 201. The italics are Belknap's.

18. Max Farrand, ed., *The Records of the Federal Convention of 1787* (2d ed.; New Haven, Conn., 1937), 1:178. For a similar position taken by Madison respecting the most sensible manner of selecting United States senators, see *Federalist* number 62, in Jacob E. Cooke, ed., *The Federalist* (Middletown, Conn., 1961), 416.

19. Quoted in Catherine Drinker Bowen, *Miracle at Philadephia: The Story of the Constitutional Convention, May to September 1787* (Boston, 1966), 114.

Hamilton was not so unrealistic and oblivious to public opinion as he is customarily depicted, however. He differed from most of his contemporaries only in wishing to shape and lead rather than consistently follow public opinion. In *Federalist* number 70 he positively acknowledged "the restraints of public opinion" as a safeguard "for the faithful exercise of any delegated power."[20] And in *Federalist* number 84 he insisted that freedom of the press ultimately depended not so much upon constitutional clauses as it did upon "public opinion, and on the general spirit of the people and of the government."[21]

Soon after Hamilton's idiosyncratic (though apparently uninterrupted) speech on June 18, he left the Convention for a period in order to return to New York. On July 3 he explained to George Washington in a letter that during his travels, and ever since reaching New York City, he had "taken particular pains to discover the public sentiment." He then revealed that he, for one, would be content to placate whatever appeared to be the public will. "The prevailing apprehension among thinking men," he observed, "is that the Convention, from a fear of shocking the popular opinion, will not go far enough."[22]

In *Federalist* number 49, first published on February 2, 1788, Madison offered one of the shrewdest commentaries on the fundamental character of public opinion (see figure 12). He followed up a very sweeping generalization with an important qualification based upon his keen understanding of human nature.

> If it be true that all governments rest on opinion, it is no less true that the strength of opinion in each individual, and its practical influence on his conduct, depend much on the number which he supposes to have entertained the same opinion. The reason of man, like man himself is timid and cautious, when left alone; and acquires firmness and confidence, in proportion to the number with which it is associated.[23]

20. Cooke, ed., *The Federalist,* 477.

21. Ibid., 580.

22. Hamilton to Washington, July 3, 1787, in Harold C. Syrett, ed., *The Papers of Alexander Hamilton,* 4 (New York, 1962), 223–24.

23. Cooke, ed., *The Federalist,* 340.

Early in 1792, when Madison published his essay entitled "Charters" [i.e., constitutions], he elaborated this theme of public opinion in the context of republican government. "All power has been traced up to opinion," he wrote.

> The stability of all governments and security of all rights may be traced to the same source. The most arbitrary government is controuled where the public opinion is fixed. . . . The most systematic governments are turned by the slightest impulse from their regular paths, where public opinion no longer holds them in it. . . . How devoutly is it to be wished, then, that the public opinion of the United States should be enlightened; that it should attach itself to their governments as delineated in *great* charters, derived not from the usurped power of kings, but from the legitimate authority of the people.[24]

Although Madison's positions in 1787–88 and 1792 are consistent, his *tone* had changed from one that was speculative and analytical to one that seems at once hortatory yet a bit apprehensive. What had happened during that four-year span to alter his tone? We do not know with assurance, but one expert on the period, Jack N. Rakove, has persuasively suggested that the state ratification campaigns in 1788 had been designed to activate public opinion, and succeeded beyond anyone's wildest imagination. Constituent impact promptly became more important than leaders had anticipated; and by 1790 coping with the pressures of public opinion turned out to be much more problematic for elected officials than delegates to the Convention envisioned in 1787.[25]

During the decades that followed, two lines of discourse emerged. The first, and the less important one in my view, celebrated in a rather mindless (and sometimes insincere) manner the emergence of public opinion as a sign of the progress of civilization.[26]

24. Hunt, ed., *Writings of Madison*, 6:85. The italics are Madison's.

25. Rakove, "The Structure of Politics at the Accession of George Washington," in Richard Beeman et al., eds., *Beyond Confederation: Origins of the Constitution and American National Identity* (Chapel Hill, N.C., 1987), 290–91, 293.

26. See Edward Everett, "The History of Liberty," an oration delivered at Charlestown, Massachusetts, July 4, 1828, in Everett, *Orations and Speeches on Various Occasions* (9th ed.; Boston, 1878), 1:168–69. See Thomas Jefferson to Joseph Priestley, March 21, 1801, in Paul Leicester Ford, ed., *The Works of Thomas Jefferson*, 9 (New York, 1905), 218: "This whole chapter in

The alternative response revealed a deepening of Madison's concern, and it cut across ideological lines. An arch-Federalist like Fisher Ames, for example, worried that public opinion would "govern rulers," and he urged that it "be purified from the dangerous errors from which it is infected."[27] Thomas Jefferson, however, the founder and figurehead of Democratic-republicanism, expressed concern in 1818 during his retirement because "public opinion erects itself into an inquisition, and exercises its office with as much fanaticism as fans the flames of an auto da fe."[28]

When the Revolutionary generation was supplanted by several sorts of successor groups during the middle third of the nineteenth century, that apprehensiveness about public opinion gave way to a determination to guide or even control public opinion. To achieve such ends was challenging enough. In 1835, for example, the executive committee of the Female Moral Reform Society determined that "public opinion must be operated upon by endeavoring to bring the virtuous to treat the guilty of both sexes alike, and exercise toward them the same feeling."[29]

The toughest tests arose, however, when Americans disagreed strenuously—when public opinion was fundamentally divided—concerning an issue that was overtly constitutional or else required constitutional

---

the history of man is new. . . . The mighty wave of public opinion which has rolled over it [the republic] is new."

27. Ames, "Eulogy on Washington," Delivered at the Request of the Legislature of Massachusetts, Feb. 8, 1800; Ames to Christopher Gore, Dec. 13, 1802; Ames to Josiah Quincy, Nov. 19, 1807, in Seth Ames, ed., *Works of Fisher Ames* (Boston, 1854), 1:310, 400; 2:82.

28. Jefferson to Rabbi Mordecai M. Noah, 1818, quoted in Anson Phelps Stokes and Leo Pfeffer, *Church and State in the United States* (rev. ed.; New York, 1964), 244. Compare those sentiments with ones that Jefferson articulated thirty-three years earlier in a letter that explicitly anticipated the imminent inevitability of constitutional change. "The want of power in the federal head was early perceived, and foreseen to be the flaw in our constitution which might endanger its destruction. I have the pleasure to inform you that when I left America in July the people were becoming universally sensible of this, and a spirit to enlarge the powers of Congress was becoming general. . . . The happiness of governments like ours, wherein the people are truly the mainspring, is that they are never to be despaired of. When an evil becomes so glaring as to strike them generally, they arouse themselves, and it is redressed." Jefferson to Richard Price, Feb. 1, 1785, in Julian P. Boyd, ed., *The Papers of Thomas Jefferson*, 7 (Princeton, N.J., 1953), 630–31.

29. Quoted in Carroll Smith-Rosenberg, *Disorderly Conduct: Visions of Gender in Victorian America* (New York, 1985), 117.

resolution, such as chartering a national bank,[30] federal regulation of slavery in the territories, or a proposal from the National Liberal League in 1876 to seek a constitutional amendment for "the total separation of Church and State."[31]

An unusual (in fact, rare) response to situations of that sort has been to seek a constitutional referendum. When repeal of the Eighteenth Amendment (Prohibition) remained a bitterly contentious political issue in 1932–33, Congress wanted to utilize the constitutional process that seemed most indicative of the majority voice in public opinion. Consequently, it required that specially elected state conventions be chosen to ratify the Twenty-first Amendment (repeal of Prohibition), rather than using the existing state legislatures.[32] So far, that has been the *only* occasion in our history when Congress opted for the selection of special state conventions. The point, however, is that mechanisms do exist so that if the Constitution is altered, it can happen (as closely as possible) in accordance with the popular will.

The value of mobilizing public opinion in order to assist or impede constitutional change has not been lost upon political activists. In February 1937, for example, after Franklin D. Roosevelt announced his "Court-packing" plan, a New York–based group that opposed the plan asked Frank Gannett, the conservative newspaper magnate, to energize and lead a public opinion crusade against it. As Senator William E. Borah of Idaho wrote to Gannett: "With your newspaper training and your background you can inform the people back home of the dangers of this bill."[33]

Gannett formed a National Committee to Uphold Constitutional

---

30. For the national bank issue, so volatile throughout the 1830s, see Martin Van Buren's Message to a special session of Congress, Sept. 4, 1837: "It cannot be concealed that there exists in our community [i.e., the nation] opinions and feelings on this subject in direct opposition to each other." James D. Richardson, comp., *A Compilation of the Messages and Papers of the Presidents, 1789–1897*, 3 (Washington, D.C., 1896), 330.

31. See William M. Wiecek, *The Sources of Antislavery Constitutionalism in America, 1760–1848* (Ithaca, N.Y., 1977); S. Cushing Strout, "Jeffersonian Religious Liberty and American Pluralism," in Merrill D. Peterson and Robert C. Vaughan, eds., *The Virginia Statute for Religious Freedom* (New York, 1988), 201–35.

32. See Robinson, ed., *Reforming American Government*, 267.

33. Samuel T. Williamson, *Frank Gannett: A Biography* (New York, 1940), 177–80.

Government. The size of his mailings increased from an initial test probe of ten thousand persons spread across all forty-eight states to nearly fifteen million envelopes sent from New York City during the most crucial six months of the struggle. It was the largest mailing effort ever mounted in connection with any legislative struggle in American history. Gannett also mobilized a shrewd telegram campaign directed at key senators who appeared to be wavering. He provided carefully selected information for the writers of newspaper editorials; and his committee prepared thirteen recordings (mostly speeches) for release to radio stations. The intensive use of public opinion to achieve political and constitutional purposes in 1937 was unprecedented.[34] It is difficult to imagine that process happening on such a scale (under non-authoritarian auspices) anywhere else in the world at that time.

III

Perhaps the most frequent and visible interaction between public opinion and constitutional change has involved the United States Supreme Court. The lessons of history that emerge from this nexus are anything but clear-cut, however. Alexis de Tocqueville once remarked of the justices that "their power is immense, but it is power springing from opinion." He then added, in two sentences that are rarely quoted: "Of all powers, that of opinion is the hardest to use, for it is impossible to say exactly where its limits come. Often it is as dangerous to lay behind as to outstrip it."[35] How prophetic Tocqueville turned out to be with respect to the desegregation of public facilities, school busing to achieve racial balance in the schools, affirmative action programs, abortion, capital punishment, and school prayer.

---

34. Ibid., 182–85, 188–89, 191–92, 196–98.

35. Alexis de Tocqueville, *Democracy in America*, ed. by J. P. Mayer (Garden City, N.Y., 1969), 150. In support of Tocqueville's observations, note this comment made by Justice Samuel F. Miller in his 1873 opinion for the Court in the *Slaughter-House Cases:* "In the early history of the organization of the government, its statesmen seem to have divided on the line which should separate the powers of the National government from those of the State government, and though this line has never been very well defined in public opinion, such a division has continued from that day to this." 16 Wallace 36 (1873), at 81–82.

During the past generation, scholars have scarcely neglected the interaction between public opinion and the Supreme Court. Predictably, given the abundance of polls that have been taken concerning the Court in general as well as particular issues that it has decided, we know a fair amount about American attitudes toward the Court[36] (and, to a lesser degree, toward the Constitution itself[37]).

What remains neglected, however, is the "flip side" of the coin: namely, the attitudes of the justices themselves toward public opinion and its relationship — real and perceived — to their roles. This is a matter of some consequence because most of the justices have held strong views concerning public perceptions of their work — and how responsive they ought to be to those perceptions.[38] There have been occasions, for example, when the Court was so concerned about the state of public opinion that it delayed the announcement of decisions.[39] Even more important, there have been times when the Court became less activist (in 1937 and 1968, for example) in order to minimize damage to the institution's prestige.

When we look to the justices themselves, however, we swiftly find that they have been of several minds concerning the proper relationship between public opinion and Supreme Court deliberations. The earliest position, so far as I can tell, as well as the most persistent, assumes that public opinion will play a major role whether we want it to or not; but that in a democratic system, public opinion is likely to enjoy

36. See David G. Barnum, "The Supreme Court and Public Opinion: Judicial Decision Making in the Post-New Deal Period," *Journal of Politics* 47 (May 1985): 652–66; Walter F. Murphy and Joseph Tanenhaus, "Public Opinion and Supreme Court: The Goldwater Campaign," *Public Opinion Quarterly* 32 (Spring 1968): 31–50. The second essay, based upon a long-term survey of public opinion in relation to the judiciary, is particularly sophisticated and informative.

37. Kammen, *Machine That Would Go of Itself,* chs. 11–13, passim; Adam Clymer, "Opinion Narrows Over High Court," *New York Times,* July 13, 1986, p. A15.

38. For fascinating instances involving Justices John Marshall in 1831 and Owen Roberts in the years following 1937, see Philip Bobbitt, *Constitutional Fate: Theory of the Constitution* (New York, 1982), 39–40, 116–17.

39. The Court's decision in *State of Georgia v. Staunton,* 73 U.S. 50 (1867), was announced on May 13, 1867, but was not read until February 10, 1868, in part because of the intensity of public opinion concerning aspects of Reconstruction at that time. See Carl B. Swisher, *Stephen J. Field: Craftsman of the Law* (Washington, D.C., 1930), 158.

a degree of power that may be inappropriate because it is excessive. In an 1829 address, for instance, Justice Joseph Story put it this way: "Our government is emphatically a government of the people, in all its departments. It purports to be a government of law, and not of men; and yet, beyond all others, it is subject to the control and influence of public opinion."[40] This apprehensive outlook, widely shared among moderates and conservatives, is notable for its emphasis upon American exceptionalism as well as for its concern about the impact of public opinion upon American law and constitutionalism.

In 1837, when Story found himself a distressed dissenter in the Charles River Bridge case, he denounced the Taney Court (pro-Democrat) for placing the whims of public opinion above the obligations of law.[41] That has been the essential attitude ever since of Justices Oliver Wendell Holmes and Robert H. Jackson,[42] and, most recently, of Chief Justice William H. Rehnquist. Rehnquist presented his position with cautious restraint in 1976 and once again a decade later: "A mere change in public opinion since the adoption of the Constitution, unaccompanied by a constitutional amendment, should not change the meaning of the Constitution."[43]

Many of the justices, particularly during the past half-century, have argued with intense feeling that the Bill of Rights, above all, ought to be insulated from the passions and prejudices of an ill-informed public. Justice Jackson epitomized this view in a major opinion written for the Court in 1943. The occasion was the second of the well-known flag salute cases involving Jehovah's Witnesses. "The very purpose of the Bill of Rights," Jackson wrote, "was to withdraw certain subjects from the vicissitudes of political controversy, to place them beyond the

40. Quoted in R. Kent Newmyer, *Supreme Court Justice Joseph Story: Statesman of the Old Republic* (Chapel Hill, N.C., 1985), 247.

41. Stanley I. Kutler, *Privilege and Creative Destruction: The Charles River Bridge Case* (New York, 1978), 121.

42. Edmund Wilson, *Patriotic Gore: Studies in the Literature of the American Civil War* (New York, 1962), 784–91; Richard Kluger, *Simple Justice: The History of Brown v. Board of Education and Black America's Struggle for Equality* (New York, 1975), 690.

43. Rehnquist, "The Notion of a Living Constitution," *Texas Law Review* 54 (May 1976): 606–7; Rehnquist, "Constitutional Law and Public Opinion," address delivered at the Suffolk University School of Law, Boston, April 10, 1986 (41-page unpublished typescript by courtesy of Chief Justice Rehnquist).

reach of majorities and officials and to establish them as legal principles to be applied by the courts."[44]

Although such attitudes, ranging from cautious to critical, have dominated, they have not always prevailed and they certainly do not represent the entire spectrum of the justices' views of, or responses to, public opinion. There have been occasions when the Court has obviated a constitutional or legal response by invoking the popular will. Here is an example articulated by Justice William Johnson in 1812, for example: "Although this question [whether the federal courts possessed a power to try offenses made criminal by English common law] is brought up now for the first time to be decided by this Court, we consider it as having been long since settled in public opinion."[45]

In a closely related approach, the Court from time to time has developed jurisprudence grounded in a historical assessment of public opinion at a critical and seemingly pertinent historical moment. To cite the most notorious instance, in 1857 Chief Justice Roger B. Taney's *Dred Scott* opinion for the Court relied, in part, upon his insistence that between 1776 and 1787, when the United States constitutions were first written, public opinion perceived Negroes as "beings of an inferior order" of humankind, and hence not entitled to the same legal status and rights as whites.[46]

By contrast, Justice John Marshall Harlan utilized a similar mode of reasoning—but exactly in reverse. He insisted that judicial precedents that had been created in a climate of opinion no longer acceptable did not and could not carry constitutional weight. His famous dissent in

---

44. *West Virginia State Board of Education v. Barnette*, 319 U.S. 624 (1943), the quotation at 638.

45. *United States v. Hudson and Goodwin*, 7 Cranch 32 (1812), quoted in Robert H. Jackson, *The Supreme Court in the American System of Government* (Cambridge, Mass., 1955), 31. See also Leon Friedman and Fred L. Israel, eds., *The Justices of the United States Supreme Court, 1789–1978: Their Lives and Major Opinions* (New York, 1980), 1:362–63.

46. See *Dred Scott v. Sandford*, 19 Howard 393 (1857), the quotation at 407; and Judith A. Baer, *Equality Under the Constitution: Reclaiming the Fourteenth Amendment* (Ithaca, N.Y., 1983), 70. Taney began the central contention of his opinion with the sentence: "It is difficult at this day to realize the state of public opinion in relation to that unfortunate race, which prevailed in the civilized and enlightened portions of the world at the time of the Declaration of Independence, and when the Constitution of the United States was framed and adopted."

Plessy v. Ferguson (1896) charged the Court's majority with invoking inappropriate references to state cases.

> Some, and the most important, of them are wholly inapplicable, because rendered prior to the adoption of the last amendments of the Constitution, when colored people had very few rights which the dominant race felt obliged to respect. Others were made at a time when public opinion was dominated by the institution of slavery; when it would not have been safe to do justice to the black man. . . . Those decisions cannot be guides in an era introduced by the recent amendments [Thirteenth, Fourteenth, and Fifteenth] of the supreme law.[47]

In modern times the justices have acknowledged that public opinion affects the acceptability of some of their most difficult choices, including the decision concerning whether or not to hear a controversial case or appeal. Felix Frankfurter became exceedingly apprehensive about public perceptions of the Rosenberg spy case in 1952–53. He and Hugo Black believed that the issue of appeal and possible stay of execution might ultimately threaten or undermine the Court's moral authority.[48]

When the High Court upheld the convictions of eleven prominent leaders of the Communist Party in 1951, the infamous *Dennis* case, Justices Black and William O. Douglas dissented on the grounds that the Smith Act (1940) permitted unjustified invasions of free speech. Black's dissent acknowledged the role of public opinion in affecting both the Court as well as popular reactions to its work.

> These petitioners were not charged with an attempt to overthrow the Government. They were not charged with overt acts of any kind designed to overthrow the Government. They were not even charged with saying anything or writing anything designed to overthrow the Government. The charge was that they agreed to assemble and to talk and publish certain ideas at a later date. . . . Public opinion be-

47. *Plessy v. Ferguson*, 163 U.S. 537 (1896), the quotation at 563. For a fine example of public opinion affecting constitutional policy and behavior during the 1890s, see Kluger, *Simple Justice*, 73.

48. Michael E. Parrish, "Cold War Justice: The Supreme Court and the Rosenbergs," *American Historical Review* 82 (October 1977): 805–42.

ing what it now is, few will protest the conviction of these Communist petitioners.[49]

It has often been said—sometimes without serious reflection—that democracy as a just and good form of government works most effectively when public opinion is aroused. The unfortunate examples of Communist witch-hunting in the years following World War II, and of widespread support for the internment of Japanese-Americans during that war, should give us pause as well as cause us to qualify such a sweeping generalization.[50]

If it is valid to say, as an American did in 1948, that "only an aroused public opinion can persuade our Congress to do justice to the American Indian and redress our national guilt as exploiters and treaty breakers,"[51] it is equally true that an aroused public opinion has occasionally been responsible for some very unjust coercion. Alexis de Tocqueville anticipated this democratic dilemma 150 years ago. Can we move a step beyond what by now must seem a banal truism? I believe that we can.

IV

Others have demonstrated in considerable detail that at least *some* constitutional issues and pressures have a persuasive effect upon public opinion. I have tried to suggest that the judiciary, in its turn, responds to public opinion in various ways, some of them more self-aware than others. What new light, if any, do these findings shed upon the problem of American exceptionalism? Paradoxically, two different sorts of conclu-

49. *Dennis v. United States*, 341 U.S. 494 (1951), the quotation at 581. See also William O. Douglas, *The Right of the People* (Garden City, N.Y., 1958), 84: "What we have witnessed during the last decade is not a new but a recurring problem. Each generation must deal with it. The only protection is an enlightened public opinion forged by men who will stand against the mob. . . . The remedy is in making public opinion everybody's business and in encouraging debate and discourse on public issues."

50. See Mark Silverstein, *Constitutional Faiths: Felix Frankfurter, Hugo Black, and the Process of Judicial Decision Making* (Ithaca, N.Y., 1984), 195–202; Peter Irons, *Justice at War: The Story of the Japanese-American Internment Cases* (New York, 1983), 43.

51. Oliver LaFarge to James Truslow Adams, March 15, 1948, Adams Papers, Butler Library, Columbia University, New York.

sions seem appropriate, even though they lead us in opposite directions.

First of all, for more than a decade now some innovative scholars have been asking whether, in a very real sense, we do not have an unwritten national constitution?[52] The question seems almost impertinent if not absolutely un-American. My own view is that we actually have a distinctive amalgam. But I would add to the aspects of an unwritten constitution already acknowledged by others[53] the powerful role played by public opinion in gradually yet continuously aerating our constitutional system.[54]

Consequently we share a fundamental similarity with others among the older democratic political cultures in the modern world. I emphasize the contrast between earlier governmental systems and those that have achieved independence since 1945, because most of the latter are closer to the circumstances of the United States during the half-century following 1789, when we expected to be governed by a blend of natural law, common law, legislative statutes, and our newly minted national Constitution.[55] With the passage of two centuries, our system has added

52. See Thomas C. Grey, "Do We Have an Unwritten Constitution?" *Stanford Law Review* 27 (February 1975): 703–18; David A. J. Richards, "Sexual Autonomy and the Constitutional Right to Privacy: A Case Study in Human Rights and the Unwritten Constitution," *Hastings Law Journal* 30 (March 1979): 957–1018.

53. Consider, for example, the increased national attention given during the past decade to state constitutions and state constitutional law. The complexity and creativity of what has been called "horizontal federalism" may very well cause our system to function in a manner that is less distinctive than Madison and his contemporaries envisioned. See, for example, William J. Brennan, "State Constitutions and the Protection of Individual Rights," *Harvard Law Review* 90 (January 1977): 489–504; symposium issue, "The Emergence of State Constitutional Law," *Texas Law Review* 63 (March–April 1985).

54. See the interesting letter written by Logan Hay, member of a law firm in Springfield, Illinois, to Andrew C. McLaughlin, Dec. 3, 1935, McLaughlin Papers, box 2, Regenstein Library, University of Chicago. McLaughlin had just published his 800-page synthesis titled *A Constitutional History of the United States* (New York, 1935). "We have in the constitutional history," Hay wrote, "the story of the building of the framework of a democracy institutionalizing that framework in a written constitution. . . . All this, however, is mere framework and machinery. After all, the motive force is the force of public sentiment, almost necessarily slow moving in a constitutional democracy and yet at times running with a strong and rapid current and subjecting the machinery to violent strains and breaks."

55. See Seymour Martin Lipset, *The First New Nation: The United States in Historical and Comparative Perspective* (New York, 1963); Clifford Geertz, "After the Revolution: The Fate of Nationalism in the New States," in Geertz, *The Interpretation of Cultures: Selected Essays* (New

other components that diminish the validity of a clear-cut distinction between written and unwritten constitutions. We need not shift all the way to a parliamentary set-up to be more like the British than we once were a century or two ago.

My second conclusion pertaining to the relationship between public opinion, constitutionalism, and American exceptionalism leads in the opposite direction. We have reason to believe that public opinion emerged throughout the Western world as a force in domestic as well as international affairs late in the eighteenth century.[56] If we look at the records of the Constitutional Convention in 1787, however, we find a sense of despair (or call it realistic frustration) about the prospects of "knowing" public opinion well enough to be properly responsive. As Gouverneur Morris declared on July 5, 1787: "Much has been said of the sentiments of the people. They were unknown. They could not be known."[57] In 1791, however, James Madison wrote a brief editorial titled "Public Opinion." In it he proposed a series of important distinctions that we have tended to overlook or ignore. His thoughts are so germane to the subject of this essay that I shall quote a lengthy extract:

> Public opinion sets bounds to every government, and is the real sovereign in every free one.
>
> As there are cases where the public opinion must be obeyed by the government; so there are cases, where not being fixed, it may be influenced by the government. This distinction, if kept in view, would prevent or decide many debates on the respect due from the government to the sentiments of the people.
>
> In proportion as government is influenced by opinion, it must be so, by whatever influences opinion. This decides the question concerning a *Constitutional Declaration of Rights,* which requires an influence on government, by becoming a part of public opinion.
>
> The larger a country, the less easy for its real opinion to be ascer-

---

York, 1973), 234–54; Edward Shils, "The Fortunes of Constitutional Government in the Political Development of the New States," *Center and Periphery: Essays in Macrosociology* (Chicago, 1975), 456–82.

56. See Richard Buel, *Securing the Revolution: Ideology in American Politics, 1789–1815* (Ithaca, N.Y., 1972), Part III; Speier, "Historical Development of Public Opinion," 376–88.

57. Farrand, ed., *Records of the Federal Convention,* 1:529.

tained, and the less difficult to be counterfeited; when ascertained or presumed, the more respectable it is in the eyes of individuals. —This is favorable to the authority of government. For the same reason, the more extensive a country, the more insignificant is each individual in his own eyes. —This may be unfavorable to liberty.[58]

The passage of time and the experience of just a few years under the new government enabled Madison to offer insights more complex and, in certain respects, less pessimistic than those of Gouverneur Morris.

The United States was then, and has remained, a large and diverse country. Public opinion regarding constitutional issues is not easy to ascertain, least of all when the issues at hand are controversial.[59] Consequently there are cases where government may seek to influence public opinion—"influence" in the sense of inform and reorient—as was the case with racial desegregation (1954–55) or one person, one vote (1962–64). In other instances, where the nature of public opinion is less ambiguous, such as broad national approval of New Deal measures for economic recovery (the later 1930s), or anxiety about the expansion of protection for the rights of suspected criminals (the later 1960s), public opinion has, as Madison suggested, helped to redefine the scope of acceptable government policy or decision-making by the judiciary.

Enter (or re-enter) American distinctiveness, if not outright exceptionalism. Two points must be made: one having to do with origins, and the other with on-going developments. When Madison wrote his intriguing essay on "Public Opinion" in 1791, it was unexceptionable in a very real sense. It may have been unusually astute; but in a new republic where everyone, irrespective of partisan affiliation, paid lip service to popular sovereignty, few if any would dispute Madison's emphasis upon and concessions to public opinion.

In Great Britain, by contrast, even though theirs was the closest political culture to our own, the recognition that PUBLIC OPINION (it often appeared in capitals during the 1790s in order to acknowledge

58. "Public Opinion," first printed in *The National Gazette,* Dec. 19, 1791, reprinted in Hunt, ed., *Writings of Madison,* 6:70.

59. See, for example, Edward J. Larson, *Trial and Error: The American Controversy Over Creation and Evolution* (New York, 1985); Eva R. Rubin, *Abortion, Politics, and the Courts: Roe v. Wade and Its Aftermath* (Westport, Conn., 1982).

the relative novelty of the concept) had recently become a potent force elicited a very substantial body of literature (pamphlets, tracts, and newspaper essays) that called for governmental restraint or resistance in responding to public opinion—particularly where calls for constitutional reform were concerned.[60]

The historical legacy of this fundamental divergence between American and European political cultures (ca. 1790–1832) provides the core of my second contention. Public opinion emerged and mattered elsewhere; but only in the United States was there a growing consensus that it was *appropriate* for it to matter; and only in the United States was its impact upon the judiciary (and hence upon questions requiring constitutional interpretation) so palpable. James Bryce summarized the situation toward the close of the nineteenth century.

> The Supreme Court feels the touch of public opinion. Opinion is stronger in America than anywhere else in the world, and judges are only men. To yield a little may be prudent, for the tree that cannot bend to the blast may be broken. There is, moreover, this ground at least for presuming public opinion to be right, that through it the progressive judgment of the world is expressed. Of course, whenever the law is clear, because the words of the Constitution are plain or the cases interpreting them decisive on the point raised, the court must look solely to those words and cases, and cannot permit any other consideration to affect its mind. But when the terms of the Constitution admit of more than one construction, and when previous decisions have left the true construction so far open that the point in question may be deemed new, is a court to be blamed if it prefers the construction which the bulk of the people deem suited to the needs of the time? A court is sometimes so swayed consciously, more often unconsciously, because the pervasive sympathy of numbers is irresistible even by elderly lawyers.[61]

Bryce returned to this theme with some frequency throughout *The American Commonwealth*, and never diminished his insistence upon the

60. See Gunn, *Beyond Liberty and Property*, 287, 289–90, 292. For France and Germany in the same period, see Palmer, "The Concept of Public Opinion in Political Theory," 239–43, 247–49.

61. Bryce, *The American Commonwealth* (2d ed.; London, 1891), 1:267.

distinctively potent and central role of public opinion in American political culture.[62] Other observers have composed variations on his theme ever since.

Over the past two centuries, needless to say, the American press and the media have played an increasingly important role in shaping public opinion concerning a broad range of constitutional questions. It all started with "Publius" and the *Federalist* papers, perhaps, and was perpetuated by newspaper editorials, by the droll craft of political cartoons, and now by investigative journalism that is undertaken with a competitive intensity previously unknown in American history. Most Americans do not read either the Constitution or the texts of Supreme Court decisions. They do, however, notice cartoons that depict justices as baby-killers (in abortion decisions) or as hangmen (the issue of capital punishment). Most likely those caricatures reinforce existing attitudes rather than form them *de novo*. Nevertheless, they imprint images and unquestionably affect or perpetuate attitudes.[63]

Public opinion has clearly played a complex role in shaping the character of American constitutionalism. We must never forget, however, that public opinion in a large, diverse, and free society is not a monolith. The implications of that unexceptionable assertion are important. Perhaps I can best explain why by comparing two national mottoes.

The Indonesian national motto, *Bhinneka Tunggal Ika*, is customarily translated as Unity in Diversity. Consequently it is sometimes viewed as a rough equivalent to the American motto *E Pluribus Unum*. There is a significant nuance of difference between them, however. The American motto is understood to mean a process of unification from (and

62. Ibid., especially 1:6, 376, 437; 2:239–40, 243, 248–49, 251–53, 257, and ch. 78 passim. Cf. A. V. Dicey, *Lectures on the Relation between Law and Public Opinion in England during the Nineteenth Century* (2d ed.; London, 1914).

63. For some prime examples, see Jim Berryman, "Another Deserter!" in the *Washington Evening Star,* July 20, 1935, p. 1; Harold M. T. Talburt, "Widen the Road or Else!" *Washington Daily News,* June 3, 1935, p. 16; and the Herblock cartoon, "We Were Told They Were 'Strict Constructionists'," discussed in Bob Woodward and Scott Armstrong, *The Brethren: Inside the Supreme Court* (New York, 1979), 505.

despite) divergent elements, whereas the Indonesian motto suggests the inseparability of unity and diversity.[64]

Given the range of diversity in American society and in public opinion concerning constitutional issues, and yet viewing that diversity in the context of our truly remarkable history of stability under a single Constitution, I cannot help wondering whether *Bhinneka Tunggal Ika* wouldn't be closer to the bull's-eye as the American national motto. Unity and diversity inseparable: that may sound, at first, like an oxymoron. It is, nevertheless, an accurate summation of our paradoxical historic experience with constitutionalism and public opinion.

64. See Ben R. O. Anderson, "The Idea of Power in Javanese Culture," in Claire Holt, ed., *Culture and Politics in Indonesia* (Ithaca, N.Y., 1972), 15.

This essay was presented in compressed format on May 21, 1987, in Washington, D.C., at an International Symposium, "Constitutional Roots, Rights, and Responsibilities," co-sponsored by the Smithsonian Institution and the American Bar Association.

I am especially glad to thank the co-organizers of that six-day extravaganza, Professor A. E. Dick Howard and Robert S. Peck, Esq., for all that they did to make the symposium so stimulating and cosmopolitan. It started with a splendid reception at Monticello, in Charlottesville, Virginia, followed by an elegant dinner in Mr. Jefferson's Rotunda. Subsequent evenings included memorable dinners in Statuary Hall at the United States Capitol and at the Supreme Court building. All in all, it became a many-splendored marathon of the mind.

11. "Washington Presiding in the Convention 1787"; popular engraving by J. Rogers (ca. 1820–40). (Collection of the author.)

12. "James Madison" by Thomas Sully (ca. 1809). It is possible, though not certain, that the document beneath Madison's left hand is meant to be the United States Constitution. (In the collection of The Corcoran Gallery of Art, Washington, D.C. Gift of Frederic E. Church, 1877.)

13. "George Washington" by John Vanderlyn (1834), located in the United States Capitol, Chamber of the House of Representatives. Although the document beneath Washington's right hand is the Constitution, the text inexplicably begins with the words "We the Delegates," a curiosity that went unnoticed until May 1987, perhaps because the words appear nearly upside down to the viewer. (United States Capitol Art Collection. Architect of the Capitol.)

14. Creamware jug decorated with transfer-printed black patriotic scenes, including "Washington Securing Liberty to America"; probably made in Liverpool, England, ca. 1795. (Division of Ceramics and Glass, National Museum of American History, Smithsonian Institution, Washington, D.C. Gift of Robert H. McCauley.)

15. Liberty and the American Eagle; liquor flask probably made by the Union Glass Company, Philadelphia (ca. 1826–35). (Courtesy of the Corning Museum of Glass, Corning, N.Y.)

16. "The Residence of David Twining 1787," by Edward Hicks (ca. 1845–48). The Twinings, a Quaker family, raised Hicks on their prosperous farm in Bucks County, Pennsylvania. Hicks, the popular folk artist, deliberately chose to connect this rural scene to 1787 — perhaps because Americans during the first half of the nineteenth century attributed their affluence and comfortable standard of living to the form of government made possible by the United States Constitution. (Courtesy of the Abby Aldrich Rockefeller Folk Art Center, Williamsburg, Va.)

17. "Justice" by David Gilmour Blythe (oil on canvas, ca. 1859–62). Workers, who may have been beaten, are being brought before a magistrate, who has law books near his right hand. An eagle holds the scales of justice over his head, but the scales are not in balance. An elderly Negro holding a banjo sits on the shadowy bench. The likelihood that any of these defendants will receive justice seems to be dim; and the concept of justice itself appears in a sardonic light. (The Fine Arts Museums of San Francisco. Gift of Mr. and Mrs. John D. Rockefeller 3d.)

18. The grave of President Andrew Johnson, Greenville, Tennessee. On the monument, erected by Johnson's family in 1878, the eagle and flag symbolize Johnson's loyalty to the Union; the open Bible his faith in God and man; and the scroll his esteem for the Constitution of the United States. When Johnson was buried on August 3, 1875, he was wrapped in the American flag and his head rested on a copy of the Constitution—as he had requested. (Courtesy of the Andrew Johnson National Cemetery.)

19. "Constitution" bread tray; clear pressed glass made by Gillinder and Sons, Philadelphia (ca. 1870s). (Courtesy of the Sandwich Historical Society/Glass Museum, Sandwich, Mass.)

20. "Drafting the Constitution in Franklin's Garden," a charcoal drawing by the muralist Allyn Cox (1896–1982). The figures are, from left to right, Alexander Hamilton, James Wilson, James Madison, and Benjamin Franklin. (Prints and Photographs Division, Library of Congress.)

Five

"A Vehicle of Life"

*Continuity and Change in Americans' Perceptions
of Their Living Constitution*

I

IN 1971, when the Judiciary Committee of the United States
Senate conducted hearings concerning the nomination of William H.
Rehnquist to become an associate justice of the Supreme Court, one
senator asked Mr. Rehnquist whether he believed in the concept of a
"living Constitution." The good-natured nominee parried by quipping
that a living Constitution was surely more desirable than a dead one.
He quickly added, however, that a permanent and stable Constitution
seemed preferable to an excessively flexible one that might be rendered
less effective by its situational variability.[1]

That seemingly innocuous interchange was symptomatic of a significant tension that has been prominent in American constitutionalism ever since the 1920s: namely, whether or not ours ought to be,
or was meant to be, a "living Constitution." The issue has never been
livelier than at the present moment. It is important to note, however,
that scholars and judges do not agree now any more than they did a
generation or two ago, when Professor William W. Crosskey of the

1. Rehnquist recounted this episode in his essay, "The Notion of a Living Constitution,"
Texas Law Review 54 (May 1976): 693.

University of Chicago Law School, an extremely learned yet peculiarly literal-minded man, fired more than one heavy salvo at the devotees of a "living document."[2]

Even more noteworthy, perhaps, distinguished jurists and the nation's leading law enforcement officials disagree as well. On July 9, 1985, Attorney General Edwin Meese III called for a "jurisprudence of original intention," a position advocated one year earlier from a different perspective by Judge Robert H. Bork of the United States Court of Appeals (District of Columbia Circuit).[3] Speeches meant as rebuttals to Meese—and reminiscent in some respects of the didactic role performed by an ancient Greek chorus—by Justices William J. Brennan and John Paul Stevens have stressed the need for a living Constitution. "The ultimate question must be," Justice Brennan believes, "what do the words of the text mean in our time?"[4]

Although the so-called "Meese-Brennan debate" (a simplistic yet convenient form of shorthand) has received considerable press coverage as well as serious analysis, the attitudes of other justices toward this issue have not been widely noticed. One result is that public perceptions of the polemic tend to assume that two clear-cut positions exist, polar opposites, with no middle ground. Another result is that shades of difference among the more conservative justices—differences that matter—are largely ignored.

We might look, for example, at the views of Justices White and Rehnquist, both of whom in 1973 opposed the majority opinion concerning a woman's right to have an abortion, and both of whom dissented in 1986 when the High Court declared Pennsylvania's Abortion Control Act of 1982 unconstitutional. In his 1986 dissent, Justice By-

---

2. See Crosskey, *Politics and the Constitution in the History of the United States* (Chicago, 1953), 2:1171–72; Paul Finkelman, "Can We Know the Intentions of the Framers? The Case of the Bank of the United States," *The New Federalist Papers*, no. 114 (April 17, 1986), 3; Herman Belz, "Judicial Power and American Politics: The Original Intention," *The New Federalist Papers*, no. 117 (May 9, 1986), 3.

3. Address of Attorney General Meese before the American Bar Association, July 9, 1985, Washington, D.C. (published text by courtesy of the Department of Justice), 3, 15; Bork, *Tradition and Morality in Constitutional Law* (Washington, D.C., 1984), 11-page address.

4. Brennan, "The Constitution of the United States: Contemporary Ratification," *The*

ron R. White articulated what I would call a carefully modulated, or cautious, affirmation of the living Constitution outlook.

> This Court does not subscribe to the simplistic view that constitutional interpretation can possibly be limited to the "plain meaning" of the Constitution's text or to the subjective intention of the Framers. The Constitution is not a deed setting forth the precise metes and bounds of its subject matter; rather, it is a document announcing fundamental principles in value-laden terms that leave ample scope for the exercise of normative judgment by those charged with interpreting and applying it.[5]

In 1976 Justice Rehnquist published an essay, titled "The Notion of a Living Constitution," which has been cited with some frequency ever since in opinions written by judges at various levels of our legal system. Rehnquist's formulation is more aggressive than White's, and he defends it (with some casuistry, it seems to me) by appealing to democratic theory. Rehnquist basically reifies a straw concept (a caricature of an idea, that is, comparable to a straw man) which he repeatedly refers to as "the brief writer's version of the living Constitution." He argues that "however socially desirable the goals sought to be advanced by the brief writer's version, advancing them through a freewheeling, non-elected judiciary is quite unacceptable in a democratic society."[6]

Elsewhere in this article, however, Rehnquist pursues a line of argument I find unpersuasive. Two illustrative sentences may suffice.

- A mere change in public opinion since the adoption of the Constitution, unaccompanied by a constitutional amendment, should not change the meaning of the Constitution.

- The brief writer's version of the living Constitution, in the last analysis, is a formula for an end run around popular government.[7]

New Federalist Papers, no. 95 (Nov. 29, 1985), 3–4; Stevens, "The Supreme Court and the Framers," *The New Federalist Papers,* no. 106 (Feb. 21, 1986), 3.

5. *Thornburgh, Governor of Pennsylvania, et al. v. American College of Obstetricians and Gynecologists, et al.,* 106 S. Ct. 2169 (1986), at 2193–94.

6. Rehnquist, "Notion of a Living Constitution," 699.

7. Ibid., 696–97, 706.

I cannot resist the observation that Chief Justice Roger B. Taney's insistence that public opinion as it existed in 1787 must control national jurisprudence in 1857 provided a major prop for his rationale in the disastrous decision concerning *Dred Scott v. Sandford.*[8]

On September 26, 1986, just moments before former Chief Justice Warren E. Burger relinquished his office to Rehnquist, Burger said to four hundred people crammed into the solemn courtroom that justices would always disagree about the meaning of the Constitution; nevertheless, alterations in the Court's composition would not alter its commitment to the United States Constitution as "a living document."[9] Using baseball parlance, one might say that Justices White, Burger, and Rehnquist were playing center, right center, and shallow right field, respectively.

II

Although the particular phrase "living Constitution" dates largely from the later 1920s and '30s, the general concept first appeared at the turn of the century when a Darwinian notion of our Constitution as a living organism supplanted the popular nineteenth-century metaphor of the Constitution as some sort of mechanism — perhaps even a perpetual motion machine.[10]

The pivotal figure in proselytizing for and popularizing the idea of America's Constitution as a "vehicle of life" was Woodrow Wilson: first as a prolific political scientist, then in lectures and addresses that he gave as the president of Princeton University, and ultimately as Governor of New Jersey and as President of the United States. At first he

8. See Stanley I. Kutler, ed., *The Supreme Court and the Constitution: Readings in American Constitutional History* (2d ed.; New York, 1977), 152–53.

9. *New York Times,* Sept. 27, 1986, p. A8. Berger's predecessor, Earl Warren, wrote the following for a lay audience in 1955: "Our judges are not monks or scientists, but participants in the living stream of our national life, steering the law between the dangers of rigidity on the one hand and of formlessness on the other." Warren, "The Law and the Future," *Fortune* 52 (November 1955): 107.

10. See Michael Kammen, *A Machine That Would Go of Itself: The Constitution in American Culture* (New York, 1986), 17–20, 140–41, 177.

referred to the Constitution's elasticity as its greatest virtue.[11] In 1908, however, when his book *Constitutional Government in the United States* appeared, Wilson worked out a formulation he liked so well that he used it, with only slight variation, three times in the same slim volume. Here is version number three.

> The Constitution cannot be regarded as a mere legal document, to be read as a will or a contract would be. It must, of the necessity of the case, be a vehicle of life. As the life of the nation changes so must the interpretation of the document which contains its change, by a nice adjustment, determined, not by the original intention of those who drew the paper, but by the exigencies and the new aspects of life itself.[12]

After 1920 the revisionist movement known among jurists and scholars as legal realism gave great impetus and meaning to the concept of a living Constitution. In an important opinion written for the Court, Justice Oliver Wendell Holmes explained how to handle an issue that is not explicitly dealt with in the Constitution itself.

> The case before us must be considered in the light of our whole experience and not merely in that of what was said a hundred years ago. The treaty in question [made in 1916 with Great Britain to protect migratory birds in the United States and Canada] does not contravene any prohibitory words to be found in the Constitution. The only question is whether it is forbidden by some invisible radiation from the general terms of the Tenth Amendment. We must consider what this country has become in deciding what that Amendment has reserved.[13]

Some of the legal realists seemed at least as notable for cynicism as for realism; but following the lead of Benjamin N. Cardozo, venerated as a judge's judge, they gladly rejected the "tyranny of concepts."[14]

11. Arthur S. Link, ed., *The Papers of Woodrow Wilson* (Princeton, N.J., 1966–), 15:537; 16:364; 20:467.

12. Wilson, *Constitutional Government in the United States* (New York, 1908), 192; see also 69, 157.

13. *State of Missouri v. Holland*, 252 U.S. 416 (1920), at 433–34.

14. Cardozo, *The Paradoxes of Legal Science* (New York, 1928), 60–61.

The belief that ours is a living Constitution achieved considerable popularity with the lay public during the 1920s and '30s. Newton D. Baker, who had been Woodrow Wilson's Secretary of War, developed the notion in a nationally broadcast speech on Constitution Day in 1932 — the very year that H. Arnold Bennett, a prominent authority on constitutional education in the public schools, posed this question: "Are we not a bit too prone to teach the Constitution as a finished document — as the last word in government, as embodying certain principles which under no conditions should be modified?"[15]

Meanwhile, in 1927 Howard Lee McBain, the Ruggles Professor of Constitutional Law at Columbia University, reached out to the mass culture with a compact, easy-to-read book that was part of The World Today Bookshelf, and said on its spine: "Workers Bookshelf." Titled *The Living Constitution: A Consideration of the Realities and Legends of Our Fundamental Law,* it lucidly explained the nature of American government as a whole. What McBain seems to have meant by the phrase "living Constitution" was really a British sort of system, the whole of which completes, alters, and if necessary may even override, the written document.[16]

During the 1930s, particularly on account of the Great Depression, growing numbers of people came to believe that severe conditions the founders could not have foreseen required a highly adaptable fundamental law. Hence the radical insistence in 1939 by Maury Maverick, a populistic Congressman from San Antonio, Texas, that the Constitution written in 1787 "is not the sole constitution of our American liberties. It is not in itself the Living Constitution, but only a part of it."[17]

Ever since 1939, however, opinion polls indicate that the general public is far more comfortable contemplating gradual change by fine-tuning rather than making any major overhaul in the United States Constitution.[18] It is my impression that, for more than a generation now, the idea of a living Constitution has had greater appeal among liberal scholars and social critics than among the public at large.[19]

15. Kammen, *Machine That Would Go of Itself,* 227, 233.

16. McBain, *The Living Constitution* (New York, 1927).

17. See Kammen, *Machine That Would Go of Itself,* 34, 397.

18. Ibid., 331–32, 383, 388.

19. See Saul K. Padover, *The Living U. S. Constitution* . . . (New York, 1953); Arthur

III

Given the current absence of consensus, even among constitutional law-yers, judges, and law enforcement officials, it might be meaningful as well as appropriate to ask whether the framers themselves can illumi-nate the issue. I am not persuaded that a jurisprudence of original in-tention ought to be the primary criterion in determining whether the concept of a living Constitution deserves an energizing role in Ameri-can political culture. If the founders turned out to be categorically op-posed to "original intent," however, that would be extremely problem-atic for proponents of such a position.

The most sensible approach, therefore, is to draw a sampling of their views from a diverse range of ideological and temperamental dis-positions. We should start with George Washington, who put his enormous prestige at risk by agreeing to preside over the Philadelphia Convention. Although he felt fully committed to the instrument that resulted, less than two months after the Convention adjourned he wrote the following (in private) to his nephew: "I do not think we are more inspired, have more wisdom — or possess more virtue than those who will come after us."[20] That candid admission surely carried the impli-cation that wise and disinterested citizens might help to execute and even interpret the Constitution in future generations.

Whenever the Convention sat as a committee of the whole, Wash-ington left the chair, joined the Virginia delegation, and the savvy Na-thaniel Gorham of Massachusetts presided. Gorham's recognition that any document they fabricated would have to be flexible is clearly re-flected in his observation that "the vagueness of the terms constitutes the propriety of them."[21] James Madison, moreover, addressing the Con-vention, made an unequivocal statement that he and others would sub-sequently reiterate: "In framing a system which we wish to last for

Selwyn Miller, *Social Change and Fundamental Law: America's Evolving Constitution* (Westport, Conn., 1979), esp. ch. 1, "The Need for a 'Living' American Constitution," and ch. 10, "Notes on the Concept of the 'Living' Constitution."

20. Washington to Bushrod Washington, Nov. 10, 1787, in John P. Kaminski and Gas-pare J. Saladino, eds., *The Documentary History of the Ratification of the Constitution.* Volume 14, *Commentaries on the Constitution: Public and Private,* 2 (Madison, Wis., 1983), 86.

21. Quoted in Catherine Drinker Bowen, *Miracle at Philadelphia: The Story of the Constitu-tional Convention, May to September 1787* (Boston, 1966), 241.

ages, we should not lose sight of the changes that ages will produce."[22]

Alexander Hamilton echoed that sentiment in *Federalist* number 34: "We must bear in mind, that we are not to confine our view to the present period, but to look forward to remote futurity. Constitutions of civil government are not to be framed upon a calculation of existing exigencies; but upon a combination of these, with the probable exigencies of ages, according to the natural and tried course of human affairs."[23] Stephen Cabarrus, a delegate to the ratifying convention in North Carolina, made a similar point more pithily on June 29, 1788: "This is a Constitution for the *future* government of the United States. It does not look back."[24]

Thomas McKean, who served as chief justice of Pennsylvania from 1777 until 1799, worked very actively on behalf of ratification. He reminded members of his state convention that they had under consideration a matter of vast importance, "not only to the present generation, but to posterity."[25] Charles Willson Peale successfully captured that sentiment in his 1787 portrait of McKean and his son, which hangs in the Philadelphia Museum of Art (see figure 9). In addition to the adolescent Thomas Jr., who obviously represents posterity, the painting shows the lawyer's table covered and surrounded by the books and papers of his profession. To complete the symbolism, Peale has placed an allegorical figure of Justice, holding her scales and a sword, near the corner of a rooftop that we notice through a window behind the boy's head.

22. Ibid., 122. For additional evidence of Madison's anticipation of change, future needs, and the wisdom of flexibility, see his remarks on June 22, 1787, in Max Farrand, ed., *The Records of the Federal Convention of 1787* (2d ed.; New Haven, Conn., 1937), 1:378. A famous passage included by Madison in *Federalist* number 14 certainly suggests that he believed the delegates had been more responsive to present needs than to custom or to the past for its own sake. "Is it not the glory of the people of America," he asked, "that whilst they have paid a decent regard to the opinions of former times and other nations, they have not suffered a blind veneration for antiquity, for custom, or for names, to overrule the suggestions of their own good sense, the knowledge of their own situation, and the lessons of their own experience?" Jacob E. Cooke, ed., *The Federalist* (Middletown, Conn., 1961), 88.

23. Cooke, ed., *The Federalist*, 210.

24. Jonathan Elliot, comp., *The Debates in the Several State Conventions on the Adoption of the Federal Constitution* . . . (2d ed.; Philadelphia, 1876), 4:184. Italics in original.

25. Bernard Schwartz, ed., *The Roots of the Bill of Rights* (2d ed.; New York, 1980), 3: 640–41.

Finally, we should recall the words that Thomas Jefferson wrote to James Madison from Paris in 1789, that "no society can make a perpetual constitution, or even a perpetual law." Jefferson was not present at the Philadelphia Convention, nor can we call his constitutional ideas at all represenatative. He was a maverick on these matters, much more radical than his close friend Madison, for example. Nevertheless, Jefferson *shared* with Chief Justice John Marshall, a political foe whose ideas and tactics he detested, a strong belief in the necessity of a living Constitution—a belief that they both acted upon when they occupied positions of power and responsibility.[26]

Two related points of a more general nature might be mentioned before we move away from the world of the founders. First, as further evidence that they envisioned a living Constitution, consider the momentous matters that they left for the first Congress to resolve. To cite only three of the most weighty: (1) the structure and nature of the entire federal judiciary; (2) what to do about the huge debt that had accumulated under the Confederation government; and (3) whether to promulgate a Bill of Rights and if so, what to include.[27] Those were not *simply* issues appropriate for legislative action. They were constitutional problems; and each one subsequently generated constitutional issues that became highly political as well.

The second point is scarcely new, yet it requires reiteration in this context. Those who signed the Constitution knew that they had been obliged to make a series of compromises, some of which, at the very least, would require major adjustments at some future time. Theodore Roosevelt summarized this imperative extremely well in 1917, and in so doing communicated his own sense of the Constitution as a living entity:

---

26. Jefferson to Madison, Sept. 6, 1789, in Julian P. Boyd, ed., *The Papers of Thomas Jefferson,* 15 (Princeton, N.J., 1958), 395–96; Kammen, *Machine That Would Go of Itself,* 15, 37, 59–60; Francis N. Stites, *John Marshall: Defender of the Constitution* (Boston, 1981), 98–108, 129–33.

27. See Charles Warren, "New Light on the History of the Federal Judiciary Act of 1789," *Harvard Law Review* 37 (November 1923): 49–132; Janet A. Riesman, "Money, Credit, and Federalist Political Economy," in Richard Beeman et al., eds., *Beyond Confederation: Origins of the Constitution and American National Identity* (Chapel Hill, N.C., 1987), 153; Robert Allen Rutland, *The Birth of the Bill of Rights, 1776–1791* (Chapel Hill, N.C., 1955).

I am certain that if the people who framed the constitution of the United States, and that was a matter of compromise from first to last, had adjourned midway, and gone back to their respective States to explain the various proposals and why they were for or against this or that proposal, there never would have been a constitution adopted. What they did was to meet, debate, agree, compromise and vote for a constitution. It was a patchwork and it was nothing but compromise. But it has lived, and under it, as interpreted by our Supreme Court, this country has grown to a hundred million, and has fought three small wars, and one of the greatest wars in history, abolished slavery and now, thank God, is taking its part in this war. Even that constitution was reluctantly adopted by the necessary two thirds. But it was put up to them either to take that or anarchy.[28]

Political anarchy, American style, did occur in 1860–65; and the pertinent point in this context is that extra-constitutional artifices had to be contrived in order to reconcile all the governmental "loose ends" once the fighting stopped. In order to regain admission to the Union, and its seats in Congress, each state that had seceded was required to summon a constitutional convention that would do three things: repeal its act of secession; repudiate the Confederate debt; and abolish slavery in conformity with the Thirteenth Amendment. When the Constitution is silent, creativity becomes inevitable. That is yet another aspect of a living Constitution.

IV

Although Americans suffered a severe political and constitutional rupture at the time of the Civil War, they subsequently managed to paper it over by means of a judicial fiction, the Supreme Court's decision in the case of *Texas v. White*. As Chief Justice Salmon P. Chase wrote in 1869: "The Constitution, in all its provisions, looks to an indestructible Union, composed of indestructible States."[29] That maxim, and the

28. Roosevelt to George William Russell, Aug. 6, 1917, in Elting E. Morison et al., eds., *The Letters of Theodore Roosevelt,* 8 (Cambridge, Mass., 1954), 1219.

29. *Texas v. White,* 7 Wallace 700 (1869), in Kutler, ed., *The Supreme Court and the Constitution,* 181.

organicism for which it stands, is yet another aspect of the American commitment to a living Constitution. Combining with that belief the boast that ours is the oldest written national constitution in continuous existence in the world, Americans historically sustained more than a modicum of chauvinism along with skepticism concerning the constitutional capabilities of other nations.[30]

Although the framers expressed admiration for the British constitution in 1787, it is important to note that, having rejected the very concept of an unwritten constitution, Americans deviated a major step further when they affirmed the right to change a written constitution and institutionalized not just one, but several, means of doing so. The method of calling a second constitutional convention has never been tried, even though Jefferson liked the idea as a matter of principle and Abraham Lincoln expressed a preference for it in his First Inaugural Address.[31] James Madison, John Marshall, William Howard Taft, and Warren E. Burger were entirely hostile to the idea; and with every additional year, decade, and century that passes, the likelihood of our ever seeing a second convention recedes.

Although only sixteen amendments have been added since the Bill of Rights was ratified in 1791, the reality remains that our Constitution is a living one—owing above all to the on-going activity of constitutional interpretation by the Supreme Court. The number and variety of major theories or concepts that lack intrinsic constitutional validation, yet have acquired it by application and usage, is intriguing. To list only a selection of them may sound like legal mumbo-jumbo to the non-specialist. Nevertheless, it is worth doing in order to drive home the point, in yet another way, that ours has indeed been a living Constitution. The following doctrines have come and (for the most part) gone: substantive due process; clear and present danger; preferred freedoms (referring to the First Amendment); ordered liberty; suspect classification; freedom to contract; separate but equal; wall of separa-

30. See John Quincy Adams, *An Oration Addressed to the Citizens of the Town of Quincy, on the Fourth of July, 1831* . . . (Boston, 1831), 32–33.

31. Willi Paul Adams, *The First American Constitutions: Republican Ideology and the Making of the State Constitutions in the Revolutionary Era* (Chapel Hill, N.C., 1980), 139; Roy P. Basler, ed., *The Collected Works of Abraham Lincoln* (New Brunswick, N.J., 1953), 4:270.

tion; compelling state interest; the silver platter doctrine; the exclusionary rule; the fair trial doctrine; the special circumstance doctrine; the content-neutrality rule; the doctrine of non-superfluousness; the fighting words doctrine; and the child-benefit theory.[32] There will, I am certain, be no end of successors.

Should we be dismayed, or even embarrassed, by this plethora of extant and discarded doctrines? Of course not. Such a pattern is the inevitable consequence of our functioning under a fundamental law that is both written and relatively brief. (By comparison, for example, the Constitution of India, prepared in 1949, requires 130 pages [amended through 1963].[33])

And besides, the necessity for interpretation emerged at the very outset under eminent auspices, to say the least. Late in 1790 Alexander Hamilton, then Secretary of the Treasury, presented Congress with his plan for the establishment of a national bank. President Washington wondered whether such a measure might be illegal, because the Constitution included no provision for Congress to charter a corporation. So he asked Hamilton and Jefferson, the Secretary of State, to prepare opinions in defense of their broad and strict constructionist positions. Hamilton's proved to be the more persuasive, and has been regarded ever since as one of his most brilliant state papers. The core of Hamilton's rationale also contained the seed that would eventually germinate as the concept of a living Constitution.

> Every power vested in a government is in its nature *sovereign,* and includes, by *force* of the *term* a right to employ all the *means* requisite and fairly applicable to the attainment of the ends of such power, and which are not precluded by restrictions and exceptions specified in the Constitution, or not immoral, or not contrary to the *essential ends* of political society. . . . If the *end* be clearly comprehended within

32. For explications of quite a few of these doctrines, see Richard C. Cortner, *The Supreme Court and the Second Bill of Rights: The Fourteenth Amendment and the Nationalization of Civil Liberties* (Madison, Wis., 1981), 57, 109, 112, 120, 124–25, 133, 177, 186; Judith A. Baer, *Equality Under the Constitution: Reclaiming the Fourteenth Amendment* (Ithaca, N.Y., 1983), 140, 233–34, 276; Carl B. Swisher, *Stephen J. Field: Craftsman of the Law* (Washington, D.C., 1930), 372–74; Anthony Lewis, *Gideon's Trumpet* (New York, 1964), 188–89, 191.

33. See Amos J. Peaslee, ed., *Constitutions of Nations* (3d ed.; The Hague, 1966), 2:308–438.

any of the specified powers, and if the measure have an obvious relation to that *end,* and is not forbidden by any particular provision of
the Constitution, it may safely be deemed to come within the compass of the national authority.[34]

A combination of broad construction when appropriate and new
amendments when necessary has kept the United States Constitution
very much a living charter. Slavery was abolished by amendment. Women
were enfranchised by amendment. But racial segregation became unconstitutional by amendment *and* by judicial interpretation; and by the
latter process state legislatures were directed to reapportion their electoral districts so that one person's vote would be worth as much as any
other's.

These are all signs of constitutional vitality. It can legitimately be
argued that they occurred slowly—much too slowly. For better and for
worse, that is the nature of our republican system. Although it may
not be swiftly responsive, neither is it precipitous. With a few significant exceptions, such as Prohibition and McCarthyism, the tyranny of
public opinion that Tocqueville so feared has not been such a terrible
problem, at least not in the realm of constitutionalism. Moreover, public opinion is remarkably resilient. It got us into Prohibition and Mc-
Carthyism; but it also got us out.

V

Having suggested various reasons why the Constitution may properly
be considered a living document, and having offered diverse sorts of
evidence, I now feel obliged to acknowledge an area of ambiguity. The
problem becomes apparent when we compare American attitudes toward
the federal Constitution with their behavior in regard to state constitutions. We find a curious double standard; for Americans have replaced,
revised, and amended their state constitutions much more readily than
they have the national charter.

Among the papers of Governor Edmund Randolph of Virginia, there

34. For both positions, see Henry Steele Commager, ed., *Documents of American History*
(7th ed., New York, 1963), 156–60, the quotations at 156 and 158. Hamilton's italics.

exists the unpublished draft of a national constitution that he prepared in about 1787. The document begins with a general suggestion that we have subsequently been much more inclined to follow at the federal level. I have in mind Randolph's caution "to insert essential principles only, lest the operations of government should be clogged by rendering those provisions permanent and unalterable which ought to be accommodated to times and events."[35]

A comprehensive history of our state constitutions is neither appropriate nor possible here. Two types of question, however, are highly germane to the focus of this essay. The first: Have state constitutions been "living constitutions" to the same degree or in the same manner as the federal one? The second: What impact, if any, have our state constitutions, and *their* interpreters, had upon the "living" attributes of our federal Constitution?

First things first. A tendency developed during the course of the nineteenth century for state constitutions to get longer and longer, like endless freight trains hauling ever larger amounts of ordinary cargo. Ignoring the prescient warning by James Madison that "these political scriptures" should not be too easy to alter or amend,[36] state legislators and voters tended to approve the inclusion of enactments — that is, conventional statutes — that simply did not belong in any text intended to serve as fundamental law. Many of these provisions eventually got to be archaic, with the consequence that too many state constitutions became burdened by the dead hand of the past. James Bryce commented upon this phenomenon extensively in his *American Commonwealth.*

> The influences at work, the tendencies which the constitutions of the last forty years reveal, are evidently the same over the whole Union. What are the chief of those tendencies? One is for the constitutions to grow longer. This is an absolutely universal rule. Virginia, for instance, put her first constitution, that of 1776, into four closely printed quarto pages, that is, into about three thousand two hundred words. In 1830, she needed seven pages; in 1850, eighteen

35. Moncure D. Conway, *Omitted Chapters of History Disclosed in the Life and Papers of Edmund Randolph* (New York, 1888), 73–74.

36. Madison, "Charters," *The National Gazette,* Jan. 19, 1792, in Gaillard Hunt, ed., *The Writings of James Madison,* 6 (New York, 1906), 85.

pages; in 1870, twenty-two pages, or seventeen thousand words. Texas has doubled the length of her constitution from sixteen quarto pages in 1845 to thirty-four in 1876. Pennsylvania was content in 1776 with a document of eight pages, which for those times was a long one; she now requires twenty-three. The constitution of Illinois filled ten pages in 1818; in 1870 it had swollen to twenty-five. These are fair examples, but the extremes are marked by the constitution of New Hampshire of 1776, which was of about six hundred words (not reckoning the preamble), and the constitution of Missouri of 1875, which has more than twenty-six thousand words. The new constitutions are longer, not only because new topics are taken up and dealt with, but because the old topics are handled in far greater detail. Such matters as education, ordinary private law, railroads, State and municipal indebtedness, were either untouched or lightly touched in the earlier instruments. The provisions regarding the judiciary and the legislature, particularly those restricting the power of the latter, have grown far more minute of late years, as abuses of power became more frequent, and the respect for legislative authority less. As the powers of a State legislature are *prima facie* unlimited, these bodies can be restrained only by enumerating the matters withdrawn from their competence, and the list grows always ampler.[37]

In our own time this tendency has become highly problematic. A few state constitutions (such as New Jersey's in 1947 and Virginia's in 1970) have been revised or replaced on a bipartisan basis by very carefully building a consensus and avoiding potentially explosive issues.[38] Other attempts, however, have ended in dismal failure (such as New York's abortive constitution in 1967); and still other attempts are proceeding at present. According to the chairman of Mississippi's current commission to draft a new state constitution, the state is determined to draw "a new constitutional blueprint that will allow us to face the future instead of hanging on to the past."[39]

The second of my questions—what impact has state constitution-

---

37. Bryce, *The American Commonwealth* (2d ed.; London, 1891), 1:438–39.

38. See A. E. Dick Howard, "Constitutional Revision: Virginia and the Nation," *University of Richmond Law Review* 9 (Fall 1974): 1–48.

39. See Vernon A. O'Rourke and Douglas W. Campbell, *Constitution-Making in a Democ-*

alism had upon federal? — really requires a whole book for an appropriate answer. I shall simply suggest four illustrative themes that might be pursued in order to elucidate the question.

1. There is evidence that passages from the Massachusetts constitution of 1780 anticipated and may have helped to shape the Equal Protection Clause of the Fourteenth Amendment.[40]

2. A reading of the *Federalist* papers suggests that delegates to the Philadelphia Convention in 1787 were aware of certain features in New York's constitution of 1777, and that its successful arrangements provided effective ammunition for advocates of ratification in 1788.[41]

3. So-called "legislative experiments" conducted by the states, particularly during the first third of this century, which were challenged yet ultimately received constitutional approval, had a profound effect, in the final analysis, upon both national legislation and constitutional law.[42]

4. In 1977 Justice William J. Brennan asserted that recent adverse decisions by the Supreme Court in the field of civil liberties justified those who are concerned about preserving the achievements of the 1960s in looking more and more to state constitutions for protection. He observed that many state courts already extended to their citizens broader protections than the Supreme Court had held are applicable under the federal Bill of Rights. Brennan lauded the implications of this new state court activism — for a healthy federalism in particular — and others have since noticed the development of a trend, known as "horizontal federalism," in which some of the state supreme courts scrutinize the decisions made by others as care-

racy: Theory and Practice in New York State (Baltimore, Md., 1943); *New York Times,* April 4, 1964, p. 1; ibid., Nov. 8, 1967, p. 1; ibid., Dec. 12, 1985, p. B25, and Oct. 19, 1986, p. E4.

40. Ronald M. Peters, Jr., *The Massachusetts Constitution of 1780: A Social Compact* (Amherst, Mass., 1978), 196–201; Richard Kluger, *Simple Justice: The History of Brown v. Board of Education and Black America's Struggle for Equality* (New York, 1975), 75–76.

41. See Cooke, ed., *The Federalist,* 167, 328–39, 411, 446, 533, 575.

42. For the sheer complexity of this dynamic relationship, see *Bunting v. Oregon,* 243 U.S. 426 (1917); *New State Ice Co. v. Liebmann,* 285 U.S. 262 (1932), covering 262–311 passim; Thomas Reed Powell, "The Supreme Court and State Police Power, 1922–1930," *Virginia Law Review* 17–19 (1930–33), passim; "Can States Act Without Federal Permission? Dialogue: The Uncertain Status of Federalism," *New York Times,* Nov. 16, 1986, p. E5.

fully as they watch determinations made by the High Court in Washington.[43]

VI

A number of our most distinguished historians and political scientists have been inclined to minimize the impact of the United States Constitution upon American democracy. Frederick Jackson Turner, for instance, once insisted: "Not the Constitution, but free land and an abundance of natural resources open to a fit people, made the democratic type of society in America for three centuries." Robert A. Dahl has provocatively turned the conventional wisdom inside out: "To assume that this country has remained democratic because of its Constitution seems to me an obvious reversal of the relation; it is much more plausible to suppose that the Constitution has remained because our society is essentially democratic."[44]

Once upon a time I found such statements somewhat troublesome — not because they seemed less than reverent, but because the assumptions that underpin them have become less valid with the passage of time, thereby leaving their iconoclasm somewhat in limbo — not to mention where it may leave the Constitution. After all, free land and abundant resources have been diminishing, if not vanishing, for a long time now. And various studies have indicated that our society may be less democratic than Dahl would like to believe.

Where, then, does that leave a Constitution that the likes of Turner and Dahl suggest is "merely" an epiphenomenon rather than a prime mover of American democracy? I would answer that question in several ways. First, very few astute observers ever claimed democracy for the Constitution. Perhaps we ought to say that it is neither democratic nor anti-democratic. Rather, both tendencies have in fact flourished under

43. William J. Brennan, "State Constitutions and the Protection of Individual Rights," *Harvard Law Review* 90 (January 1977): 489–504; symposium issue, "The Emergence of State Constitutional Law," *Texas Law Review* 63 (March–April 1985); Robert Pear, "State Courts Move Beyond U.S. Bench in Rights Rulings," *New York Times,* May 4, 1986, p. 1.

44. Turner, "The West and American Ideals," in Turner, *The Frontier in American History* (New York, 1920), 293; Dahl, *A Preface to Democratic Theory* (Chicago, 1956), 143.

its auspices. Fortunately, because of the value system that we have long subscribed to as a people, the Constitution has been more than compatible with democracy. The two have developed *pari passu,* with happy consequences for both. Such developments, in my view, would seem to provide important evidence that ours is a living Constitution.

Second, if the Constitution is really based upon popular sovereignty — as the framers claimed in theory, and subsequent implementation over time has augmented in actuality — then it can only be described as a living Constitution. Despite spasmodic resistance, the democratization of American political values has occurred. As assumptions and goals of the populace change, so does the operative nature of the Constitution.

So, perforce, do the views of the ultimate custodians of that Constitution: the United States Supreme Court. Justice Harold H. Burton, a Republican politician turned jurist, exemplified that in 1952 when he responded to oral arguments before the Court concerning the issue of racial desegregation. Burton put this question to counsel for the state of Kansas, an attorney defending the status quo. "Don't you recognize it as possible," Burton asked, "that within seventy-five years the social and economic conditions and the personal relations of the nation may have changed so that what may have been a valid interpretation of them seventy-five years ago would not be a valid interpretation of them constitutionally today?" Subsequently, while Burton was interrogating John W. Davis, chief counsel for the "separate-but-equal" defense team, the following interchange occurred.

> DAVIS: "Changed conditions may affect policy, but changed conditions cannot broaden the terminology of the Constitution. The thought is an adminstrative or a political one, and not a judicial one."
>
> BURTON: "But the Constitution is a living document that must be interpreted in relation to the facts of the time in which it is interpreted."[45]

If Burton, who has been described as a fair-minded, middle-of-the-road conservative, could publicly express such a view; and if Justice

45. See Kluger, *Simple Justice,* 568, 572–73.

Lewis F. Powell, a moderate (joined by three others), could conclude an important dissent in 1980 with the reminder to his brethren that "We are construing a living Constitution"; and if the ofttimes radical though sometimes unpredictable Hugo Black developed a philosophy of judicial interpretation best defined in terms of the concept of a "living Constitution," then the notion must surely have more substance than shadow, both historically as well as in the present.[46]

And what of the future? As one possible litmus of our living Constitution, the notion of "constitutional morality" ought to be kept in mind. Although it does not qualify as a familiar household phrase, it recurs with some frequency in the history and language of American constitutionalism. Predictably, perhaps, its meaning has changed over time. When Chancellor Kent of New York used it in 1837, for example, it essentially referred to sanctity of contract—a phase in the intellectual history of property rights and possessive individualism.[47] When Willmoore Kendall used it in 1964, however, he had in mind the assumptions of "Publius" concerning the capacity of the American people for co-operation, self-restraint, and doing what best promotes the true interests of the community.[48]

Although conservative constitutional scholars today tend to reject morality as a proper basis for sound jurisprudence,[49] I wish to close with the prediction that constitutional morality—that is, the inclusion

---

46. For Burton, see ibid., 610–11; for Powell, see *Rummel v. Estelle, Corrections Director,* 445 U.S. 263 (1980), at 307; and Charles A. Reich, "Mr. Justice Black and the Living Constitution," *Harvard Law Review* 76 (February 1963): 673–754, esp. at 727–50.

47. See R. Kent Newmyer, *Supreme Court Justice Joseph Story: Statesman of the Old Republic* (Chapel Hill, N.C., 1985), 228, 233.

48. Kendall, "Constitutional Morality and *The Federalist*," in Kendall and George W. Carey, *The Basic Symbols of the American Political Tradition* (Baton Route, La., 1970), 96–118. This posthumously published volume originated as lectures delivered at Vanderbilt University in 1964.

49. See Henry P. Monaghan, "Our Perfect Constitution," *New York University Law Review* 56 (May 1981): 353–96. But compare the emphasis upon "general moral purposes" in *The New Right v. the Constitution* (published in 1986 by the Cato Institute), reported in *New York Times,* Aug. 7, 1986, p. A22; and Ronald Dworkin's belief that judicial interpretation is "inevitably a reflection of moral philosophy" (symposium on constitutional interpretation held at Harvard University in September 1986, reported in *Harvard Magazine,* January–February 1987, p. 52).

of social justice and fairness as legitimate criteria—will one day, not far distant, be broadly accepted as an appropriate underpinning for American jurisprudence.[50] Such a prospect would come as no surprise to anyone who has customarily and correctly regarded the United States Constitution as a "vehicle of life."

50. See William O. Douglas, *The Right of the People* (Garden City, N.Y., 1958), 89; "Group Marks 20 Years of Fighting for Rights" [the Center for Constitutional Rights], *New York Times,* Dec. 28, 1986, p. 37.

This essay was presented in Philadelphia on April 24, 1987, at the annual meeting of the American Philosophical Society. I must express particular appreciation to Professor Arthur S. Link (who supplied my assignment), and to Drs. Whitfield J. Bell, Edward C. Carter II, and Randolph S. Klein for making my visit such a congenial one.

The essay was published promptly in the *Proceedings* of the American Philosophical Society, volume 131 (September 1987), 325–40, ably edited by Miss Carole N. Le Faivre; and that special issue subsequently appeared as a casebound book titled *A More Perfect Union: Essays on the Constitution* (Philadelphia, 1987).

Six

The Revival of States' Rights in American Political Culture, ca. 1918–1938

Reflections on the Ambiguities of Ideological Constitutionalism

JAMES TRUSLOW ADAMS, who may have been the most widely read historian of the United States during the 1920s and '30s, was also regarded by many as a wise interpreter of contemporary affairs. In 1933, Adams explained to a friend that he had long been fascinated by the issue of states' rights,[1] but he went on to lament that states' rights was ideologically defunct: "The future lies with sections," he explained, "such units as the Federal Reserve districts etc."[2]

At about the same time, in 1932, a politically active Virginian named

1. Throughout this essay I shall use the spelling "states' rights"; but readers should be aware that people have been extraordinarily inconsistent with respect to both orthography and usage. As a devoted Confederate historian and publicist wrote in 1932: "There is one thing, however, which I am surprised you do not do and that is spell States with a capital "s" as our forefathers did, not necessarily because they did, but because it gives these great commonwealths a distinction they deserve and differentiates these ancient and honorable commonwealths from the abstract noun meaning state or condition. Somewhere or other I have seen the argument brought forward by some distinguished authority that we should always say State rights rather than States' rights. I don't know the argument but it was convincing to me when I saw it." Mathew Page Andrews to Lyon G. Tyler, June 27, 1932, Tyler Papers, Group I (Family), box 20, Swem Library, College of William and Mary, Williamsburg, Va.

2. Adams to Stringfellow Barr, Sept. 5, 1933, Adams Papers, Butler Library, Columbia University, New York.

Mary Carter, every bit as traditional as James Truslow Adams, received a disconcerting letter from a gentleman who declared that "States Rights are all but a buried memory." She responded promptly by quoting to him the current slogan of the American Taxpayers League, that "States Rights is the most vital issue now before the public." Simultaneously she wrote to her good friend Lyon G. Tyler, retired president of the College of William and Mary, marvelling at the phenomenon of a "nation-wide States' Rights Renaissance."³

Mary Carter could not have been more correct, nor James Truslow Adams more wrong. Nevertheless, historians ever since have followed his example by ignoring the entire phenomenon, despite the wonderful opportunity that it provides to explore a variety of important issues involving federalism and state sovereignty in American politics during the inter-war years.⁴ I cannot explain with any assurance why American scholars have so neglected this major episode, except to say that by comparison with the states' rights crises that preceded the American Civil War, developments of the 1920s and '30s are (1) quite confusing in their own right; (2) an inversion in many respects of the ante-bellum issues and positions; and (3) chock full of vacillation and ambiguity. On the side of absolute consistency we have Albert C. Ritchie, Democratic Governor of Maryland,⁵ as a less cerebral successor to John C. Calhoun. On

3. Carter to M. C. McConkey, Jan. 22, 1932, Tyler Papers, Group V, box 7; Carter to Lyon G. Tyler, n.d., ibid., Group V, unsorted box. See also Carter to Tyler, July 29, 1930, ibid., Group V, box 6: "Dr. M. D. Boland is keeping me in touch with this States Rights movement in the West. Am enclosing a copy of an editorial from *The Tacoma Times*—which has some pretty stiff States Rights dope in it, that Mr. Boland sent me recently. . . . This statement in this article pleases me muchly: 'The founders of this nation did not found a republic; they founded a union of republics, each sufficient unto itself, handling its own peculiar problems according to the popular will'."

4. For some very limited exceptions, see Arthur M. Schlesinger, *New Viewpoints in American History* (New York, 1928), ch. 10, "The State Rights Fetish"; Charles Warren, *The Supreme Court and Sovereign States* (Princeton, N.J., 1924), 31–52, 69–97; Edward S. Corwin, "Constitution v. Constitutional Theory: The Question of the States v. the Nation" (1925), in Alpheus T. Mason, ed., *American Constitutional History: Essays by Edward S. Corwin* (New York, 1964), 99–108.

5. Ritchie's statements and speeches on the topic are seemingly interminable. For a summary view, published soon after his death in 1935, see Ritchie, "The Constitution and the States," *Annals of the American Academy of Political and Social Science* 185 (May 1936): 16–21. For his remarkably consistent usage, see Ritchie, "The Eighteenth Amendment an Invasion

the side of inconsistency we have Franklin Delano Roosevelt. And as exemplars of ambivalent vacillation we have, to cite just a few, Woodrow Wilson, Herbert Hoover, the United States Supreme Court, and the *New York Times*.

Consequently I must insist that there is, indeed, a states' rights story to be told for this period; but more often than not it is a topsy-turvy story. Its genesis prior to 1924 is multi-faceted, yet comprehensible. Its waning after 1937 is rather more complicated, yet equally comprehensible. Between 1925 and 1936, however, when the states' rights saga reached rather sizable proportions, it contained some predictable aspects, but a good many surprises as well. Accordingly, the structure of this essay is embodied in four sections: first, background and predictable stimuli for the states' rights movement; second, surprising, or less predictable, stimuli; third, basic issues and manifestations of the movement; fourth, changes, the resolution of ideological tensions, and consequences.

I

Some historical provocations for the states' rights movement, but only some, seem in retrospect to have been almost inevitable. For the sake of convenience they can perhaps be clustered into five categories: first, the Southern tradition of states' rights; next, provocatively nationalizing tendencies in Supreme Court decisions made between the later 1880s and the early 1920s; third, manifold (and often contradictory) aspects of Progressivism; fourth, the imperative of wartime mobilization in 1917–18; and finally, passage of the Eighteenth Amendment to the Constitution (Prohibition) in January 1919.

A strong sense of state sovereignty was never suppressed entirely in what had been the Confederacy. In 1866 Robert E. Lee explained to Lord Acton that "while I have considered the preservation of the constitutional power of the General Government to be the foundation

---

of State Rights," *Current History* 28 (April 1928): 35: "The term State Rights today involves the right of the States to local self-government as against the tendency of the Federal Government to deprive them of it more and more, and to centralize in the Federal Government more and more of the functions which constitutionally and traditionally belong to the States."

of our peace and safety at home and abroad, I yet believe that the maintenance of the rights and authority reserved to the states and to the people, not only essential to the adjustment and balance of the general system, but the safeguard to the continuance of a free government."[6] Echoes of that utterance, though not always so eloquent, would be heard for several generations, but especially after the mid-1920s, from the likes of Carter Glass and Harry F. Byrd, senators from Virginia, and Governor Eugene Talmadge of Georgia.[7]

Nevertheless, it is only the first among our surprising "inversions" that Southerners were occasionally criticized, by their own intellectuals and politicians as well as by the Northern press, for neglecting their heritage, supporting such national controls as the Volstead Act, and all too eagerly accepting federal subsidies. As a *New York Times* editorial put it on July 4, 1930: "There is no doubt that the Federal government has been washing away State lines. But the South, which once went to war to resist the process was foremost in voting this new power to Washington. Eagerly it accepts Federal road-building money and aid—a partnership its forefathers once raised an awful row against entering."[8]

During the period from 1888 until 1921, when Chief Justices Melville W. Fuller and Edward D. White presided over the Supreme Court, that body frequently invoked the federal Constitution "to strike at state

6. Lee to Acton, Dec. 15, 1866, in John N. Figgis and R. V. Laurence, eds., *Selections from the Correspondence of the First Lord Acton* (London, 1917), 303.

7. See *New York Times*, June 9, 1927, p. 6; ibid., July 5, 1935, p. 2; ibid., Jan. 30, 1936, p. 8; and ibid., Dec. 5, 1936, p. 20. Southerners were most likely to invoke states' rights when federal anti-lynching legislation was proposed. Controversy over such a law reached peak intensity in 1934–35. See James Weldon Johnson, "Lynching: America's National Disgrace," *The Current History Magazine* 19 (January 1924): 596–601; "Lynching Shows Need for Federal Law," *The Christian Century* 51 (Jan. 24, 1934): 133; "Federal Action Coming Against Lynching," ibid. (Nov. 14, 1934): 1444; "Should the Costigan-Wagner Anti-Lynching Bill be Passed by Congress?" *The Congressional Digest* 14 (June–July 1935): 172–92; "Should America Have a Federal Anti-Lynching Law?" *The Literary Digest* 124 (Dec. 4, 1937): 12; James R. McGovern, *Anatomy of a Lynching: The Killing of Claude Neal* (Baton Rouge, La., 1982), 115–17, 123–25, 136–39.

8. *New York Times*, Aug. 13, 1927, p. 12; ibid., July 4, 1930, p. 12; Philip A. Bruce to Lyon G. Tyler, Jan. 28, 1931, Tyler Papers, Group V, box 3; Bishop Charles B. Galloway, "Jefferson Davis and State Sovereignty," *Dallas Morning News*, June 2, 1930, copy, ibid., box 6.

interests. It also sustained Federal statutes over against the states and their interests."⁹ During the decade from 1920 until 1930, moreover, the Court determined that nearly 140 state laws were unconstitutional. Justices from both ends of the ideological spectrum, such as Oliver Wendell Holmes and Willis Van Devanter, joined this nationalizing tendency; and in the famous case of *Near v. Minnesota* (1931), Chief Justice Charles Evans Hughes led the Court in using the Due Process Clause of the Fourteenth Amendment to protect freedom of speech and of the press against restrictive action by the states.¹⁰

Here again, however, the story is so complex that it seems to meander rather than to measure a neat, straight line. In 1918 the Court nullified a federal child labor law; and a furious editorial in *The New Republic* condemned the Court for asserting "that such a grave issue as the protection of children must be left to the diverse judgments of the legislatures of the forty-eight states." When a Child Labor Amendment to the Constitution began to receive national consideration in 1924 and '25, one critic correctly diagnosed the essential basis for opposition: "The real issue is the old one of states rights, the most momentous domestic issue in our history."¹¹

Throughout 1925 various state legislatures angrily rejected the proposed amendment. Tennessee's rationale was read into *The Congressional Record:* "That the people of each state of the United States of America is a sovereignty, all inherent powers of the several peoples being vested in these several sovereignties, the States; that the United States of America is not a sovereignty, but is a federation or association of these states, the said sovereignties. . . ." Eight years later, in 1933, the president of the American Bar Association would denounce the Child Labor Amend-

9. Unpublished comments (p. 3) by Russell K. Osgood on April 7, 1983, at the annual meeting of the Organization of American Historians, Cincinnati, Ohio. For contemporary corroboration, see *The Outlook* 99 (Sept. 23, 1911): 145–46; *The Literary Digest* 46 (May 10, 1913): 1049; *The Nation* 96 (June 12, 1913): 587–88; *The Independent* 74 (June 19, 1913): 1368–69.

10. See Paul L. Murphy, *The Constitution in Crisis Times, 1918–1969* (New York, 1972), 37, 50, 63, 119; Murphy, "*Near v. Minnesota* in the Context of Historical Developments," *Minnesota Law Review* 66 (November 1981): 95–160.

11. "States' Rights vs. the Nation," *The New Republic* 15 (June 15, 1918): 194–95; "Child Labor: Why They Invoke States Rights," ibid., 41 (Dec. 24, 1924): 108–9.

ment as "a communist attempt to nationalize children, making them responsible to the government instead of their parents."[12]

During the twenty years that followed World War I, the Court upheld states' rights, and particularly the police power of the states, with sufficient frequency so that it appeared to be highly cognizant, if not outright sympathetic, to the ever more vocal states' rights movement. Such a perspective underpinned Chief Justice William Howard Taft's widely noticed decision in *Bailey v. the Drexel Furniture Company* (1922); and Taft's successor, Charles Evans Hughes, declared in 1930 that "encroachments upon State authority, however contrived, should be resisted with the same intelligent determination as that which demands that the national authority should be fully exercised to meet national needs."[13]

The legacy of Progressivism was every bit as ambiguous for states' rights as the Supreme Court's record during the half-century following 1888. On the one hand, Theodore Roosevelt and *The Outlook* (a journal that may fairly be called his "mouthpiece"), were not sympathetic to states' rights. In an editorial about dual sovereignty, published in 1913, *The Outlook* observed that recent policies had "produced a borderland between the jurisdiction of the one and that of the other, so that there has been doubt as to whether there was any power, either of the Nation or of the State, to settle certain questions. It has also resulted in a tendency to exalt too highly the power of the local authorities, especially

12. *New York Times,* Jan. 24, 1926, section 8, p. 14; ibid., April 6, 1925, p. 18; ibid., Aug. 31, 1933, p. 11; William L. Chenery, "Children in Politics: The Rights of States and the Rights of Children," *The Century Magazine* 109 (March 1925): 599–605; and Glenn Frank, "Is States' Rights a Dead Issue?" ibid. (April 1925): 839–42.

13. See Zechariah Chafee, Jr., "Freedom of Speech and States Rights," *The New Republic* 25 (Jan. 26, 1921): 259–62; David E. Lilienthal, "The Tennessee Case and State Autonomy," *The Outlook* 140 (July 29, 1925): 453–54; *New York Times,* March 13, 1930, p. 13; ibid., Aug. 22, 1930, p. 1; ibid., Jan. 7, 1936, p. 1; ibid., May 19, 1936, p. 1; ibid., June 2, 1936, p. 1; ibid., May 23, 1937, section 8, p. 7; Corwin, "Constitution v. Constitutional Theory," 103 ; Murphy, *Constitution in Crisis Times,* 114, 156–57; and Michael E. Parrish, *Felix Frankfurter and His Times: The Reform Years* (New York, 1982), 263–64, where the author notes that although Justice Owen Roberts supported states' rights, the six conservative justices remained quite likely to strike down state laws as unconstitutional. For the famous decision in *Erie Railroad v. Tompkins,* (1938) as a boost for states' rights, see Alfred H. Kelly et al., *The American Constitution: Its Origins and Development* (6th ed.; New York, 1983), 521.

in matters which vitally concern the Nation as a whole."[14] In 1916 *The New Republic* complained, characteristically, that "the majority of American lawyers and publicists still like to celebrate states' rights as the chief legal bulwark of the American democracy." British commentators with similar points of view expressed themselves freely during these years.[15]

Other popular journals of opinion, however, including liberal ones, perceived the states as "laboratories in which industrial and political experiments can be worked out on [an ideal] scale. . . . It means the relieving of the nation as a whole from many of the pangs necessary in the growth of democracy." Consequently the states should not be regarded "as mere administrative units, subject to the direction and domination of a federal authority thousands of miles away. . . . They are rather constituent parts of the union, self-directive, and capable of maintaining their own autonomy and of carrying on their own functions within their own boundaries."[16]

In 1913, when Woodrow Wilson first assumed the presidency, he rejected national regulation of the economy, opposed the uplifting of impoverished groups through ambitious projects requiring federal intervention, and explained to a group of social workers that "my own party in some of its elements represents a very strong state's rights feeling." Writing privately to a young professor he had hired at Princeton, Wilson allowed himself to be more direct: "I do not feel by any means as confident as you do as to the power of the Federal Government in the matter of overriding the constitutional powers of the states through the instrumentality of treaties. . . ." In 1914 he explained to a large delegation of woman's suffrage leaders at the White House that his "pas-

14. Roosevelt, "Nationalism and Progress," *The Outlook* 97 (Jan. 14, 1911): 57–59; "The Governors and the Judge," ibid., 99 (Sept. 30, 1911): 266–68; "The Borderland and the Nation," ibid., 104 (June 21, 1913): 363–64.

15. "The Failure of the States," *The New Republic* 9 (Dec. 16, 1916): 170–72; Harold J. Laski, "Sovereignty and Centralization," ibid., pp. 176–78; Gerald B. Hurst, "Federal Devolution," *The Contemporary Review* 116 (October 1919): 383–87; Raymond L. Buell, "The New States-Rightism," *The Nation* 113 (Aug. 17, 1921): 173–74.

16. "The Conflict of Administrations," *The Popular Science Monthly* 80 (February 1912): 142–50, the quotation at 147; "Where There Are No States' Rights," *The World's Work* 26 (September 1913): 501–2; Bentley W. Warren, "Destroying Our 'Indestructible States'," *The Atlantic Monthly* 133 (March 1924): 370–78.

sion" was for local self-government "and the determination by the great communities into which this nation is organized of their own policy and life."[17]

Wilson's most controversial appointee to the Supreme Court, Louis D. Brandeis, may have been more liberal on social issues than his patron, yet he shared Wilson's states' rights sympathies. From his first year on the Court in 1917 until his twilight years of retirement (1939–41), one of Brandeis's guiding maxims was "Thank God for the limitations inherent in our federal system." This Progressive jurist was profoundly apprehensive about the danger of federal centralization, especially during the years 1925–36, years that significantly spanned the presidencies of Coolidge, Hoover, and Roosevelt, years when Republicans as well as Democrats dominated the Congress. The liberal Brandeis could decide against a widow, an orphan, or a workingman if a problem of federalism caused him to feel cautious about treading upon states' rights. In 1922, explaining to a friend an opinion by Chief Justice Taft with which he heartily disagreed, Brandeis lamented that "State Rights succumbed to the Rights of Nations. State Duties were ignored and state functions atrophied. . . . The new Progressivism requires local development—quality not quantity."[18]

The provocation provided by Progressivism for states' rights during the decade following World War I involved even more than Teddy Roosevelt's nationalism versus the commitment of Wilson and Brandeis to decentralization. It developed from a whole panoply of programs and issues—mostly, in fact, unrealized programs—that seemed to threaten state sovereignty by aggrandizing the national government. Federal regulation of child labor, already mentioned, was only one of these. An-

17. Arthur S. Link, *Wilson: The New Freedom* (Princeton, N.J., 1956), 241, 256–58, 293, 300 n. 81; Wilson to Edward S. Corwin, April 19, 1913, in Link, ed., *The Papers of Woodrow Wilson*, 27 (Princeton, N.J., 1978), 336.

18. Alpheus T. Mason, *Brandeis: A Free Man's Life* (New York, 1956), 515, 545, 567, 569. The quotations are from pp. 558 and 621; Parrish, *Frankfurter: The Reform Years*, 208–9, 260–61. The Brandeis legacy, favoring states' rights and fearing centralization, was perpetuated for more than a generation by two disciples, Felix Frankfurter and James Landis. See their book, *The Business of the Supreme Court: A Study in the Federal Judicial System* (New York, 1927), and Frankfurter's condensed version, "The Distribution of Judicial Power between the United States and State Courts," *Cornell Law Quarterly* 13 (June 1928): 449–530.

other concerned the possible creation of a federal Department of Education. In Governor Ritchie's horrified words, it seemed "bent on nationalizing the teaching of the young, with the deadening results that it would be sure to have."[19] A third arose from opposition to any federal inheritance or estate tax.[20]

A fourth, which remains problematic to this day, concerned the problem of control over natural resources and the public domain. The issue arose during the Progressive era, and initially the states most directly affected, often in the West, were more likely to oppose federal regulation, whereas the older states and their journals of opinion were most inclined to regard the invocation of states' rights as a euphemism for possessive exploitation.[21] During the period from 1927 until 1936, however, these controversies involved a broad range of problems and geographic areas: resentment by a senator from Utah at interference from the Department of the Interior in a Colorado River project; Alabama's insistence that the War Department pay state taxes on electric power produced at Muscle Shoals; a protest by Western governors against federal control over mineral and oil rights on unappropriated lands; a Texas governor's determination to prevent intervention by a federal court concerning the development of East Texas oil fields; and an attack upon provisions of the Federal Water Power Act by five southeastern states seeking to develop an Appalachian Electric Power Company.[22]

Between 1916 and 1919, United States involvement with World War I, in terms of economic and military preparations as well as domestic security issues, obliged both the President and the Supreme Court to extend and justify the expansion of federal authority—and not

19. *New York Times* Aug. 15, 1926, section 2, p. 7; ibid., May 1, 1927, p. 15; ibid., March 7, 1928, p. 3.

20. Ibid., Oct. 30, 1926, p. 5; ibid., Jan. 4, 1927, p. 24; ibid., Jan. 30, 1927, section 8, p. 16; and ibid., Dec. 17, 1933, section 4, p. 4.

21. "The Conservation Split," *The Literary Digest* 47 (Dec. 6, 1913): 1103–4; "A New Water-Power Policy," ibid., 48 (March 7, 1914): 476. See William E. Leuchtenburg, *Flood Control Politics: The Connecticut River Valley Problem, 1927–1950* (Cambridge, Mass., 1953), 1–2, 11–13, 18, 37, 41–42, 50, 59–62, 70–73, 77, 79, 82, 84–87, 89, 96, 101.

22. *New York Times*, April 19, 1927, p. 3; ibid., Oct. 11, 1927, p. 36; ibid., July 2, 1930, p. 17; ibid., Oct. 15, 1931, p. 2; ibid., Feb. 17, 1931, p. 37; and ibid., March 6, 1932, section 3, p. 6.

merely powers of the presidency or of executive agencies. Chief Justice Edward D. White, a Louisiana man who had fought for the Confederacy and states' rights, stood firm as a nationalist in 1916–17. Two years later he justified Wilson's seizure and operation of the railroads. White insisted that federal encroachment upon state authority was legitimate in war time.[23]

Moreover, patterns and precedents created during the war were not easily obliterated during the 1920s, so that still another refrain of states' rights advocates took the form of hostile opposition to federal commissions. Addressing the Springfield, Massachusetts, Chamber of Commerce in 1929, the president of the Radio Corporation of America likened the United States Constitution to a marriage contract between the states and the national government. Fulminating against the Federal Radio Commission and the Interstate Commerce Commission as principal violators of states' rights, he complained that such bodies, "either by default of proper supervision run wild with uncontrolled power or they become a tool of an irresponsible and somewhat unscrupulous fraction of our national legislature."[24]

The fifth "predictable" stimulus to states' rights sentiment during the 1920s, Prohibition, has received extensive attention elsewhere. No single issue can compare with it as a persistent source of acrimony, or for constitutional complexity, because opponents of the Eighteenth Amendment invariably felt obliged to explain that their hostility had absolutely nothing whatsoever to do with a personal fondness for liquor.[25] An essay in *The North American Review* typified more than a decade of passionate hostility: "Take away the sense that each State has a right to order its purely internal affairs according to its own desires, and you condemn to inevitable decay . . . the public life of every one of them."[26]

23. Robert B. Highsaw, *Edward Douglass White: Defender of the Conservative Faith* (Baton Rouge, La., 1981), ch. 9; Murphy, *Constitution in Crisis Times,* 12, 21.

24. *New York Times,* Oct. 5, 1926, p. 2; ibid., May 5, 1927, p. 29; ibid., April 9, 1929, p. 51.

25. "States Rights Today," *The North American Review* 211 (April 1920): 438–43; John Philip Hill, "A States Rights Remedy for Volsteadism," ibid., 221 (June 1925): 635–40.

26. Fabian Franklin, "Prohibition and the States," ibid., 207 (February 1918): 231–38, the

No spokesman for states' rights was more relentless than Governor Ritchie of Maryland in manipulating this issue for purposes that reached well beyond its immediate significance: namely, to reformulate and thereby "modernize" the meaning of states' rights, and to demonstrate that Prohibition exemplified a broad cluster of encroachments by the national government. "The term State Rights is not a particularly well chosen one in connection with Prohibition," he observed in 1928. "It harks back to the Civil War and bears the label of a lost cause, a cause no one would revive today. Yet it is the term which has always been applied to those who take the side of the States against advancing and encroaching Federalism of any kind, the side of less government against more government." He concluded, quite correctly, with a reminder that "it has meant different things at different periods of our history."[27] Concerning states' rights, Ritchie can only be described as a fanatic; yet unlike many who shared his views (as we shall see below), he sought to be candid in his use of language and in his reading of American history.

II

Still other stimuli for the upsurge in states' rights intensity during the 1920s came from less obvious sources, and are likely to surprise all but a few scholars who specialize in American politics during the inter-war era. These stimuli emanated from every branch of the federal government. We have already seen that the Supreme Court did not behave as a consistent monolith; it alternately infuriated and then encouraged states' rights enthusiasts. Congress as well as every president who served between World War I and 1938 behaved in ways that seemed equally erratic. To add a final irony, who would have expected that more states' rights rhetoric would emanate from New York than from any other state during these years?

---

quotation at 235; Ralph R. Lounsbury and Archibald E. Stevenson, "Prohibition and the Constitution: A Debate," *Current History* 28 (July 1928): 585–98; *New York Times*, Jan. 9, 1918, p. 12; ibid., June 17, 1923, section 8, p. 8; ibid., Jan. 13, 1926, p. 4; ibid., Sept. 21, 1927, p. 3.

27. *New York Times*, March 8, 1926, p. 1; ibid., April 23, 1926, p. 13; Ritchie, "The Eighteenth Amendment an Invasion of State Rights," 34.

By 1925 the criticism became commonplace that Congress was passing too many "national" laws, thereby usurping responsibilities and decisions best left to the state legislatures. These laws required an expansion of federal enforcement networks (involving, for example, child labor, narcotics control, and larceny in interstate commerce.) As Governor George S. Silzer of New Jersey stated — and his was a comparatively moderate position — "It is quite clear that we have gone too far to wholly abandon all of the activities taken over by the Federal government but we can and should retrace our steps and start afresh under the compact clause and recapture so much as is possible."[28]

A closely related criticism, voiced with even greater frequency and bitterness, declared that Congress essentially bribed, seduced, or anaesthetized the states with subsidies enacted by law — a lament that began in 1924 and hence had a steady ten-year history even prior to the New Deal. Alfred B. Johnson, president of the Pennsylvania State Chamber of Commerce, exhorted a convention of the National Association of State Chambers of Commerce, held at Atlantic City in 1928: "Under the guise of assisting the poorer and backward States, with help from the National Treasury, five laws have been enacted which have the effect of extending the national authority over important matters which belong within the sole jurisdiction of States. These laws are socialistic."[29]

Despite the fact that Presidents Coolidge and Hoover made a series of statements on behalf of states' rights, supporters of the movement felt dissatisfied, and understandably spotted ambiguities in those statements. On Memorial Day in 1925, and once again by means of a message to Congress in December of that year, Coolidge supplied major support for state sovereignty. Editorial sources that one would expect to be critical, such as *The New Republic*, found no ambiguity at all. It simply emphasized Coolidge's remark that "the greatest solicitude

28. *New York Times,* Dec. 1, 1925, p. 3; ibid., Dec. 18, 1925, p. 15; ibid., Nov. 18, 1927, p. 40; John M. Egan, "The Case for Decentralization," *The Commonweal* 20 (July 13 and 20, 1934): 283–85, 301–2.

29. Albert C. Ritchie, "Back to States' Rights!" *The World's Work* 47 (March 1924): 525–29; *New York Times,* April 27, 1924, p. 10; ibid., Jan. 11, 1925, p. 21; ibid., June 1, 1925, p. 14; ibid., July 5, 1925, p. 1; ibid., Feb. 25, 1926, p. 13; ibid., Dec. 18, 1927, section 3, p. 1; and ibid., Feb. 26, 1928, p. 13, for the quotation from Johnson.

should be exercised to prevent any encroachments on the rights of the states."[30]

But true believers remained discontented. Governor Ritchie called the Memorial Day address "unsound and unfortunate" because he understood Coolidge actually to mean "that the federal government would have the final say in every state question." Governor Al Smith of New York declared that Coolidge's speech had really repudiated states' rights because the President's plan would compel each state to pass separate laws in order to enforce federal legislation. Governor Silzer gibed that Coolidge only wished to give back to the states those responsibilities that seemed burdensome to the federal government.[31]

Coolidge and then Hoover, time after time, continued to invoke all the appropriate clichés. Let one brief example suffice for each.

> *Coolidge in 1928*: [States'] rights ought always to be scrupulously regarded. Unless their actions are such as to violate the Constitution and seriously interfere with the rights of other States, they should be left to solve their own problems in their own way under the pressure of public opinion rather than have outside authority step in to attempt to solve it for them.[32]

> *Hoover in 1936*: Something should be done to give back to the States the powers they thought they already had.[33]

Despite the apparent sincerity of their statements, however, these conservative presidents felt obliged, more often than not, to take a national view of issues; and consequently they became targets for the most pejorative accusation in the entire states' rights vocabulary: that they were *centralizers*. Critics and cynics—right, left, and center—were likely to note that traditional ideological alignments had turned all topsy-turvy. Many Democrats hailed Coolidge's 1925 Memorial Day address as a vin-

30. "Stand-pattism and States' Rights," *The New Republic* 45 (Dec. 23, 1925): 126–27.

31. *New York Times*, May 31, 1925, p. 1; ibid., June 1, 1925, p. 1; ibid., June 7, 1925, section 9, p. 5; ibid., Dec. 18, 1925, p. 15; ibid., April 25, 1928, p. 26.

32. Ibid., April 17, 1928, p. 1, the quotation at 17. See also ibid., May 16, 1926, p. 20; ibid., Aug. 4, 1926, p. 10; ibid., April 25, 1928, p. 26.

33. *Newsweek* 7 (June 13, 1936): 12. See also *New York Times*, Dec. 7, 1930, section 2, p. 9; ibid., Oct. 14, 1932, p. 18; Parrish, *Frankfurter: The Reform Years*, 265.

tage Grover Cleveland/Woodrow Wilson declaration;[34] and late in 1934, well after FDR's New Deal had begun to emerge, an editorial in the widely read *Saturday Evening Post* pointed out that "the centralization of government did not begin on March 4, 1933; it began long before that, and if it is to be discussed in terms of political-party guilt, the Republicans have many sins to answer for during their long reign, whatever may be the more recent responsibilities of the New Dealers."[35]

Although leaders of both parties espoused states' rights in the 1928 elections, Democrats made this one of their central themes quite early in the campaign. Party leaders received clear signals from the grassroots level of their organization that national hegemony over state functions was unacceptable. And ultimately, the platform adopted by the Democratic National Convention, in Houston, contained this ringing resolution: "We demand that the constitutional rights and powers of the States shall be preserved in their full vigor and virtue. These constitute a bulwark against centralization. . . ."[36]

To complete our list of unexpected twists—Democrats sounding like Republicans, and Westerners more vocal about states' rights than Southerners—it should be pointed out that no place seems to have produced more ardent advocates of states' rights than New York, regardless of party affiliation or social status.[37] We may not be startled to find

34. *New York Times,* June 1, 1925, p. 1; ibid., Jan. 9, 1926, p. 19. See "Centralization of Power in the Federal Government," Purdue University *versus* Iowa State College, in Edith M. Phelps, ed., *University Debaters' Annual . . . 1925–1926* (New York, 1926), 195–235.

35. "Swallowing the States," *The Saturday Evening Post* 207 (Dec. 8, 1934): 22. Eight months later George Soule asked: "What brought about this remarkable change of clothing? Why are Republicans now acting like Democrats? It is not mere lack of knowledge of history. Leading Republicans are not unaware that their party's historic role has been to oppose rather than to emphasize the doctrine of States' rights. This is not merely a question of abstract political philosophy. It is a question of interests and economic forces. On no other basis can the reversal be explained." Soule, "Back to States' Rights," *Harper's Magazine* 171 (September 1935): 485. Despite its title, Soule's essay opposed states' rights and accused FDR's administration of not pushing far enough in the direction of nationalization.

36. Le Roy Hodges to O. K. Brown, Sept. 8, 1927, John D. Rockefeller, Jr., Papers, Group II, box 190, Rockefeller Archive Center, Pocantico Hills, N.Y.; *New York Times,* Sept. 1, 1927, p. 5; ibid., Jan. 13, 1928, p. 1; ibid., June 20, 1928, p. 52; ibid., June 29, 1928, p. 5.

37. See, e.g., the letters to the editor, *New York Times,* June 4, 1925, p. 18; ibid., Feb. 6, 1934, p. 20; ibid., June 27, 1935, p. 20.

Republican United States Senator James Wadsworth, or President Nicholas Murray Butler of Columbia University, or Congressman Ogden Mills (Secretary of the Treasury during the final year of Hoover's presidency) all highly protective of states' rights, for they are regarded historically as having been quite conservative.[38]

By contrast, however, what a difference a decade can make—1926 to 1936—when we find a startling shift in the political circumstances and ideological imperatives of New Yorkers. In 1926 Judge Robert F. Wagner promised that, if elected to the United States Senate, he would guard against federal "encroachment." Throughout the 1920s Franklin Delano Roosevelt hoped for "less governing from Washington with a decrease in the existing functions of the national government. . . ." Governor Al Smith, to whom FDR wrote those words in 1925, would hold that same view steadfastly for the remainder of his career. Speaking in 1936 to the Independent Coalition of American Women, Smith lamented that the New Dealers were entirely "unwilling to meet the issue of states' rights. They preferred to go up a dark alley and do it under cover, and do it in spite of and not with the consent of the people's Constitution."[39]

As Governor of New York, 1929–33, Roosevelt frequently warned against a tendency for the national government to encroach upon state sovereignty, especially with respect to police powers and the administration of justice. Early in 1931, admittedly, he started to move toward a somewhat more nationalistic position. Nonetheless, as late as 1934 he hoped to maintain a major role for the states in the area of business regulation.[40]

Finally, just to complete this litany of New Yorkers devoted to states' rights, so late as 1938 the Solicitor General of the state of New York, addressing the annual convention of the National Association of Attorney-Generals, announced that "we are concerned today primarily with a fed-

38. *New York Times,* March 10, 1922, p. 14; ibid., Jan. 11, 1925, p. 21; ibid., April 20, 1925, p. 7; ibid., May 16, 1926, p. 20.

39. Ibid., Oct. 30, 1926, p. 3; ibid., Oct. 2, 1936, pp. 1, 4; Frank Freidel, *Franklin D. Roosevelt: The Ordeal* (Boston, 1954), 205, 210.

40. *New York Times,* March 3, 1930, p. 1; ibid., July 3, 1930, p. 2; ibid., July 4, 1930, p. 14; Freidel, *Franklin D. Roosevelt: The Triumph* (Boston, 1956), 71, 74–75, 196; Parrish, *Frankfurter: The Reform Years,* 245.

eral invasion of state sovereignty, that goes to the very foundation of the power to govern." At the outset he had wondered whether the American people were "beginning to forget the part which the states must play to preserve our form of government?" After less than six years of Roosevelt's New Deal program, the Solicitor General may well have had cause to wonder. On September 17, 1937, known then as Constitution Day, a *New York Times* editorial enjoyed twitting Roosevelt by reminding him of an aggressively states' rights speech that he had made back in March 1930.[41]

III

In the process of examining the context, stimuli, and momentum of the states' right movement, I have touched upon some of its central issues. I must now turn to an assessment of its major concerns. Most of them are manifest in key phrases that recur constantly in editorials, speeches, and appeals by its devotees; "our dual form of government," "state sovereignty," and "individual liberty."[42] Even more revealing, perhaps, are those key words that had pejorative connotations, the worst and most persistent, as I have already indicated, being "centralization." Others included bureaucracy, aggrandizement and aggrandizing the nation, interference, regimentation, encroachment, standardization, usurpation, collectivism, impotent states, uncontrolled power, and finally, "federal" as an adjective: e.g., a federal yardstick, federal aid, federal bureaucrats, and federal monster (which first appeared in 1918).[43]

41. Henry Epstein, "The States—At the Cross-Roads: Facing a Great Crisis," *Vital Speeches of the Day* 4 (Sept. 1, 1938): 675, 678: *New York Times*, Sept. 17, 1937, p. 24.

42. Critics of the states' rights position took pleasure in pointing out that aggrandizing or maintaining state power often meant diminishing the *county's* role, thereby reducing the citizen's direct participation in government. See Paul W. Sager, "State Centralization in the South," *Annals of the American Academy of Political and Social Science* 207 (January 1940): 144–50, as well as James Harlean, "Seven Southern State Capitals," *Social Forces* 4 (December 1924): 394; and William Cox Redfield, "Federal Usurpation," *The Forum* 73 (January 1925): 89.

43. John Hemphill, "The Constitutional Pendulum," *The American Mercury* 24 (December 1931): 434–39; Virgil Jordan, "The Flight from the Centre," *Scribner's Magazine* 91 (May 1932): 262–65; "Swallowing the States," 22; *New York Times*, June 19, 1923, p. 3; ibid., April 5, 1925, p. 1; ibid., June 17, 1925, p. 23; ibid., Jan. 20, 1926, p. 9, ibid., March 28, 1926, sec-

It should come as no surprise that between 1918 and 1938 many of those who felt most apprehensive about "centralization" and "collectivism" expressed their support for states' rights by proclaiming the need to halt Bolshevism, "semi-socialism," fascism, and communism.[44] Far more interesting, however, were the games of historical semantics and word-twisting utilized mostly by states' rights advocates, just as the Federalists of 1787 (who were actually nationalists) had unfairly labelled their opponents Anti-Federalists (who were actually federalists). Perhaps four illustrations of states' rights double-talk, drawn from as many prominent exponents, will suffice.

- *Governor Albert C. Ritchie of Maryland (1926):* It was the principle of self-government which saved the South and made possible a re-united and happy nation.

- *President Nicholas Murray Butler of Columbia University (1926):* The best minds in the Republican Party today are doing their best to resist this centralization and are doing it in the name of union of the States rather than States' rights.

- *Senator James Wadsworth of New York (1926):* There is no place for appeal to purely local or selfish interest. We are a nation and in deciding upon the future of the Federal Government we must think nationally.

- *President Herbert Hoover (1930):* I have in a previous message recommended effective regulation of interstate electrical power. Such regulation should preserve the independence and responsibility of the States.[45]

As a historical accompaniment to such rhetoric, a repudiation of Hamiltonianism, connoting big government, blossomed as early as 1918, followed by a gradual (but selective) revival of Jeffersonian ideals. This

---

tion 9, p. 12; ibid., Nov. 27, 1926, p. 6; ibid., Feb. 26, 1927, p. 1; ibid., June 3, 1927, p. 11; ibid., Jan. 24, 1932, p. 22; ibid., May 22, 1935, p. 2; ibid., July 16, 1935, p. 2; ibid., Oct. 5, 1937, p. 24.

44. *New York Times*, April 3, 1919, p. 19; ibid., Feb. 26, 1928, p. 3; ibid., Dec. 4, 1935, p. 7; ibid., Jan. 19, 1936, p. 38; ibid., Oct. 13, 1937, p. 35.

45. Ibid., March 6, 1926, p. 32; ibid., Oct. 28, 1926, p. 5; ibid., Oct. 31, 1926, p. 2; ibid., Dec. 7, 1930, section 2, p. 9.

took various organizational forms: a revitalized Democratic Party in Illinois devoted to restoring the Jeffersonian doctrine of states' rights (1925), or the formation of a nationwide Thomas Jefferson League in 1926 to oppose federal paternalism and incursions upon the states' power of taxation. Most commonly, however, it followed hyperbolic and anomalous lines: in 1927, for example, when Senator Robert F. Wagner of New York promoted Al Smith's candidacy for president. "There is one man in the country today," he proclaimed, "who stands out as a defender of democracy in the same manner in which did Thomas Jefferson and the other great figures of the past."[46]

Yet another manifestation of states' rights anxiety, particularly during the years 1925–37, took the form of varied proposals for inter-state co-operation as an alternative to federal intervention or actual control. Some of these proposals had a positive genesis in the partiality toward regionalism that flourished during the inter-war years,[47] whereas others were utterly negative: desperate attempts to stave off control by Congress or by special commissions. In 1925, for example, the State Controller of New York called for a States' Rights Conference whose goal would be to "establish a well-defined line of demarcation between State and Federal authority and to put a stop to the trend of centralization of government. . . ." Two years later Governor Ritchie proposed the formation of a "House of Governors, a League of States, so to speak,

---

46. Ibid., April 15, 1918, p. 14; ibid., Aug. 31, 1925, p. 2; ibid., Jan. 27, 1926, p. 14; ibid., Jan. 7, 1927, p. 1; and ibid., Feb. 1, 1931, p. 19. See also Merrill D. Peterson, *The Jefferson Image in the American Mind* (New York, 1960), esp. 347–79; Hemphill, "Constitutional Pendulum," 434–35; "Coolidge, the Jeffersonian," *The Outlook* 143 (Aug. 18, 1926): 529–30; and Senator William H. King, "The Vanishing State," *National Republic* 22 (May 1934): 2.

47. For an example of the connection, see Parrish, *Frankfurter: The Reform Years*, 169–70. For a fascinating debate over the viability of "state compacts," generated by the Boulder Dam project on the Colorado River, see "An Interstate Compact Fails," *The New Republic* 42 (April 1, 1925): 144–45, and James Landis's reply, ibid. (April 29, 1925): 265–66. The editors of *The New Republic* insisted that "doctrinaire anti-federalism in such a situation is little less than absurd. It was wise to try to negotiate a state compact. But there is no wisdom in allowing its possible abstract desirability to obscure its obvious failure." In response to Landis's hopefulness about the possibility of an interstate compact, the editors added: "We do not argue that the federal government is immune to mistakes, delays and failures to which the states are liable. We argue simply that we should do our best to improve the operation of all agencies of government whether state or national. . . ."

which could so function as to become in effect almost a third house in the republic."[48]

Although most of these suggestions of the mid-1920s never got beyond the planning stage, opposition to the New Deal would lead, a decade later, to the actual creation of a Conference of Commissions on Interstate Cooperation (based in the Northeast); a Council of State Governments (designed to provide mechanisms so that states could resolve mutual problems without turning to the federal government for help); a New England Council; an American Legislators Association; and an Interstate Commission on the Delaware River Basin. The executive director of the last-mentioned organization expressed concerns that were characteristic of all these groups. If federal authorities were permitted to control pollution in navigable waters and their tributaries, it would mean "the virtual destruction of the States and the fusing of American sovereignty into one gigantic all-powerful sovereignty centered in Washington."[49]

By 1934–35 the states' rights movement had acquired its second wind, so to speak. In addition to the organizational efforts just mentioned, it now generated more polemical fireworks through the media than at any time since the peak years, 1925–28. The basic stimulus for this revival, needless to say, was Roosevelt's New Deal program, a source of utter despair for those committed to the cause of state sovereignty. James M. Beck, for example, former Solicitor General of the United States and a Congressman from Philadelphia, declared at the end of 1934 that "in my judgment the Union will not survive the present centralization of political power in Washington."[50] Similarly, in a speech de-

48. *New York Times*, Nov. 19, 1925, p. 5; ibid., July 27, 1927, p. 23; the *Times* responded to Ritchie with skepticism on July 28, 1927, p. 18.

49. Ibid., Nov. 23, 1935, p. 4; ibid., April 18, 1936, p. 4; ibid., Nov. 21, 1937, section 8, p. 4; ibid., Dec. 12, 1937, p. 34. For a droll example of double-talk by a centralizer, see David E. Lilienthal, "The TVA and Decentralization," *Survey Graphic* 29 (June 1940): 335–37.

50. Beck to Edward S. Corwin, Dec. 15, 1934, Corwin Papers, box 1, Seeley G. Mudd Manuscript Library, Princeton University. In a complex and curious way, the deeply conservative Beck had moved from a dual, nationalist–states' rights position in 1926 to passionate localism at the time of his death ten years later. Because Beck was one of the most widely read exponents of states' rights, the trajectory of his outlook, although not entirely representative of the movement as a whole, is worth tracing. See Beck, *The Vanishing Rights of the*

livered on Constitution Day in 1934, Ogden Mills disparaged "a nation temporarily unmindful of its ancient virtues and apparently willing to follow a leadership . . . that stands ready to substitute the sovereignty of the State for that of the citizen, collectivism for individualism, bureaucracy for democracy."[51]

In so far as the 1936 elections can be considered a referendum on the New Deal, they also supplied what turned out to be the penultimate serious referendum on states' rights in American history (the last occurring in 1948). Once again journalists noted that traditional party ideologies had been turned inside out. The situation was even more complicated than that, however, because numerous Southern Democrats, who supported their party but not the President, shared the belief of Georgia's Governor Eugene Talmadge, expressed early in 1936, that "if the present program is continued for four more years, the lines between the States will be only a shadow on paper, and the government of the separate States will be subservient to the will of a central power in Washington."[52]

Parallel to the electioneering of 1935–36, moreover, there was yet another sort of referendum on states' rights. It took the form of sustained public controversy over various constitutional amendments, most of which never got beyond the discussion stage and generated considerably more heat than light. In 1935 conservatives began to talk about

---

States (New York, 1926); *New York Times,* April 3, 1926, p. 16; ibid., April 10, 1926, p. 16; ibid., May 3, 1926, p. 20; Beck to Senator William H. King, Feb. 9, 1927, Beck Papers, box 1, Seeley G. Mudd Manuscript Library, Princeton University; and Morton Keller, *In Praise of Yesterday: James M. Beck and the Politics of Conservatism, 1861–1936* (New York, 1958).

51. *New York Times,* Sept. 18, 1934, p. 2. For a fierce attack upon the New Deal in the name of states' rights, see Albert C. Ritchie, "The Threatening Destruction of Self Government among the American States," *Vital Speeches of the Day* 1 (April 22, 1935): 456–59. Opposition to the New Deal with a states' rights rationale was especially strong in Texas. See Judge Joseph C. Hutcheson, "The March of the Federal Constitution," a Constitution Day address given in Houston on Sept. 17, 1933 (printed pamphlet); *New York Times,* June 16, 1935, section 4, p. 6; ibid., June 22, 1935, p. 13; Palmer Hutcheson to Edward S. Corwin, Sept. 18, 1936, Corwin Papers, box 2.

52. "Who Owns States' Rights," *The Nation* 142 (May 20, 1936): 632–33; *New York Times,* July 14, 1935, section 4, p. 8; ibid., Jan. 7, 1936, p. 12; ibid., Jan. 30, 1936, p. 8 (for the Talmadge quotation); ibid., Aug. 2, 1936, section 4, p. 8; ibid., Aug. 11, 1936, p. 9; ibid., Aug. 13, 1936, p. 2.

the need for some sort of amendment that would formally return power to the states, and in the same breath expressed apprehension that liberals intended to respond to the Supreme Court's rejection of New Deal legislation, particularly the National Recovery Act, by achieving the same result through a constitutional amendment enhancing executive authority and/or curtailing the Court's powers. As Frank Lowden, a former Governor of Illinois explained: "it is sought in this way to acquire power that was denied by the Supreme Court in the Schechter case. If such an amendment should prevail, in the language of the court, 'there would be virtually no limit to the Federal power, and for all practical purposes we should have a complete centralized government'."[53]

Curiously enough, the only amendment formally introduced for consideration came from Senator William E. Borah late in February 1937, an amendment that would have redefined the Due Process Clause of the Constitution in order to clarify and enhance the states' power to respond to economic and social problems. Borah's proposal is doubly interesting. First, because it reminds us that by 1936–37 the conflict was not simply between liberal activists in Washington and do-nothing conservatives in the provinces. There were, in fact, advocates of states' rights in the Progressive, Wilson-Brandeis tradition, who preferred, for example, the passage of state minimum wage laws to federal ones.[54]

And second because Borah's own zig-zag course from a moderate states' rights position in the 1920s to an extreme one by 1937 is symptomatic of many others who vacillated between ideological and more purely expedient motives. In 1922 Borah had helped to block a federal anti-lynching law on the grounds that it required an unconstitutional redistribution of governmental powers. In 1923, however, addressing the Citizens Conference on Law Enforcement, Borah took a judicious, centrist position:

53. See Lowden, "The Federal Principle," *Vital Speeches of the Day* 1 (June 17, 1935): 595–97; *New York Times*, June 8, 1935, p. 7; ibid., June 13, 1935, p. 4; ibid., June 15, 1935, p. 7; ibid., June 21, 1935, p. 20; ibid., June 23, 1935, section 4, p. 7; ibid., Aug. 4, 1935, section 4, p. 8; ibid., Jan. 19, 1936, section 4, p. 9; ibid., Feb. 16, 1936, section 4, p. 9.

54. See *New York Times*, Feb. 26, 1937, p. 1; and William E. Leuchtenburg, "The Origins of Franklin D. Roosevelt's 'Court-Packing' Plan," *The Supreme Court Review, 1966* (Chicago, 1966), 399.

The State is an integral part of the American Union. The whole purpose, the very existence of the Union requires and depends upon concerted action in carrying out the aims and purposes of the Union as expressed in the Federal Constitution. We live under two sovereignties. We seek to combine and utilize local and national interests in one grand purpose. We are endeavoring in this way to work out the great problem of representative government. Is not every State a part, and anxious to be considered a part, of the purpose?[55]

In 1927–28, as a strong supporter of Prohibition and as a presidential aspirant, Borah took his most "nationalistic" stance. Ten years later, however, he had returned to the fold of states' rights and strict constructionism.

IV

We should, finally, inquire into the changes, consequences, and ultimate resolution of these issues. What was the essential outcome of this peculiar chapter in American political history? Who spoke up against states' rights; and why did they, eventually, carry the day? Why should we regard 1934–36, despite all the constitutional acrimony and uncertainty of those years, as the determinative phase in the triumph of American federalism (viz., nationalism)? Why had many in the business community essentially made an ideological about-face by 1937–39? And what residue of states' rights feeling remained as the United States re-elected Franklin D. Roosevelt to a third term in the White House?

If we ask who opposed states' rights, the obvious answer is, a growing number of Americans and journals of opinion between the mid-1920s and later 1930s. The more surprising response, however, is that their motives and political persuasions were diverse. They did not constitute any sort of ideological monolith. Editorials and signed articles in *The New Republic* and *The Outlook* consistently opposed — indeed scorned — states' rights.[56] National newspapers, like the *New York Times,* initially

55. See LeRoy Ashby, *The Spearless Leader: Senator Borah and the Progressive Movement in the 1920's* (Urbana, Ill., 1972), 253–54; Borah, "Shall the Constitution of the United States Be Nullified?" in Borah, *American Problems: A Selection of Speeches and Prophecies* (New York, 1924), 318–19.

56. See Curtis Nettels, "The Plea for States' Rights," *The New Republic* 41 (Jan. 14, 1925):

responded on an *ad hoc* basis, issue by issue and one proposal at a time. As early as 1926, however, its editorials advised that "it is no more possible to get 'back to the Constitution' than it is to get back from the twentieth century to the eighteenth"; and sometimes even responded with ridicule: "'States' Rights' is just as blessed as 'Mesopotamia'. And just about as powerful in legislation; good to make speeches about, pretty sure to be thrown away when the vote comes." During Roosevelt's first administration the *Times* offered qualified approval. In a special feature tracing the growth of federal governmental power, for example, it argued that "the administration has been scrupulous in observing the legal rights of States. Secretary Ickes and other officials have been hampered in their work by the care they have exercised in not overstepping the wall that protects the machinery of these subdivisions." It went on to concede, however, that "a quilt of Federal activities has nevertheless been laid over the nation."[57]

New Deal officials as moderate as Attorney General Homer Cummings, and as radical as Secretary of Agriculture Henry A. Wallace, declared that the nation's problems had ceased to be "local and isolated." Wallace warned in 1936 that the states no longer demarcated "economic boundaries that make sense, and they provide only limited instruments for action to meet modern problems."[58] The positive notions for such men were national standards, co-operation, the nation as a whole, and, as one put it, the "authority to speak as a single nation." Their pejorative phrases were likely to be "American provincialism" and the "anarchy of particularist legislation"; they tended to refer to the states as "arbitrary and antiquated political sub-divisions."

As early as 1925, however, former members of Wilson's cabinet and conservative Democrats like William G. McAdoo had asserted that the so-called "usurpation" of federal power was more apparent than real. McAdoo, for example, protested the abolition of national agencies and accused his opponents of hypocrisy:

191–92; Don C. Seitz, "Whence Cometh Federalism?" *The Outlook* 146 (July 13, 1927): 350–51, and the editors' reply on 337.

57. *New York Times,* Jan. 8, 1926, p. 18; ibid., Jan. 28, 1926, p. 22; ibid., Feb. 4, 1926, p. 2; ibid., April 15, 1928, section 3, p. 4; ibid., Sept. 2, 1934, section 4, p. 7.

58. Ibid., Sept. 1, 1933, p. 9; ibid., June 28, 1936, p. 5.

These people are not interested in States' rights because they honestly desire to see the powers of the State Governments protected or extended. The best proof of this is that when the States act to control them, they fly for refuge in the Fourteenth Amendment to the Constitution, which gives the Federal Supreme Court authority to set aside regulatory legislation.[59]

In 1928 the National Municipal League issued a qualified report declaring that "Federal aid has been consistently administered without unreasonable interference in State affairs"; and Charles Evans Hughes, former Republican Governor of New York and Wilson's presidential opponent in 1916, blamed the inadequacies of state government for the decline of state sovereignty.[60]

Those opposed to states' rights on account of the Prohibition question ranged along a fairly broad ideological spectrum. A leader of the Anti-Saloon League asserted that "State frontiers are but nominal," particularly because "communication is so developed that no State can protect or cultivate any evil thing and confine it within its borders." A clergyman at Miami University in Ohio argued that "the increasing surrender of state powers to the government at Washington is not a tragedy. As long as individual states maintain different codes on important practical social and economic issues it is a necessity." And a college president (Republican and Presbyterian) declared that he was neither for nor against Prohibition. He simply favored consistency, and considered the implications if adjacent states had divergent regulations with respect to liquor: "The highest right any state has is to recognize the right of another state. If by the theory of state rights one state would make it difficult or impossible for another state to maintain a code of morals, it must be very evident no progress could be made in advancing any reform."[61]

59. William Cox Redfield, "Federal Usurpation," *The Forum* 73 (Jan. 1925): 88–95; McAdoo is quoted in the *New York Times*, May 26, 1926, p. 20.

60. *New York Times*, May 23, 1928, p. 27; ibid., Oct. 14, 1928, section 3, p. 4; ibid., Oct. 27, 1928, p. 29.

61. Ibid., Sept. 19, 1926, section 2, p. 5; Howard G. Lytle, "Prohibition and Jeffersonian Doctrine," *The Christian Century* 47 (Sept. 24, 1930): 1151–53; W. W. Boyd, "State Rights: A Wet Error," *The Review of Reviews* 83 (March 1931): 47–48.

In March 1932, one year after those words appeared, but a year before Franklin Roosevelt took office, an editorial in *The Christian Century* offered a modest suggestion: namely, that before federal agencies spent any more money, and before politicians offered any more hyperbole, "it would be better, before either expanding or contracting the federal goverment's functions, to have some sober consideration of the relations of national to state governments under contemporary conditions."[62]

During the mid- and later 1920s, a few figures had called for a genuine reconsideration of the nature and potential meaning of federalism. For the most part, however, these had been scholars and jurists — not necessarily from ivory towers, but not exactly voices widely listened to at the time. Brandeis tended to be a lonely dissenter on the Court. His disciples, Frankfurter and Landis, were not yet very influential outside of academe. Charles Warren's *The Supreme Court in United States History* (1922) contained considerable food for revisionist thought; but its three weighty volumes were not easily accessible to even the more cerebral citizen. Edward S. Corwin could compare theories of "competitive federalism" and "co-operative federalism," but did so in the *American Political Science Review*, a journal not widely read beyond professional circles.[63]

Beginning late in 1934–35, however, accelerating the next year, and continuing steadily thereafter, calls for a reconsideration of federalism came from popular as well as from academic sources, from conservatives as well as liberals, from sardonic journalists as well as sober judges. One letter to the editor of the *New York Times* in 1936 even talked about the "full realization" of "the New Federalism," as did Irving Brant's best-selling volume, *Storm Over the Constitution*, later that same year.[64]

62. "State Rights Doctrine Needs to Be Restudied," *The Christian Century* 49 (March 9, 1932): 309.

63. See Parrish, *Frankfurter: The Reform Years*, 169–70; Senator Henry Cabot Lodge to Charles Warren, July 19, 1923, Warren Papers, box 2, Library of Congress, Manuscript Division, Washington, D.C.; Judge George W. Anderson to Charles Warren, Jan. 5, 1923, ibid.; Horace J. Fenton, "Federal Encroachments on State Rights," *Current History* 22 (July 1925): 613–17; Corwin's essay (1925) is reprinted in Mason, ed., *American Constitutional History*, 99–108, see esp. 103. Clyde A. Beals, "State Governors Challenge Federal Encroachments," *Current History* 22 (August 1925): 793–95, reports on the 17th annual Governors' Conference, held late in June 1925. The tone of the Conference seems to have been fairly balanced and judicious.

64. John G. Brunini, "States' Rights and Divorce," *The Commonweal* 20 (Oct. 19, 1934):

This does not mean that a consensus, or anything close to one, had been achieved by 1936. The letter-writer to the *Times* seems to have been a frustrated devotee of states' rights whereas Brant delighted in labelling such people "the New Antifederalists";[65] and regarded Roosevelt's program itself as "the New Federalism" incarnate.

What *was* happening, however, involved a lessening of polarization, as people who had been at opposite ends of the spectrum edged closer to the center. Such flexible types did not seem either to dread federal centralization or to despise those who harbored residual sympathy for states' rights. They felt a degree of optimism about the potential for intergovernmental cooperation. R. Walton Moore, for example, had sat in Congress as a conservative Democrat from Virginia (1919–31), and between 1933 and 1937 he served as an assistant secretary of state under FDR. In 1935 Moore wrote to Douglas Southall Freeman, the prominent biographer of George Washington and Robert E. Lee, historian of the Confederacy, and editor of the *Richmond News Leader*, to remind him that

> five years ago I tried to indicate the impossibility of applying the doctrine of states' rights with great strictness in an emergency period. All of us who consistently favor the maintenance of our dual system of government, it seems to me, recognize that unless the states themselves are able and willing to function more actively in various directions, the solution of some present and prospective problems cannot be found under the existing constitutional situation.[66]

577–79; "At the Observation Post," *The Literary Digest* 119 (March 9, 1935): 15; *New York Times*, Feb. 16, 1936, section 4, p. 9; John M. Gaus to Edward S. Corwin, June 12, 1936, Corwin Papers, box 2; Brant, *Storm Over the Constitution* (Indianapolis, Ind., 1936), 42–43; Jane Perry Clark, *The Rise of a New Federalism: Federal-State Cooperation in the United States* (New York, 1938); Felix Frankfurter, *Mr. Justice Holmes and the Supreme Court* (1938; 2d ed., Cambridge, Mass., 1961), 88–112, "The Federal System." In October 1941 the 175th anniversary celebration at Rutgers University strongly emphasized federalism. On June 5, 1942, Edward S. Corwin delivered a nationwide radio address entitled "The Federal Idea, Especially as It Has Evolved in the United States." The text will be found in the Corwin Papers, box 3.

65. *Storm Over the Constitution*, 51, 52, 57, 108 n. 180.

66. Moore to Douglas Southall Freeman, July 15, 1935, Freeman Papers, box 25, Library of Congress, Manuscript Division, Washington, D.C. For contextual developments, see James T. Patterson, *The New Deal and the States: Federalism in Transition* (Princeton, N.J., 1969), 194–207.

Throughout 1935 and '36 one finds, time and again, individuals and the press paying lip service to certain customary and formulaic phrases about states' rights, all the while acknowledging that economic and political realities had changed beyond recall. The results varied. In some instances, as we have noted, there was an inclination to soften hitherto inflexible positions.[67] In others, we can see the emergence of substantial support for what I would call *modified* conservatism.[68] And in still others we witness a willingness to concede ambiguities and to enter into genuine dialogue with the opposition. Here is just one illustration, a *New York Times* editorial from June 1935:

> There must be Liberals who find themselves in a painful dilemma on this new issue of States' rights. As politicians, they no doubt want a strongly centralized America with full powers in Congress to tame the ravening appetites of the profit-motive system. As champions of a richer national culture, they are not so sure about centralization. It was their greatest grief for years that America had been standardized and ironed out into a flat uniformity. Of late they have rejoiced to find our writers mirroring the sections and regions and localities and diversities that after all make up America. Wage differentials between Georgia and Indiana ought to be flattened out. But can this be done without flattening out the differential between Erskine Caldwell and Booth Tarkington?[69]

During the mid-1930s, a few spokesmen for the business sector expressed concern that if regulatory agencies in divergent states could es-

---

67. See e.g., the speech of Governor Martin L. Davey, Democrat of Ohio, reported in the *New York Times,* June 2, 1935, p. 26; a major feature essay on states' rights, ibid., June 9, 1935, section 7, p. 1; John Corbin, "What Is a United State?" *Scribner's Magazine* 98 (November 1935): 257–61; and George R. Farnum, "States' Rights, Nationalism, and the Supreme Court," *Vital Speeches of the Day* 3 (Nov. 2, 1936): 46–48.

68. *New York Times,* June 9, 1935, section 4, p. 8; ibid., Jan. 9, 1936, p. 20; ibid., July 24, 1936, p. 1, for Governor Alf Landon's speech accepting the Republican presidential nomination; ibid., March 15, 1937, p. 22; and William L. Ransom, "The Rights Reserved to the States and the People," *Annals of the American Academy of Political and Social Science* 185 (May 1936): 170–81. Ransom was then president of the American Bar Association.

69. *New York Times,* June 9, 1935, section 4, p. 8; ibid., Jan. 26, 1936, p. 7; John M. Egan, "State Power and Freedom," *The Commonweal* 23 (Nov. 29, 1935): 117–19; a reply to

tablish minimum rates on nationally merchandised goods, then catalogues and price lists would be confusing, and national marketing campaigns hopelessly ruined. In 1936 the states of Indiana and New Mexico conceded their inability to control the soft coal industry within their borders, and therefore asked the Supreme Court to sustain the Guffey Act as the only means of achieving effective regulation.[70]

By 1938–39 an even stronger swing occurred. Railroad companies disliked the proliferation of state railroad commissions and preferred exclusive federal jurisdiction. In 1938 an editorial in *Business Week* responded critically to a Supreme Court decision upholding a Minnesota law imposing restrictions upon liquor brought into that state. *Business Week* anticipated, as a consequence, even more barriers to interstate trade, and remarked that "great importance is attached to the decision of the growing disposition on the part of the states to protect their own industries by border barriers." In 1939 *Business Week* launched what amounted to a major offensive in opposition to state protectionism.[71]

It would be naive to expect states' rights sentiments to have disappeared entirely by the close of the 1930s. They lingered on in various quarters—some public, political, and volatile; others more private, and often within the groves of academe. Once again, many of the most recalcitrant voices came from northern New England and upstate New York. Governor George Aiken of Vermont fulminated throughout 1938–39 against federal involvement in flood control programs for the Connecticut River Valley; and incidentally elicited snide or disparaging comments from Southerners in the process.[72] As late as 1940 an occasional

---

Egan by Victor S. Yarros, ibid. (Jan 24, 1936), p. 358; and "Resolved: That the Power of the Federal Government Should Be Increased," *Vital Speeches of the Day* 7 (Jan. 1, 1941): 169–73, a four-person debate aired on NBC radio, Nov. 22, 1940.

70. *Business Week,* June 16, 1934, p. 12; *New York Times,* March 5, 1936, p. 31.

71. Pierce Williams, "State Walls and Economic Areas," *Survey Graphic* 26 (April 1, 1937): 192–96, 240–41; "States' Rights Win," *Business Week,* June 4, 1938, pp. 39–40; "State Rights—Interstate Wrongs," ibid., Jan. 28, 1939, p. 48.

72. "In the Name of the Great Jehovah," *The Commonweal* 29 (Jan. 27, 1939): 383–84; George D. Aiken, "State Rights the Real Issue," *Vital Speeches of the Day* 5 (Feb. 15, 1939): 271–72; Aiken, "Fear and Its Effects: The States Must Stand Shoulder to Shoulder," ibid., 5 (March 1, 1939): 300–304.

journalist would raise the question, rhetorically and sympathetically, of whether states' rights could be preserved. Or a Bostonian, appropriately named T. Jefferson Coolidge, who had served as Undersecretary of the Treasury (1934–36), poignantly lamented that "no longer is any state self-supporting. Think of your sovereign states depending not on their own citizens but on favors from the Washington political administration to carry out their duties."[73]

Nevertheless, nationwide discussion of states' rights waned after 1937 and had virtually disappeared by 1940. Public opinion polls were quite new in the later 1930s, and several Gallup Polls taken during 1937–38 are indicative of the closure that took place on this whole issue. In 1937 almost three thousand people (a national sample) were asked whether amendments to the Constitution should be placed before each state legislature or given "directly to the people of each state for approval?" Only 8 percent had no opinion, 74 percent preferred the latter, and a mere 18 percent the former. Similar polls taken late in 1937 and early the following year resulted in similar outcomes but with slightly less dramatic margins of defeat for the role of the state legislature. In mid-1938 *Fortune* magazine, which was extremely hostile to the New Deal, published the outcome of its own poll (worded more bluntly): "In the division of government power between the federal and the state governments, do you think the federal should have more power and the state less, or the state more and the federal less?"[74] Here is *Fortune's* tally, along with its editorial commentary:

73. O. K. Armstrong, "Can State Rights Be Saved?" *Nation's Business* 28 (September 1940), pp. 36, 38, 66, 69; Coolidge, "Remember the States," *The Atlantic Monthly* 165 (January 1940): 89–93. For academic advocacy of states' rights, see the convocation address by the president of Colgate University, George B. Cutten, "Your Freedom at Stake," *Vital Speeches of the Day* 6 (Oct. 1, 1940): 738–42; and the correspondence of Dixon Ryan Fox, president of Union College in Schenectady, N.Y. See E. Parmalee Prentice to Fox, Nov. 8, 1940; Fox to Carroll Osborn, March 11, 1941, with the typescript of Fox's essay attached; and George W. Robnett to Fox, Dec. 11, 1944, Fox Papers, Schaffer Library, Union College.

74. The Gallup Polls are located at The Roper Center, Office of Archival Development, The University of Connecticut, Storrs, Conn., nos. AIPO0072 Q4, 4A; AIPO0107 Q5 x-ray; and AIPO0112 Q9A, 9B x-ray. The *Fortune* Quarterly Survey, "Sovereign States vs. the Nation," appeared in *Fortune* 18 (July 1938): 76, 79.

	TOTAL	PACIFIC COAST	SOUTHEAST	NORTHWEST PLAINS
State more power. . . .	31.8%	22.3%	30.1%	41.1%
Federal more power. . .	27.2	42.3	21.5	20.3
Same as now	20.4	20.0	25.4	21.3
Don't know.	20.6	15.4	23.0	17.3

Thus about one-fifth of the public has no opinion, another fifth is satisfied with the status quo between state and federal power, and of the remaining three-fifths a good majority would reverse the trend toward the federalization of power. At first glance this might seem like popular contradiction. People can't demand more local autonomy, and in the next breath ask for federal regulation of wages and hours of labor and of business and industry. But note that the status quo plus the federal-power vote add up to a total that almost equals the New Deal public. And note also that the states'-rights group numerically nearly matches the Roosevelt opposition. The illogic in the returns lies in the Southeast, which apparently is unwilling to surrender its traditional stand, yet plumps immense majorities for Mr. Roosevelt on every count, and especially for federal regulation of wages and hours. But the Southeast is nevertheless in a median position. It is the anti-Roosevelt Northwest Plains that stand conservatively upon their local rights of self-government. And from the Pacific Coast comes the greatest demand for still more federalization of government.

Quite clearly, the states' rights issue had not died by 1938, and it has resurfaced in a series of spasmodic revivals since then.[75] Each one of them, however, has been markedly unsuccessful. The three states' rights amendments proposed in 1963, for example, gathered no momentum at all. And that same year, in public opinion polls where support for school segregation was linked to states' rights, 48 percent of those

75. See, e.g., G. Edward White, *Earl Warren: A Public Life* (New York, 1982), 109, 133, 153; Thomas Wilcox, *States' Rights vs. the Supreme Court* (Boston, 1960); and the brief flurry of interest in 1963 in a cluster of so-called states' rights amendments. See "States' Rights?" *The Commonweal* 78 (May 31, 1963): 269; "A Crowd of Umbrella Heads," *The Reporter* 28 (June 6, 1963): 10–11. For the John Birch Society's strident position on states' rights, see Robert Welch, Jr., *The White Book* (March 1961), 10.

polled opposed state sovereignty, though 45 percent expressed the belief that school integration and its implementation should be left to the states.

Writing for a general audience in 1940, Edward S. Corwin acknowledged that the Supreme Court's more liberal orientation since 1937 was causing some critics "to complain that this means the end of States' Rights." In reality, he declared, "the truth is that the states were no longer capable of exercising the powers which this conception attributed to them," a position that various commentators, conservative as well as liberal, had been expounding ever since Elihu Root's benchmark address of 1906.[76] Corwin sensibly predicted that the Court would "no longer play States' Rights against National Power and vice versa as it often did through the half-century between 1887 and 1937."[77]

Nevertheless, the fact remains that for twenty years following World War I, a genuine revival of states' rights occurred—a revival fostered by a curious mixture of localists and nationalists,[78] Democrats and Republicans, Wilsonian Progressives and apprehensive conservatives, and most certainly by Northerners as well as Southerners. Although historians have neglected this impulse and the extensive controversies that it engendered, a professor of constitutional law at Columbia University, writing in 1927, caught the most basic point concerning the revival. The doctrine of states' rights, he explained, in a popular little

76. Root, "How to Preserve the Local Self-Government of the States: A Brief Study of National Tendencies" (speech at the dinner of the Pennsylvania Society in New York, Dec. 12, 1906), in Root, *Addresses on Government and Citizenship* (Cambridge, Mass., 1916), 363–70. For explicit as well as implicit variations of Root's influential view, see the *New York Times*, April 6, 1925, p. 18; ibid., May 31, 1925, p. 1; ibid., May 17, 1926, p. 20; James M. Beck, *Our Changing Constitution* (Williamsburg, Va., 1928), esp. 27–28; and "Work Relief and States' Rights," *The New Republic* 99 (June 14, 1939): 145–46.

77. Corwin, "Statesmanship on the Supreme Court," *The American Scholar* 9 (Spring 1940): 159–63, reprinted in Mason, ed., *American Constitutional History*, 143–44. See also Corwin, "The Passing of Dual Federalism," *Virginia Law Review* 36 (February 1950): 1–24.

78. For diverse examples of states' rights nationalists, see Federal Judge Charles M. Hough, quoted in the *New York Times*, Jan. 29, 1917, p. 4; H. L. Mencken, "What Is This Talk about Utopia?" *The Nation* 126 (June 13, 1928): 662–63; and Gutzon Borglum, the sculptor of Mount Rushmore, who feared federal financing of the project [1925–28] because then "control would pass into other hands." See Gilbert Fite, *Mount Rushmore* (Norman, Okla., 1952), 67–68, 84.

book written for the general public, "knows no special sectional habitation. It is a nomad, reviving whenever and dwelling wherever toes are trod upon or feelings severely ruffled by the exercise of federal power."[79] If that was a sage observation in 1927, it seems equally applicable in the United States more than half a century later.

79. Howard Lee McBain, *The Living Constitution: A Consideration of the Realities and Legends of Our Fundamental Law* (New York, 1927), 66–67.

This essay was prepared for presentation on October 26, 1983, at a conference concerning "Regionalism and Centralization in American and Italian History," held at the University of Florence under the joint sponsorship of the American Historical Association and the Società degli Storici Italiani.

I am indebted to Professors Ennio Di Nolfo, Ira A. Glazier, Emiliana Noether, and Robert V. Remini for their superb planning of the conference; and to Professors Giuseppe Buttà and William E. Leuchtenburg for their thoughtful assessments of my paper.

My essay, along with the two critics' comments, first appeared (in Italian translation) in *Regionalismo e Centralizzazione Nella Storia di Italia e Stati Uniti* (Florence, 1986), edited by Luigi De Rosa and Ennio Di Nolfo.

Seven

Constitutional Pluralism

*Conflicting Interpretations
of the Founders' Intentions*

I

THE FORMER ATTORNEY GENERAL of the United States, Edwin Meese III, made a most valuable contribution to the Bicentennial observance of the United States Constitution. He obliged us to rethink some of the most fundamental assumptions and aspects of our constitutional system. Although I do not agree with very much that Mr. Meese has said, he confronted us with some uncomfortable truths—especially pertaining to what's happened to the concept of federalism. I can only applaud the fact that he prompted jurists, scholars, students, the media, and concerned lay people—let's call them serious citizens—to discuss governmental fundamentals.

I do regret the peculiar manner in which Mr. Meese chose to proceed, however: omitting from his oral presentations, for example, some of the most controversial points contained in texts that were released to the press by his aides, and vice versa.[1] That's a strange way to score points, and it is *not* the honorable way to play the game.

I should also acknowledge from the outset that references to the

1. Stuart Taylor, Jr., "Meese and the Supreme Court: He Deals with Critics by Softening His Remarks," *New York Times,* Nov. 19, 1986, p. A16.

so-called "Meese-Brennan debate concerning original intent" have been a convenient yet excessively reductive code-phrase for a complex cluster of issues and a remarkable roster of participants. It is extremely important for us to acknowledge the number of protagonists, the range of issues, and the reality that those issues existed well before Edwin Meese became Attorney General in 1985.[2]

Contemporary constitutional discourse can best be described in terms of a forum rather than a dialogue—which is only the first of several reasons why I have chosen to emphasize the theme of constitutional pluralism. If Meese stands quite solidly for the Constitution of 1787, for example, and Supreme Court Justice William J. Brennan for a constitution adaptable enough to "do justice" in a manner consonant with the most humane ideals of our time, then we must bear in mind that the Committee on the Constitutional System, with more than three hundred distinguished members, co-chaired by Lloyd N. Cutler and C. Douglas Dillon, urges us to contemplate fundamental changes in the United States Constitution. The Committee keeps saying that adaptability may not be sufficient to see us through to a tercentennial in 2087.[3]

The spectrum is even broader, however, than those three positions might suggest. In addition to numerous authorities whose views lie somewhere *between* those of Brennan and Meese, each one has his empathetic critics. There are scholars to the right of Meese, for example, who complain that "the liberals give us ideals without a text, and the conservatives give us a text without ideals."[4] There are also professors

2. See, e.g., Nathan Glazer, "Towards an Imperial Judiciary?" in Glazer and Irving Kristol, eds., *The American Commonwealth: 1976* (New York, 1976), 104–23. For biographical information, see John A. Jenkins, "Mr. Power: Attorney General Meese is Reagan's Man to Lead the Conservative Charge," *New York Times Magazine*, Oct. 12, 1986, pp. 18–19, 89–101. Meese submitted his resignation as Attorney General on July 5, 1988.

3. See Donald L. Robinson, ed., *Reforming American Government: The Bicentennial Papers of the Committee on the Constitutional System* (Boulder, Colo., 1985), esp. 11–32, 55–60, 68–71, 93–109, 299–312; Stuart Taylor, Jr., "Citing Chronic Deadlock, Panel Urges Altering Political Structure," *New York Times*, Jan. 11, 1987, p. A1.

4. See Thomas G. West, "How the Constitution Embodies Our Ideals," *The New Federalist Papers*, no. 144 (Nov. 21, 1986), 2; Stephen Macedo, "How Should Judges Protect Liberty?" in *Cato Policy Report* 9 (January–February 1987): 6–7.

of constitutional law, like Ronald Dworkin and Mark Tushnet, located to the left of Brennan, who offer this sort of critical commentary:

> The jurisprudence of original intent is kept alive because we don't seem to have any good alternatives. Justice Brennan's position is that the judges should do justice. A society confident that people could discover indisputable standards of justice might find that position to be an acceptable mediation between judicial power and passivity. But that's not our society. Everybody knows that Justice Brennan's enduring principles of justice are his and his political allies', not some principles immanent in the natural order. When Meese says that his adversaries are defending unbridled judicial power, he's right. But the jurisprudence of original intent also defends unbridled judicial power.[5]

Professor Tushnet balances his blast at Meese with this concession: "The dilemma is that Justice Brennan's confident liberalism, though it recognizes that governments and judges can do good, fails to express our concern that they do evil as well."[6]

If I may now abandon the image of a forum and shift to that of a contest, it might be helpful to identify some of the principal combatants. Among those who are vocally sympathetic to Justice Brennan and critical of Mr. Meese we find various chapters of the American Civil Liberties Union; some top leaders of the American Bar Association; Benno Schmidt, Jr., the president of Yale University; unsigned editorials in the *New York Times* as well as op-eds by analyst Anthony Lewis; and such prominent professors of constitutional law as Laurence Tribe of Harvard and Paul Brest of Stanford.[7]

It is more difficult to list the former Attorney General's allies — not

5. Tushnet, "The U.S. Constitution and the Intent of the Framers," *Tikkun: A Quarterly Jewish Critique of Politics, Culture & Society* 1 (1986): 35–40, the quotation at 39–40; Dworkin, *Taking Rights Seriously* (Cambridge, Mass., 1977); Dworkin, *A Matter of Principle* (Cambridge, Mass., 1985).

6. Tushnet, "U.S. Constitution and the Intent of the Framers," 35.

7. Stuart Taylor, Jr., "Meese and the Storm Over the Court," *New York Times*, Oct. 27, 1986, p. A20; Taylor, "Liberties Union Denounces Meese," ibid., Oct. 24, 1986, p. A17; letter to the editor from Gara LaMarche, executive director of the Texas Civil Liberties Union, *New York Times Magazine*, Nov. 16, 1986, p. 134; symposium held at Harvard University in September 1986, "The Constitution and What to Make of It," reported in *Harvard Magazine*, January–February 1987, pp. 50–52; "Mr. Meese's Contempt of Court," *New York Times* edi-

because he lacks them but because he has presented provocative positions on a broad range of fundamental issues. Many of his allies take a "yes, but" position; or else sympathize with some of his stands more than with others. Concerning the notion of a jurisprudence of original intention, however, Meese not only has numerous supporters, such as Charles Fried (Solicitor General of the United States) and the Heritage Foundation, but also respected constitutional lawyers and jurists (rarely mentioned by Meese in his speeches) who have developed arguments for "original intention" buttressed by serious scholarship.[8]

In a very real sense, their conservative outlook amounts to a new form of legal realism. Unlike the liberal movement that flourished during the 1920s and '30s, however, which sought to counteract the inflexibility of traditional concepts and their usage, the new variant of legal realism accepts the status quo by acknowledging that the United States Constitution does not, as Henry P. Monaghan puts it, guarantee either a perfect government or a perfect society. Judge Robert H. Bork, formerly of the United States Court of Appeals in Washington, D.C., has frequently contended that the Constitution simply does not "cover all possible or even all desirable liberties."[9]

The common denominator that I find among Mr. Meese and his allies, then, is the belief that we have an admirable but non-utopian Constitution. If the American judiciary relentlessly seeks perfect justice, or some approximation of it, judges will achieve only judicial tyranny rather than a utopian society. Not all wrongs can be rectified, at least not by the courts. According to Judge Bork: "Constitutional scholarship today is dominated by the creation of arguments that will encourage judges to thwart democratic choice."[10]

---

torial, Oct. 26, 1986, p. E22; Lewis, "Law or Power?" ibid., Oct. 27, 1986, p. A23; Brest, "Meese, the Lawman, Calls for Anarchy," ibid., Nov. 2, 1986, p. E23.

8. See Raoul Berger, *Government by Judiciary: The Transformation of the Fourteenth Amendment* (Cambridge, Mass., 1977); Henry P. Monaghan, "Our Perfect Constitution," *New York University Law Review* 56 (May 1981): 353–96; Robert H. Bork, *Tradition and Morality in Constitutional Law* (Washington, D.C., 1984), 10–11.

9. Monaghan, "Our Perfect Constitution," passim; Stuart Taylor, Jr., "U.S. Appellate Judge Criticizes Judicial Activism, *New York Times,* Nov. 19, 1985, p. A27.

10. Bork, *Tradition and Morality in Constitutional Law,* 9.

At this point I should supply the reader with a sense of direction for this essay. Where are we heading? Our itinerary can be traced through several sections: first, an extended and somewhat editorialized summary of Edwin Meese's constitutional agenda; then a précis of the responses offered by Justices William J. Brennan and John Paul Stevens; next, an effort to establish an ideological context, followed by a demonstration of the need for historical perspective; and finally, a few thoughts concerning the relationship between constitutional myths and historical realities.

Please notice that "myths" and "realities" are deliberately used in the plural. Even though pluralism has recently been tainted as a tired or even outworn concept, like liberalism, it's at the core of my rather old-fashioned response to the issues posed by Mr. Meese. Radicals and conservatives are not very fond of pluralism because they both tend to subscribe to the notion of One Great Redeeming Ideology. Quick to point out that not all persuasions are equally valid or worthy, they are likely to define a pluralist as someone too feckless to make up his mind.

Be that as it may, if we truly want to come to terms with the nature of our governmental set-up, we have to acknowledge the extent to which both the Federalists and the Anti-Federalists, for diverse reasons, were pluralists. Consequently our constitutional system, no matter what intellectual pedigree you prefer, has a pluralistic bloodline.

- Item: State sovereignty, to which the Anti-Federalists were wedded, is a fundamental form of political pluralism.
- Item: Federalism, a system of divided sovereignty to which the framers were committed, is also a form of political pluralism.
- Item: Republicanism as a mode of government extended over a vast continental expanse is viable only if geo-political pluralism is taken into account. That's what *Federalist* number 10, James Madison's most famous essay, is all about.[11]

11. Recent scholarship, by the way, suggests that while Madison may have been the most brilliant theorist of pluralism, he was not *sui generis* among politicians of the 1780s in accepting and being willing to predicate a new governmental system upon a pluralistic infrastructure. See Stephen E. Patterson, "The Roots of Massachusetts Federalism: Conservative Politics and Political Culture before 1787," and Richard A. Ryerson, "Republican Theory and Partisan Reality in Revolutionary Pennsylvania: Toward a New View of the Constitutionalist Party," in

- Item: Volatile disagreements occurred within the Constitutional Convention, within the state ratifying conventions, and within George Washington's first administration concerning the most basic constitutional matters. That's how we got the classic explications of broad and strict construction from Alexander Hamilton and Thomas Jefferson in 1791.[12] What is most fascinating, to me at least, is that both modes of interpretation have served us well over the past two centuries. I believe that our constitutional system would have been, and would still be, less stable and perhaps even impoverished without an on-going tension between the two. Call it different approaches appropriate for different people or different situations. Call it different approaches utilized by the same leader facing different dilemmas. Abraham Lincoln, for instance, relied upon strict construction in refusing to accept Southern secession, yet relied upon broad construction—some have said too broad—in using presidential powers to sustain the Union war effort.
- Item: The First Amendment of the Bill of Rights is meant to protect pluralism (unpopular faiths and opinions) if it is meant to achieve anything. To desire liberty of conscience, which increasing numbers of people did between 1776 and 1791, meant accepting the inevitability of pluralism, protected by law, in this heterogeneous society.

It is my contention, therefore, that the historical roots of political pluralism in American life render Edwin Meese's obsession with a jurisprudence of original intention an ingenuous sophistry. Consider these two sentences, for example, spoken at the Constitutional Convention on June 9, 1787, by one of the most sensible among the delegates, George Mason of Virginia: "We all agree in the necessity of new regulations; but we differ widely in our opinions of what are the safest and most effectual. Perhaps this contrariety of sentiment arises from our not thoroughly considering the peculiar circumstances, situation, character and

---

Ronald Hoffman and Peter J. Albert, eds., *Sovereign States in an Age of Uncertainty* (Charlottesville, Va., 1981), 58, 96–97.

12. See Henry Steele Commager, ed., *Documents of American History* (7th ed.; New York, 1963), 156–60.

genius of the people of America, differing materially from that of any other nation."[13]

II

On Tuesday, July 9, 1985, Edwin Meese presented an untitled address to the House of Delegates of the American Bar Association, gathered at the Sheraton Hotel in Washington, D.C. Its essential purpose and format was a report card on the 1984–85 term of the United States Supreme Court, but with particular reference to three topics: federalism, criminal law, and freedom of religion. Meese accused the Court, not unfairly, of failing to "yield a coherent set of decisions." Although he scattered some words of praise hither and yon, he concluded that "far too many of the Court's opinions were, on the whole, more policy choices than articulations of constitutional principle."[14]

Although this is the speech in which Meese called for a "Jurisprudence of Original Intention" (pp. 3, 15–17), it is noteworthy for several other reasons as well. First, because it gave advance warning of several major concerns that Meese would elaborate more fully in subsequent addresses. The importance of federalism, for example: "By allowing the states sovereignty sufficient to govern we better secure our ultimate goal of political liberty through decentralized government" (p. 8). Or the Reagan administration's opposition to the incorporation doctrine, according to which the Bill of Rights has become applicable to the states by means of the Fourteenth Amendment. Meese offered the Court moderate praise for minimizing the *Miranda* ruling (1966) by "stressing its origin in the court rather than in the Constitution" (pp. 10, 12).

13. Robert A. Rutland, ed., *The Papers of George Mason, 1725–1792* (Chapel Hill, N.C., 1970), 3:904. See also Mason's letter to Elbridge Gerry of Massachusetts, Oct. 20, 1787, ibid., 1005–6: "There is great contrariety of Opinion in Virginia upon the new Constitution of Government, & tho' in general it seems to be approved, yet even its Advocates can not deny that there are in it some very exceptionable and unsafe Articles."

14. "Address of the Honorable Edwin Meese III . . . before the American Bar Association," Washington, D.C., July 9, 1985 (text by courtesy of the Department of Justice), 6, 14. After initial citation in the notes to the various speeches by Meese that I discuss, page references to them will be incorporated into my text.

Three other attributes of this address also seem noteworthy. The first is Meese's insistence upon literalism. He declared that the justices ought to "resist any political effort to depart from the literal provisions of the Constitution" (pp. 2–3). The second is his unwillingness to acknowledge that a pluralistic political universe existed in 1787. Note his use of the singular in this key sentence: "The text of the document and the original intention of those who framed it would be the judicial standard in giving effect to the Constitution" (p. 3).

The third attribute involves Meese's frequent invocation (pp. 3, 15, 18) of an undeveloped and unexplained oxymoron: namely, that government ideally ought to be "limited but also energetic." The framers themselves often spoke of achieving a goverment that would be energetic and stable. (No oxymoron there.) But compared to what? Everyone knew the answer: compared to government under the Articles of Confederation, which was neither energetic nor stable. "Limited but also energetic," however, remains rather mysterious in Meese's political discourse. Perhaps he has in mind a government that would be limited in *some* of its parts (such as the judiciary) but energetic in others (such as the National Security Council and the C.I.A.). We can only surmise, because the former Attorney General has never elucidated this phrase.

In September 1985 Mr. Meese presented the American Enterprise Institute in Washington with a paean of praise for federalism. He appealed for a restoration of "the proper division of sovereignty between the national government and the states," which is unexceptionable; but he predicated his talk upon a definition of federalism that is historically unsound to the point of being nonsensical: namely, "the essence of federalism is the protection of liberty."[15] I beg to differ. Everything I have read during the past thirty years that is germane to this point tells me that the essence of federalism is the distribution of sovereignty within a political system.

On Friday, November 15, 1985, Mr. Meese walked across Pennsylvania Avenue a few blocks from the Department of Justice to a restaurant called the Golden Palace, where he spoke to a friendly crowd: the

---

15. Meese, "The Political Value of Federalism," issued on Dec. 4, 1985, by Public Research Syndicated (release no. 308), 1–2.

D.C. Chapter of the Federalist Society Lawyers Division.[16] Here Meese reiterated his disapproval of "judicial activism" and his anxiety about "'penumbras', somehow emanating ghostlike from various provisions —identified and not identified—in the Bill of Rights" (p. 9).

On this particular November day at the Golden Palace Mr. Meese repeated his call for "a jurisprudence of original intention" and insisted that "the meaning of the Constitution can be known" (pp. 5, 9). What's most intriguing about the speech, however, is that the Attorney General seemed to be responding rather nervously to the uproar caused by his A.B.A. address back in July. He makes reluctant concessions to his critics, especially to devotees of the concept of a living Constitution. He admits, for example, that "the disputes and compromises of the Constitutional Convention were carefully recorded" (p. 2). He concedes that the delegates intended "to write a document not just for their times but for posterity" (p. 3), and even acknowledges a lack of "unanimity among the framers and ratifiers on all points" (p. 5). And finally, he makes the surprising observation that the framers sought to create a national government "that would have the flexibility to adapt to face [*sic*] new exigencies—as it did, for example, in chartering a national bank" (p. 12).

On February 27, 1986, Mr. Meese went to Texas, where he spoke at the University of Dallas. Like the Golden Palace performance, this one did not attract a great deal of notice, but it did contain some patterns of repetition, some new inconsistencies, and some strange historical judgments that suggest someone hadn't done adequate homework.[17]

The "jurisprudence of original intention" is there (p. 5). The commitment to "limited but energetic government" is there too (pp. 3, 17), but this time that oxymoron is identified as a goal of the framers as well as of the Reagan administration. (Actually, George Washington may have been the only American president ever to put the oxymoron

16. "Address of the Honorable Edwin Meese III . . . before the D.C. Chapter of the Federalist Society Lawyers Division," Washington, D.C., Nov. 15, 1985 (text by courtesy of the Department of Justice).

17. Meese, "The Constitution as a Bill of Rights: Separation of Powers and Individual Liberty," Lecture at the University of Dallas, Irving, Texas, Feb. 27, 1986 (text by courtesy of the Department of Justice).

into practice. He asked Alexander Hamilton [Mr. Energetic] to be in charge of the Treasury, and Thomas Jefferson [Mr. Restraint-in-Government] to be in charge of the State Department.)

Perhaps sensing that he had gone too far at the Golden Palace in making concessions to the concept of a living Constitution, in Dallas Meese approvingly quoted a conservative scholar who believes that the framers' objective was *not* to keep the Constitution in tune with the times, but rather to "keep the times . . . in tune with the Constitution" (p. 6).

What's new in this address is the Attorney General's emphasis upon separation of powers as a principle cherished by the framers, which is fair enough, and his explication of how that principle "contributes to the preservation and perpetuation of individual liberty"—language and a linkage that, I believe, have their origins not in the founders but in the tradition of conservative constitutionalism that dates distinctively from David Jayne Hill and William Howard Taft during the second and third decades of this century.[18]

The real nemesis that Meese had in mind was not so much the Supreme Court, for a change, but regulatory agencies. "Are they legislative institutions? Or executive? Or judicial?" Meese specifically attacked a 1935 decision by the High Court, *Humphrey's Executor v. United States,* a case that arose when President Roosevelt tried to remove William Humphrey, a Hoover appointment, from the Federal Trade Commission.[19] The Court's decision—and bear in mind that the 1935 Court, the Nine Old Men, was controlled by conservatives—in Meese's words "spawned a radically new view of separation of powers." Meese then revealed his real concern.

> The holding posited the notion that these agencies are not purely executive in their essential functions. As a result, Congress could, by statute, restrict the President's power to remove those in the independent agencies in order to preserve their independence. The re-

18. See Michael Kammen, *A Machine That Would Go of Itself: The Constitution in American Culture* (New York, 1986), 206–8, 229.

19. *Humphrey's Executor v. United States,* 295 U.S. 602 (1935). The Attorney General incorrectly dates this case at 1936.

sult of this famous case was, in effect, to create a new and politically unaccountable "fourth branch" of the national government. Such independent regulatory agencies were held to be "quasi-legislative" and "quasi-judicial" and thus not, strictly speaking, a part of the executive branch. (Pp. 9–10.)

We could easily get sidetracked at this point onto an interesting discussion of whether or not independent agencies are more (or less) likely to behave as political loose cannons, depending upon whether they are independent or ("strictly speaking") controlled by the White House. Given the recent histories of the Environmental Protection Agency and the Commission on Civil Rights, for example, I don't have a great deal of confidence in either the empirical grounding or the motives underlying the Meese position. In theory, at least, the constitutional status of regulatory agencies is indeed a subject worthy of serious exploration; and we should feel grateful to the Attorney General for raising the issue. Unfortunately, the press did not find the Dallas address very interesting, apparently, and I have yet to see much significant analysis or commentary generated by it.

Nevertheless, Mr. Meese is wide of the mark in two key respects, at least from a historian's vantage point. The first is that he believes the framers intended separation of powers to be absolutely complete (pp. 9, 15–16, 19). That is not the case, nor is it realistic. They learned from reading Montesquieu's *Spirit of the Laws* (1748) that separation would enhance human freedom by controlling government. So they sought a greater degree of separation than was allowed by the system embodied in the British constitution—which Montesquieu along with many of the founders greatly admired. But they understood perfectly well what the Cutler-Dillon Committee on the Constitutional System has been preaching throughout the 1980s: namely, that absolute separation, especially between the executive and legislative branches, would very likely mean governmental paralysis.[20] Sometimes I get the impression that Mr. Meese has conflated in his mind separation of powers (a concept of which he is fond) and checks and balances (which he never mentions). The

20. See note 3 above, and especially James Madison, *Federalist* number 47, in Jacob E. Cooke, ed., *The Federalist* (Middletown, Conn., 1961), 325.

two are obviously related, yet in terms of the framers' objectives they are not the same.[21]

The other respect in which the erstwhile Attorney General seems wide of the mark is reflected in these two short sentences: "Our technological accomplishments over the past two hundred years have been awesome. But the fact is political life remains much the same" (p. 8). The historical ignorance revealed by the latter sentence is mind-boggling. Perhaps naiveté might be a more charitable word. In any case, the literature concerning political change between 1787 and the present is persuasive as well as voluminous. Think of major transformations in the party system alone. Consider the political impact of the media, especially television. Reflect upon the relatively recent role of political action groups. Recall changes in the dynamics of political behavior owing to the expansion of the electorate, especially in terms of ethnic groups. And think of what political historians call the great electoral re-alignments of the 1850s, 1890s, and 1930s.[22]

Meese's fifth public address, delivered in October 1986 at Tulane University, has *not* been neglected.[23] It stirred up quite a ruckus because, half-way through, Meese declared that any decision made by the Supreme Court "binds the parties in a case and also the executive branch

21. See. W. B. Gwyn, *The Meaning of the Separation of Powers* (New Orleans, La., 1965); M. J. C. Vile, *Constitutionalism and the Separation of Powers* (Oxford, 1967).

22. See, for example, Walter Dean Burnham, *The Current Crisis in American Politics* (New York, 1982); Nelson W. Polsby, *The Consequences of Party Reform* (New York, 1983); Leon D. Epstein, *Political Parties in the American Mold* (Madison, Wis., 1986); David S. Broder, *The Party's Over: The Failure of Politics in America* (New York, 1972); Everett C. Ladd, *Where Have All the Voters Gone? The Fracturing of American Political Parties* (New York, 1978); Richard P. McCormick, *The Second American Party System: Party Formation in the Jacksonian Era* (Chapel Hill, N.C., 1966); Richard L. McCormick, ed., *Political Parties and the Modern State* (New Brunswick, N.J., 1984); David M. O'Brien, "'The Imperial Judiciary': Of Paper Tigers and Socio-Legal Indicators," *The History Teacher* 19 (November 1985): 47; Michael J. Robinson, "Television and American Politics: 1956–1976," *The Public Interest,* no. 48 (Summer 1977): 3–39.

23. Meese, "The Law of the Constitution," lecture for the Tulane University Citizens' Forum on the Bicentennial of the Constitution, New Orleans, Louisiana, Oct. 21, 1986 (text by courtesy of the Department of Justice). See Stuart Taylor, Jr., "Meese Says Court Doesn't Make Law," *New York Times,* Oct. 23, 1986, p. A1. Evangelist Pat Robertson, a presidential aspirant with a huge television following, shares Meese's view on this matter. See his interview with the *Washington Post,* reported in the *Ithaca Journal,* June 28, 1986, p. 2.

for whatever enforcement is necessary. But such a decision does not establish a 'supreme law of the land' that is binding on all persons and parts of government" (p. 7). He followed up with the vague suggestion that some sort of defiance was not merely acceptable but positively appropriate. "If a constitutional decision is not the same as the Constitution itself, if it is not binding in the same way that the Constitution is, we as citizens may respond to a decision we disagree with" (p. 10). The range of permissible responses, however, is never clarified; and the Attorney General's spokesman at the Department of Justice refused to answer questions about hypothetical situations. It is clear, for instance, that Meese encourages citizens to criticize decisions they do not like. (That right is already protected by the First Amendment.) But it is not clear whether he approves of legislators voting for bills that are virtually identical to ones already declared void by the High Court.

It is unfortunate, for several reasons, that this address met with such scorn from the media and other critics; because the consequence has been failure to take Meese seriously or to read the full text of his address. That is a pity because he makes some perfectly reasonable points and reminds us of truths that we tend to forget or else gloss over, viz., that "constitutional law and the Constitution are not the same" (p. 8); that "constitutional interpretation is not the business of the Court only, but also, and properly, the business of all branches of government" (p. 11); and, closely related, a point that really does get periodically neglected, that "each of the coordinate branches of government created and empowered by the Constitution — the executive and legislative no less than the judicial — has a duty to interpret the Constitution in the performance of its official functions" (p. 11).

Curiously enough, however, critics have so concentrated their fire on Meese's "supreme law of the land" passage that they have ignored aberrations, constitutional and historical, that appear elsewhere in the address. Meese is highly critical of the Court's unanimous decision in *Cooper v. Aaron* (1958), signed by all nine justices, categorically reaffirming its desegregation decisions in 1954–55 as well as the authority of federal courts.[24] He has the effrontery to imply that "the Court seemed

24. *Cooper v. Aaron*, 358 U.S. 1 (1958), esp. at 4, 16–18.

to reduce the Constitution to the status of ordinary constitutional law, and to equate the judge with the lawgiver" (p. 12). And he compounds arrogance with historical shallowness by contending that in 1958 the Court reached "conclusions about its own power that would have shocked men like John Marshall and Joseph Story" (p. 12). That simply isn't so.[25]

III

Whether or not Marshall and Story would have been shocked may remain a moot point, perhaps; but we can say with assurance that Justices William J. Brennan and John Paul Stevens were put off by Meese's arrogance because they said so explicitly in rebuttals of their own. Since their ripostes have received reasonably comprehensive coverage, we can take note of them very briefly.

Brennan spoke out first at a symposium convened by the Georgetown University Law Center in October 1985.[26] His thoughts on that occasion actually covered a range of questions considerably broader than those raised earlier in the year by Mr. Meese. It is clear that Justice Brennan decided to avail himself of the opportunity to set the record straight, and he did so with impressive moral power and intellectual clarity. He called the doctrine of original intent "little more than arrogance cloaked as humility," and subsequently as "facile historicism." He declared that "those who would restrict claims of right to the values of 1789 specifically articulated in the Constitution turn a blind eye to social progress and eschew adaptation of overarching principles to changes of social circumstances" (pp. 4–5).

After elaborating those points, Justice Brennan made a statement that transcended his differences with Meese. It might serve as a viable creed for any advocate of a compassionate and vital jurisprudence:

25. For a scholarly presentation that implicitly refutes Meese, see R. Kent Newmyer, *Supreme Court Justice Joseph Story: Statesman of the Old Republic* (Chapel Hill, N.C., 1985), esp. 108, 190–91.

26. Brennan, "The Constitution of the United States: Contemporary Ratification," lecture presented at Georgetown University, Washington, D.C., Oct. 12, 1985 (text by courtesy of the United States Supreme Court Public Information Office; page references given in my text). See also E. R. Shipp, "Brennan Restates Views on Freedom," *New York Times*, Aug. 9, 1986, p. 46.

We current Justices read the Constitution in the only way that we can: as Twentieth Century Americans. We look to the history of the time of framing and to the intervening history of interpretation. But the ultimate question must be, what do the words of the text mean in our time. For the genius of the Constitution rests not in any static meaning it might have had in a world that is dead and gone, but in the adaptability of its great principles to cope with current problems and current needs. What the constitutional fundamentals meant to the wisdom of other times cannot be their measure to the vision of our time. (P. 7.)

Although Brennan chose to emphasize with some frequency "our amended Constitution," and stressed the significance of the Bill of Rights along with the post–Civil War amendments in a manner that Meese did not,[27] the Justice concluded on a note that is not so far removed from the Attorney General's central theme at Tulane, even though Brennan, to be sure, had a different *rationale* for acknowledging the impermanent character of constitutional law. "The unique interpretive role of the Supreme Court with respect to the Constitution," he conceded, "demands some flexibility with respect to the call of *stare decisis.* Because we are the last word on the meaning of the Constitution, our views must be subject to revision over time, or the Constitution falls captive, again, to the anachronistic views of long-gone generations" (p. 15).

When Justice Stevens spoke to the Federal Bar Association in Chicago on October 23, 1985, his angle of approach was a little less direct than Justice Brennan's. Stevens announced at the outset that he planned to tell his audience "about a few of the things that a Supreme Court justice does during his or her vacation."[28] Taken at face value, it sounds

27. Brennan reiterated and expanded upon this emphasis in a speech delivered at the New York University Law School on November 18, 1986. He praised a series of decisions made by the Supreme Court between 1961 and 1969 because those rulings "transformed the basic structure of constitutional safeguards for individual political and civil liberties in this nation and profoundly altered the character of the Federal system." E. R. Shipp, "Brennan Praises High Court of 60's," *New York Times,* Nov. 20, 1986, p. B15.

28. Stevens, "Address to the Luncheon Meeting of the Federal Bar Association, The Standard Club, Chicago, Illinois," Oct. 23, 1985 (text by courtesy of the United States Supreme Court Public Information Office), 2. Page references hereafter will be given in my text.

like the first assigned essay of the fall term that we all had to write in the seventh or eighth grade. Although much of Stevens' address was, in fact, aimed at the issue of the Court's heavy workload and what to do about it, he eventually got around to the Attorney General's speech to the A.B.A. on July 9. In rejecting Meese's appeal for a jurisprudence of original intention, Stevens, like Brennan, insisted upon "the importance of evaluating subsequent developments in the law, as well as the original intent of the Framers."

Stevens saved his heaviest fire, however, for one of the Attorney General's pet peeves—one that I have not mentioned because Meese tended to include it in written texts released to the press but then omit it from oral presentations—namely, the concept called incorporation, by which the Bill of Rights became applicable to the states by being "absorbed" into the Fourteenth Amendment. As Stevens put it, once again Meese's "argument is somewhat incomplete . . . because its concentration on the original intention of the Framers of the Bill of Rights overlooks the importance of subsequent events in the development of our law. In particular, it overlooks the profound importance of the Civil War and the post-war amendments on the structure of our government, and particularly upon the relationship between the Federal Government and the separate States" (pp. 8–9). Justices Stevens and Brennan speak as one on this matter.

Edwin Meese himself, by comparison, does *not* speak with one voice on this matter. Not only did he say one thing in his text and another to his audience, but when members of the press asked him directly whether the Court went too far in applying the Bill of Rights to the states, he replied: "No. I think this is something that's been done in 1925 and I do not have any particular quarrel at this stage of the game with what the Court has done in the intervening 60 years."[29] Now that we have been reminded of the "game" analogy, I will simply add that it is very difficult to hit a moving target. So far as the appli-

29. *New York Times,* Nov. 19, 1986, p. A16. See also ibid., Oct. 23, 1986, p. A1, and Oct. 27, 1986, p. A20. For a defense of Meese on this issue by Terry Eastland, then director of the Office of Public Affairs at the Department of Justice, see his letter to the *New York Times,* Aug. 16, 1986, p. 22.

cation of constitutional ideas is concerned, Mr. Meese is without peer as a man in motion.

IV

To provide a modicum of ideological perspective might seem like a simple matter. Surely, to use a current colloquialism, we all know where each of the combatants is "coming from." It's really not so easy, however, because there is a lot of hanky-panky with the use of language —legal as well as ordinary language. Both Brennan *and* Meese, for example, speak of "liberty and justice for all" as an imperative, even though Meese asserts that criminal suspects are guilty until proven innocent.[30]

More important than the incantation of catch phrases, however, is the odd occurrence of role reversal in the use of traditional constitutional concepts. Following the Attorney General's speech at Tulane, when he challenged the High Court's rulings as the supreme law of the land, liberal critics such as Ira Glasser of the A.C.L.U., Anthony Lewis of the *New York Times,* and Paul Brest of the Stanford University Law School all called for "the rule of law" to be maintained.[31] That phrase used to be a rallying cry, of course, for law-and-order conservatives; but just to confuse the issue a bit, it should be noted that Meese *also* used the phrase no fewer than three times in his Tulane speech.[32]

When Meese declares, as he did at Tulane, that "the rule of law is still the very fundament of our civilization" (p. 15), however, his context helps to illuminate ideological differences and divergent political agendas. The great evil cited by Meese in that context is "government by judiciary," an evil that he designated as "judicial activism" in his Golden Palace address (pp. 9, 14), and as "judicial supremacy" on other occasions.

If we shift our attention back to the late 1780s, however, and especially to the Constitutional Convention, we find two pertinent develop-

---

30. "The thing is," Meese has said, "you don't have many suspects who are innocent of a crime." Quoted in *New York Times,* Nov. 19, 1986, p. A16. For Meese's concerted attempt to reverse the *Miranda* ruling of 1966, see ibid., Jan. 23, 1987, pp. A1 and A9.

31. Ibid., Oct. 24, 1986, p. A17; ibid., Oct. 27, 1986, p. A23; ibid., Nov. 2, 1986, p. E23.

32. Both sides are also fond of the expression, "a government of laws, not of men."

ments. First, a widely shared feeling that the judiciary, even if its independence were respected, would remain the least aggressive and therefore the weakest branch of government.[33] And second, the presumption that vigorous yet prudent use of judicial review would be indispensable to any viable system of checks and balances. As James Iredell wrote in 1787, before he served on the Supreme Court, an act incompatible with the Constitution must be void, and "judges, consistently with their duties, could not carry it into effect."

> The Constitution appears to me to be a fundamental law, limiting the powers of the Legislature, and with which every exercise of those powers must, necessarily, be compared. . . . It is not that the judges are appointed arbiters, and to determine as it were upon any application, whether the Assembly have or have not violated the Constitution; but when an act is necessarily brought in judgment before them, they must, unavoidably, determine one way or another.[34]

To my way of thinking, the least attractive use of language by the ex-Attorney General and his allies appears in their casuistical insistence that they are the true champions of democracy. In July 1985 Meese claimed that "a Jurisprudence of Original Intention also reflects a deeply rooted commitment to the idea of democracy" (p. 15). In November of that year he praised the "early democrats" who wrote the Massachusetts state constitution (p. 14) — a remarkable piece of misinformation.[35] And in October 1986 he asserted that in a "constitutional democracy like ours" it is essential to uphold "the right of the people to govern themselves through the democratic branches of government" (p. 9). How are we

33. See Hamilton, *Federalist* number 78, in Cooke, ed., *The Federalist,* 522–23; John Adams to Roger Sherman, July 18, 1789, in Adrienne Koch, ed., *The American Enlightenment: The Shaping of the American Experiment and a Free Society* (New York, 1965), 197. For a modern reaffirmation of this point of view, see O'Brien, "'The Imperial Judiciary'," 37.

34. Iredell to Richard Dobbs Spaight, Aug. 26, 1787, in Griffith J. McRee, *Life and Correspondence of James Iredell,* 2 (New York, 1858), 172–73. See also Max Farrand, *The Framing of the Constitution of the United States* (New Haven, Conn., 1913), 157; George Mason to Arthur Lee, May 21, 1787, in Rutland, ed., *Papers of George Mason,* 3:882; Don Higginbotham, "James Iredell and the Origins of American Federalism," in George G. Suggs, Jr., ed., *Perspectives on the American Revolution* (Carbondale, Ill. 1977), 110–11.

35. Cf. Ronald M. Peters, Jr., *The Massachusetts Constitution of 1780: A Social Compact* (Amherst, Mass., 1978).

supposed to reconcile that sort of rhetoric with the following phrases that so clearly come from Mr. Meese's mouth with expectorant distaste: "radical egalitarianism," "expansive civil libertarianism," "creating new powers and new rights," and a "living Constitution"?

The Attorney General's repudiation of the notion of a living Constitution revealed one of several major inconsistencies in his thinking. In the Golden Palace speech, for instance, he acknowledged that precisely because the Constitution "posits so few conclusions it leaves to the more political branches the matter of adapting and vivifying its principles in each generation" (p. 13). I have never heard a more succinct definition of a living Constitution. Presumably the phrase "more political branches" refers to the Congress and the presidency; but it is difficult to be sure. Although Mr. Meese has accused the Supreme Court of being a highly political branch, and with pejorative implications, he nevertheless uttered the following in his A.B.A. address of July 1985:

> The Court is what it was understood to be when the Constitution was framed—a political body. The judicial process is, at its most fundamental level, a political process. . . . It is a process wherein public deliberations occur over what constitutes the common good under the terms of a written constitution. (P. 5.)

Because scholars, serious journalists, and diverse critics have exposed various other inconsistencies in the former Attorney General's constitutional thought,[36] I shall only observe that when so many inconsistencies emerge from the offices of a dedicated man and his devoted staff, it can only mean that an ideological agenda, addressed in an *ad hoc* or piecemeal fashion, has become the tail that wags the dog.[37]

36. In addition to the critiques cited earlier in these references, see Anthony Lewis, "Power and Triviality," *New York Times,* July 14, 1986, p. A17; and the letters from Professors Norma M. Riccucci and Jack Greenberg, ibid., Nov. 6, 1986, p. A34.

37. See Terry Eastland, "Proper Interpretation of the Constitution," ibid., Jan. 9, 1986, p. A23; Stuart Taylor, "Meese Aide Assails the Press and Law Schools on Courts," ibid., Nov. 16, 1986, p. A26. Legal counsel for the segregationist coalition conceded in 1953 that the Supreme Court had always been free to veer away from what might have been the founders' original intent—in that particular instance referring to a broad interpretation of the interstate commerce clause. See Richard Kluger, *Simple Justice: The History of Brown v. Board of Education and Black America's Struggle for Equality* (New York, 1975), 647.

Mr. Meese's agenda obviously is epitomized by a phrase that he used in Dallas early in 1986: "the preservation and perpetuation of individual liberty" (p. 3). Meanwhile, Mr. Brennan's agenda is epitomized by a phrase that he used in his remarks at Georgetown University in October 1985: "the human dignity of every individual" (p. 9). The individual may *appear* to be their common denominator; but there is a difference that supersedes numerators. Meese uses "individual" as a modifier, as an adjective, while Brennan uses it as a noun—a noun-concept that embraces humankind as ordinary rather than as privileged people. That is not a trivial difference. As a matter of preference it explains much. It is inescapably an ideological difference.

V

Once upon a time, back in 1938, Franklin D. Roosevelt began an address with the words: "Let me talk history."[38] That is my purpose at this point also; but with the caution that the historical perspective on these matters is neither predictable nor singular. Other historians have already had their say on the "Meese-Brennan" polemic, and there is a fair amount of divergence.[39] It is not yet widely obvious whose "side" History is, or ought to be, on.

I must also point out that for quite some time there have been serious scholars who care very much about the United States Constitution, yet do not believe that either history or original intent matter at all. One such scholar (a political scientist with a traditional orientation toward the value of historical context) concluded a widely read analysis in 1955 with these two sentences: "As it stands today, the Constitution has been developed through a variety of amendments, court decisions, statutes, and practices to meet the needs of the nation of today and tomorrow. Any new discovery about the intentions of the origi-

38. Quoted in Alfred Haworth Jones, *Roosevelt's Image Brokers: Poets, Playwrights, and the Use of the Lincoln Symbol* (Port Washington, N.Y., 1974), 66.

39. Compare Henry Steele Commager, "Meese Ignores History in Debate with Court," *New York Times*, Nov. 20, 1985, p. A31, with Wilcomb E. Washburn, "Justice Brennan's Challenge to Historians," *Perspectives* [American Historical Association Newsletter] 24 (December 1986): 19–20.

nal framers could have little more than antiquarian interest today."[40]

In case such agnosticism is not sufficiently exasperating to true believers like Mr. Meese, I must next point to an alternative school of thought, currently attractive to many scholars who specialize in constitutional law. A very careful study of what the founders' generation understood "original intent" to mean has revealed that the founders did not recognize the validity of such a judicial strategy. To the extent that historical evidence was deemed valuable at all, jurists preferred to rely upon what had been said in the various state ratifying conventions. Only later, during the 1840s, did the orientation of constitutional interpretation shift from the perspectives of the various sovereign states to the personal and collective intentions of individual delegates to the Convention in 1787. In other words, the framers themselves did not approve of a "Jurisprudence of Original Intention."[41]

One clear lesson of this entire inquiry is that language, like constitutional interpretation itself, is not immutable. Although political and judicial discourse in the years immediately following 1787 contained references to "original intention" and "the intent of the framers," the meaning of such phrases does not coincide with modern usage. That really should not surprise us, however, because we have known for many years that highly particular political circumstances in 1787–88 compelled the Federalists to develop arguments and use language in ways that were partially deceptive. I have in mind such key words as sovereignty, popular sovereignty, federal, national, equality, republican, consolidation, and confederation.[42] The quirky, sometimes capricious, and frequently inconsistent uses of political concepts in public discourse all combine to trap any quest for the framers' original intent in a textual quagmire.

40. William Anderson, "The Intention of the Framers: A Note on Constitutional Interpretation," *American Political Science Review* 49 (June 1955): 340–52. For a recent version of that agnosticism, from a prominent political scientist whose specialty is constitutional history and law, see the letter from John P. Roche, *New York Times*, May 18, 1986, p. E24.

41. H. Jefferson Powell, "The Original Understanding of Original Intent," *Harvard Law Review* 98 (March 1985): 885–948, esp. 888, 946–48.

42. See Gordon S. Wood, *The Creation of the American Republic, 1776–1787* (Chapel Hill, N.C., 1969), esp. chs. 7–13; Paul K. Conkin, *Self-Evident Truths* (Bloomington, Ind., 1974).

Having used the word "intent" repeatedly as a matter of convenience, however, I must now insist that "intentions" is much more appropriate — which pulls us back once again to the reality of constitutional pluralism at the time of the founding. James Madison and John Adams disagreed on many crucial constitutional issues. So did John Adams and Alexander Hamilton. So did Hamilton and Madison, who nevertheless collaborated as "Publius" to write *The Federalist*.[43]

James Madison's views did not coincide entirely with those of Thomas Jefferson, his intellectual soul-mate; and Madison said so publicly as well as privately.[44] Most symptomatic of all, however, Madison's constitutional thought and writings following the Convention did not even coincide in certain key respects with his own views on the eve and during early phases of the Convention. With all of his erudition and careful forethought, he still grew intellectually as a result of hearing and responding to other points of view.[45]

Hence my insistence upon constitutional pluralism. If we acknowledge that there were founders — and everyone does — then we must also concede that there were intentions: once again plural rather than singular. Although Alexander Hamilton's crucial defense of the national bank's legitimacy, prepared early in 1791, made reference to the views of the framers at the Convention, he nonetheless felt perfectly comfortable contending for broad construction and a living Constitution.[46]

Unlike FDR in 1938, Justice Brennan's primary concern in his

43. See Joyce Appleby, "Republicanism in Old and New Contexts," *William and Mary Quarterly* 43 (January 1986): 20–21; Patterson, "The Roots of Massachusetts Federalism," 60; Marvin Meyers, "Founding and Revolution: A Commentary on Publius-Madison," in Stanley Elkins and Eric McKitrick, eds., *The Hofstadter Aegis: A Memorial* (New York, 1974), 3–35.

44. See *Federalist* number 49 in Cooke, ed., *The Federalist*, 338–42; Madison's "Observations on Jefferson's Draft of a Constitution for Virginia [1783]," October 1788, in Robert A. Rutland et al., eds., *The Papers of James Madison*, 11 (Charlottesville, Va., 1977), 281–87.

45. Madison to Jefferson, Oct. 24, 1787, in Rutland et al., eds., *Papers of Madison*, 10 (Chicago, 1977), 205–19; Lance Banning, "The Practicable Sphere of a Republic: James Madison, the Constitutional Convention, and the Emergence of Revolutionary Federalism," in Richard Beeman et al., eds., *Beyond Confederation: Origins of the Constitution and American National Identity* (Chapel Hill, N.C., 1987), 162–87.

46. Hamilton's Opinion on the Constitutionality of the Bank, Feb. 23, 1791, in Commager, ed., *Documents of American History*, 157. See also James H. Hutson, "The Creation of the Constitution: The Integrity of the Documentary Record," *Texas Law Review* 65 (November 1986): 1–39.

Georgetown address was not to talk history. Nevertheless, he got the most germane historical lesson absolutely right.

> It is arrogant to pretend that from our vantage we can gauge accurately the intent of the Framers on application of principle to specific, contemporary questions. All too often, sources of potential enlightenment such as records of the ratification debates provide sparse or ambiguous evidence of the original intention. Typically, all that can be gleaned is that the Framers themselves did not agree about the application or meaning of particular constitutional provisions, and hid their differences in cloaks of generality. (P. 4.)

It should not surprise anyone that Brennan has taken such a position, because the Justice has very strong feelings about the method of decision-making that Mr. Meese advocates. The more broadly instructive exercise (and for me a kind of clincher) is to read what Brennan's predecessors on the Court had to say—above all, those who, by and large, were judicial conservatives. It would be an easy task to trace Brennan's intellectual genealogy back through liberals like Louis D. Brandeis.[47] But what happens when we explore the pages written by jurists who in theory *ought* to have provided grist for the Attorney General's mill? Look at Joseph Story, for example. In 1842, aging and testy with conservatism, he wrote the Court's opinion in *Prigg v. Pennsylvania,* which surely must have been one of the most difficult decisions he ever faced. Justice Story, who opposed slavery, nevertheless felt constitutionally obliged to uphold the Fugitive Slave Act against maverick personal liberty laws passed by Northern states. Though compelled by his sense of devotion to the supremacy of national law, Story decided to make a general statement, fairly early in his eighteen-page opinion, about some fundamental aspects of constitutional interpretation. Given the ambiguous character of the document itself, he explained, the powers that it confers and the rights that it secures,

> as well as the known historical fact that many of its provisions were matters of compromise of opposing interests and opinions; that no uniform rule of interpretation can be applied to it which may not

47. See especially Brandeis's dissent in *Olmstead v. United States,* 277 U.S. 438 (1928), at 471–85.

allow, even if it does not positively demand, many modifications in its actual application to particular clauses. . . . [Perhaps] the safest rule of interpretation after all will be found to be to look to the nature and objects of the particular powers, duties, and rights, with all the lights and aids of *contemporary* history; and to give to the words of each just such operation and force, consistent with their legitimate meaning, as may fairly secure and attain the ends proposed.[48]

In 1895 Justice Edward D. White, dissenting in the adverse income tax decision, argued against reliance upon original intent and preferred instead to call upon precedents that had developed *since* 1787.[49] During the difficult winter of 1953–54, when the justices agonized in conference over the pending school desegregation ruling, conservative Justice Stanley Reed firmly believed that *Plessy* remained good law. Nevertheless, he joined Justices Robert H. Jackson and Felix Frankfurter — each of them a strong advocate of judicial restraint — in voting for desegregation on grounds that the Constitution had to be a living document that could adjust to new realities by repudiating social evils.[50]

Finally, we have two interesting instances from 1986 involving prominent jurists who are not supportive of Meese. First there is Justice Byron R. White dissenting, as usual, against a pro-choice decision involving Pennsylvania's 1982 Abortion Control Act. "The Court is on relatively firm ground when it deems certain of the liberties set forth in the Bill of Rights to be fundamental and therefore finds them incorporated in the Fourteenth Amendment's guarantee that no State may deprive any persons of liberty without due process of law."[51] Clearly, even moderate conservatives categorically accept incorporation.

Second, when the Senate Judiciary Committee held confirmation hearings in August 1986 on the nomination of Antonin Scalia, he was asked for his view concerning a jurisprudence of original intent. "I'm

48. *Prigg v. Commonwealth of Pennsylvania*, 41 U.S. 539 (1842), at 610. My italics.
49. See *Pollock v. Farmers' Loan and Trust Co.*, 158 U.S. 601 (1895), at 706–15; and Carl B. Swisher, *Stephen J. Field: Craftsman of the Law* (Washington, D.C., 1930), 407.
50. See Kluger, *Simple Justice*, 680–81, 685, 689.
51. *Thornburgh, Governor of Pennsylvania, et al. v. American College of Obstetricians and Gynecologists, et al.*, 106 S. Ct. 2169 (1986), at 2193–94. See also Justice White's dissent quoted in Robinson, ed., *Reforming American Government*, 246.

a little wishy-washy" on that, he replied![52] Discretionary stonewalling by any other name is known as *politesse*.

As for the Court's traditions respecting a jurisprudence of original intent, perhaps the last word should come from Oliver Wendell Holmes —who was sometimes liberal and sometimes not, sometimes activist but more often not. His consistency lay in his common sense, realism, candor, *and* respect for the law. "When we are dealing with words that also are a constituent act," he wrote for the Court in 1920,

> like the Constitution of the United States, we must realize that they have called into life a being the development of which could not have been foreseen completely by the most gifted of its begetters. It was enough for them to realize or to hope that they had created an organism. . . . The case before us must be considered in the light of our whole experience and not merely in that of what was said a hundred years ago.[53]

VI

Although my own point of view does not correspond with that of the quondam Attorney General, it must be reiterated that his perspective is not entirely archaic. There have, undeniably, been constitutional issues about which one *can* legitimately generalize with regard to the views of the founders; and, to avoid any hint of hypocrisy, let it be said that both judges and professors have done so in the past, sometimes implicitly and sometimes explicitly.[54]

Constitutional scholars, moreover, tend to be somewhat more cautious than Justice Stevens by acknowledging that application of the federal Bill of Rights to the states by means of "incorporation" or "absorption" was a tortuous process that met with considerable resistance for fully four decades from justices of diverse judicial temperaments. It is not correct to say that no member of the Court since 1925 has

52. "Rehnquist to Scalia, Bitterness to Bonhomie," *New York Times*, Aug. 8, 1986, p. A8.

53. *State of Missouri v. Holland*, 252 U.S. 416 (1920), at 433.

54. See, e.g., Robinson, ed., *Reforming American Government*, 243, 248, 268.

resisted or rejected the doctrine of incorporation. It has been a "secure" doctrine only since the mid-1960s.[55]

I also feel that a significant silver lining can be seen in the Attorney General's rejection of High Court decisions as part of the "supreme law of the land" (Tulane speech, p. 7). When Mr. Meese asserts that "we as citizens may respond to a decision we disagree with" (ibid., p. 10), I can only add "Amen." How else could *Betts v. Brady* (1942) have been reversed by *Gideon v. Wainwright* (1963) concerning the right of an indigent person to counsel? How else could *Minersville School District v. Gobitis* (1940) have been reversed by *West Virginia State Board of Education v. Barnette* (1943) concerning Jehovah's Witnesses and the compulsory flag salute? How else could *Poe v. Ullman* (1961) have been reversed by *Griswold v. Connecticut* (1965) concerning the sale of contraceptive devices? And how else could *Plessy v. Ferguson* (1896) have been reversed by *Brown v. Board of Education* (1954) concerning racial integration in public institutions? I, for one, am not unhappy with the Attorney General's "necessary distinction between the Constitution and constitutional law" (Tulane speech, p. 4).

If we recapitulate what Mr. Meese was calling for in 1985–88 — namely, a less powerful and less intrusive national government; "individual liberty"; a restoration of responsible state sovereignty; a strong preference for legislative action over judicial activism; and a "limited Constitution" (A.B.A. speech, p. 2) — this historian has to hypothesize that Mr. Meese might have lined up with the Anti-Federalists in 1787–88. Had he been a delegate to the Constitutional Convention, he probably would have walked out and gone home, as John Lansing and Robert Yates of New York did on July 10, 1787, because the other delegates had technically exceeded their authority.

A close reading of Mr. Meese's public pronouncements over the past few years can only lead to the conclusion that he would have opposed the Constitution in 1787–88, would have fought Alexander Hamilton's

---

55. Richard C. Cortner, *The Supreme Court and the Second Bill of Rights: The Fourteenth Amendment and the Nationalization of Civil Liberties* (Madison, Wis., 1981); Harold M. Hyman, book review in *The Journal of Southern History* 52 (August 1986): 471.

fiscal policies in 1790–91, and would have joined the Jeffersonian party as a states' rights strict constructionist during the 1790s.[56] Although the Attorney General presents himself as a champion of the United States Constitution, I proclaim him to be in direct line of descent, intellectually speaking, from the fearful Anti-Federalists.[57]

Moreover, if there is a single Supreme Court opinion that Mr. Meese reviles above all others, it is the one written for the majority by Chief Justice Roger B. Taney in *Dred Scott v. Sandford* (Tulane speech, p. 14). The great irony, however, is that Taney's logic in that opinion turned upon his rejection of a living Constitution and his explicit use of a jurisprudence of original intent. Here are the pertinent extracts.

> The duty of the court is, to interpret the instrument they [the founders] have framed, with the best lights we can obtain on the subject, and to administer it as we find it, according to its true intent and meaning when it was adopted. . . . It is too clear for dispute, that the enslaved African race were not intended to be included, and formed no part of the people who framed and adopted this declaration [of Independence]. . . . This state of public opinion had undergone no change when the Constitution was adopted, as is equally evident from its provisions and language.[58]

Although I shall resist the temptation to find Mr. Meese in a direct line of descent from Taney's opinion in *Dred Scott,* I strongly urge him to re-read that opinion in order to enhance his appreciation of how bad it really was as a piece of jurisprudence. Perhaps he will then understand, through analogical reasoning, just what's wrong with "a jurisprudence of original intention."

56. An interesting litmus for purposes of historical comparison may be found in Dumas Malone, "Jefferson, Hamilton, and the Constitution," in William H. Nelson, ed., *Theory and Practice in American Politics* (Chicago, 1964), 18–19.

57. See Herbert J. Storing, *What the Anti-Federalists Were For* (Chicago, 1981); Cecelia Kenyon, "Men of Little Faith: The Anti-Federalists on the Nature of Representative Government," *William and Mary Quarterly* 12 (January 1955): 3–43.

58. *Dred Scott v. Sandford,* 60 U.S. 393 (1857), at 426, conveniently available in Stanley I. Kutler, ed., *The Supreme Court and the Constitution: Readings in American Constitutional History* (2d ed.; New York, 1977), 151, 153. The invocation of Taney's elucidation of racial attitudes

VII

When the United States Constitution was written and implemented, a commonplace belief was articulated that the founders meant the document to act directly upon the people rather than upon the states or upon the people through the mediation of the states. James Madison said so in *Federalist* number 39, and Justice James Iredell offered that view explicitly in an important 1796 opinion: "The present constitution was particularly intended to affect individuals, and not States, except in particular cases specified; and this is the leading distinction between the articles of confederation and the present constitution."[59]

When this nation came into being, however, that view embodied as much myth as it did reality—especially considering the assumptions widely shared about the importance of state sovereignty. Since that time, inexorable developments that are encapsulated in our understanding of history as a word-concept have made the Madison-Iredell formulation less of a myth and much more of a reality. There is a lesson in that transformation that can be illuminated by comparison with the curious conflation of law and history in early Jewish thought. Josef Hayim Yerushalmi has called to our attention this fascinating Talmudic aggadah:

> Rabbi Judah said in the name of Rab: When Moses ascended on high [to receive the Torah] he found the Holy One, blessed be He, engaged in affixing *taggin* [crown-like flourishes] to the letters. Moses said: "Lord of the Universe, who stays Thy hand?" [i.e., is there anything lacking in the Torah so that these ornaments are necessary?] He replied: "There will arise a man at the end of many generations, Akiba ben Joseph by name, who will expound, upon each tittle, heaps and heaps of laws." "Lord of the Universe," said Moses, "permit me to see him." He replied: "Turn thee round."
>
> Moses went [into the academy of Rabbi Akiba] and sat down behind eight rows [of Akiba's disciples]. *Not being able to follow their*

---

in 1776–87 by counsel for the District of Columbia's segregated school system backfired before the Supreme Court on December 11, 1952. See Kluger, *Simple Justice*, 580.

59. Cooke, ed., *The Federalist*, 255–56; *Hylton v. United States* (1796), in Kutler, ed., *The Supreme Court and the Constitution*, 22.

arguments he was ill at ease, but when they came to a certain subject and the disciples said to the master "Whence do you know it?" and the latter replied, *"It is a law given to Moses at Sinai,"* he was comforted.[60]

American constitutionalism, in all of its developed fullness, richness, and complexity, could not have been revealed to James Madison: not on Sinai, not at Montpelier, and not even in Philadelphia. Madison himself understood that. John Marshall understood that. Louis D. Brandeis understood that.[61] The fact that the President of the United States and his foremost legal counsel do *not* understand that offers the most serious challenge to American constitutionalism in the years of its Bicentennial.

60. Yerushalmi, *Zakhor: Jewish History and Jewish Memory* (Seattle, Wash., 1982), 19.

61. See Madison to J. G. Jackson, Dec. 27, 1821, in Max Farrand, ed., *The Records of the Federal Convention of 1787* (2d ed.; New Haven, Conn., 1937), 3:450; and Brandeis dissenting in *Olmstead v. United States,* 277 U.S. 438 (1928), at 471–85.

This essay was prepared for presentation on March 5, 1987, as the Annual Invitational Lecture of the Society for the Humanities at Cornell, and then on May 15, 1987, in New York City at the plenary luncheon of the 81st Annual Meeting of the American Jewish Committee.

My special thanks to Gary E. Rubin (Director of Programs at the AJC), and to Robert S. Rifkind, Esq., who added generous remarks as the "designated commentator."

My essay was published as a separate pamphlet in September 1987 by the American Jewish Committee. Ms. Sonya F. Kaufer prepared the manuscript for publication swiftly and meticulously.

Index

Index